DEUTSCH-CHINESISCHE PROJEKTE

ARCHITEKTUR
LANDSCHAFTSARCHITEKTUR

CHINESE-GERMAN PROJECTS

ARCHITECTURE
LANDSCAPE ARCHITECTURE

H.M.NELTE

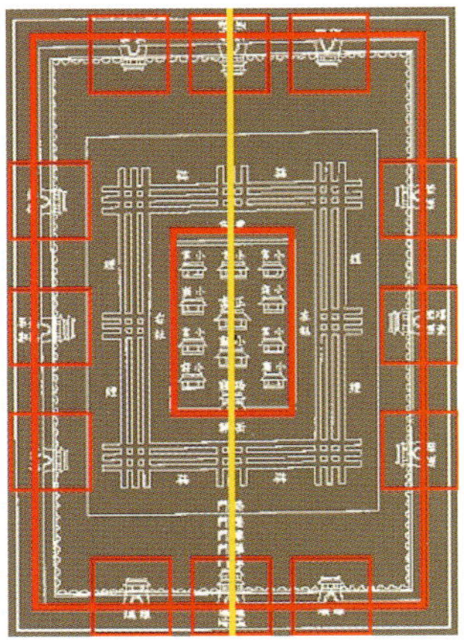

Als Grundlage für die Entwicklung des Gestaltungsrasters dieses Buches wurde der Grundriss der historischen Stadt Peking gewählt, der den über 2.000 Jahre alten traditionellen Prinzipien der chinesischen Stadtplanung folgt.

In diesem Regelwerk wurde festgelegt, wie eine „ideale" Stadt anzulegen ist: Ausgangspunkt ist der streng geometrische Stadtgrundriss, in dessen Zentrum sich die zentrale Anlage des kaiserlichen Palastes („Verbotene Stadt") befindet.

Um diesen herum liegen die Stadtquartiere, die aus den traditionellen chinesischen Hofhäusern gebildet werden. Abgeschlossen wird der Stadtgrundriss von zwölf regelmäßig angeordneten Stadttoren. Die gesamte Anlage der Stadt ist zudem entlang der zentralen Nord-Süd-Achse ausgerichtet.

The layout of this book was based on Beijing's historic urban layout according to the country's 2000-year-old tradition of urban design.

These rules determined how the 'ideal city' should be laid out. It had a strictly geometric, rectangular, grid with the imperial palace (the Forbidden City) in its centre.

The different urban quarters of traditional courtyard houses were arranged around this centre. The entire city – aligned along a north-south axis – was surrounded by walls with twelve gates spaced at regular intervals.

INHALTSVERZEICHNIS
CONTENTS

EINFÜHRUNG
INTRODUCTION

Ausländische Architekten in China

Selbst bei verlangsamtem Wirtschaftswachstum bleibt das Riesenreich China mit seinen 1,2 Milliarden Menschen der Welt größter Baumarkt. War der Urbanisierungsprozess, den die Kommunistische Partei 1978 mit der ökonomischen Öffnung des Landes und dem Weg zu einer sozialistischen Marktwirtschaft einleitete, vor allem durch seine in historischer Hinsicht einmalige Dimension und ein bisher unvorstellbares Tempo geprägt – die Zahl der Städte hat sich seit 1980 verdreifacht, darunter drei Dutzend Millionenstädte – zeichnet sich aufgrund der unübersehbaren Begleiterscheinungen des Booms allmählich ein Wandel von exzessivem zu intensivem Wachstum ab. Was das Planen und Bauen anbetrifft, ist im Gefolge des WTO-Beitritts die Tendenz zur Internationalisierung der Märkte von Interesse. Großveranstaltungen, um die sich China mit enormem Einsatz beworben hat, sorgen dafür, dass die atemberaubende Dynamik in den Metropolen Chinas anhält, aber auch hier allmählich ein Übergang von quantitativer zu qualitativer Entwicklung stattfindet.

Die Austragung der Olympischen Spiele 2008 in Peking wird von einem gewaltigen Stadtumbau begleitet, die World Expo of Leisure 2006 sorgt ebenso für weitere Impulse wie die Weltausstellung 2010 in der Metropole Shanghai, die bisher als Synonym des chinesischen Baubooms gilt. Mit diesen Ereignissen beansprucht China einen Platz auf dem Weltmarkt der Architektur. Gerade das einst konservative Peking, wo noch vor zehn Jahren Hochhäusern eine Art Pagodendach verordnet war, verpflichtet heute bei Prestigeprojekten Vertreter der internationalen Architekturavantgarde, die das Bauen in China vor kurzem noch belächelt haben mögen. Spektakuläre Entwürfe von Rem Koolhaas/OMA (Zentrale des staatlichen Fernsehsenders CCTV), Herzog & de Meuron (Olympiastadion), Paul Andreu (Opernhaus), PTW Architects, Sydney (Olympiaschwimmhalle), Norman Foster (internationaler Flughafen) sollen Peking ein modernes Erscheinungsbild und der Volksrepublik Prestige verschaffen, was aber noch lange nicht bedeutet, dass die Entwürfe tatsächlich realisiert werden.

Warum aber sollte China aufgrund seiner Vormachtstellung auf dem Weltmarkt des Bauens nicht auch eine gewichtige Rolle in der internationalen Architekturszene anstreben? Nachdem es den gesamten Welthandel auf den Kopf gestellt hat, spielt China in fast allen wirtschaftlichen Belangen längst in einer eigenen Liga und kann sich daher nur immer wieder selbst übertreffen. Auch gewinnt man die Aufmerksamkeit der Weltmedien und damit der Weltwirtschaft wesentlich einfacher mit internationalem Architekturimport als mit immer neuen Exportrekorden. In der unnachahmlichen Art das mediale Interesse der Welt stets aufs neue auf China zu lenken, spielen die geschickt inszenierten Architekturprojekte in Peking vor allem eine strategische Rolle.

Der fachliche Austausch ist bislang eher einseitig, denn während die westliche Architekturelite erfolgreich nach China vordringen konnte und dort auch in den Medien präsent ist, treten chinesische Architekten international bisher nicht in Erscheinung. Eine Ausnahme ist das Pekinger Projekt „Kommune der Großen Mauer“, das bei der Architektur-Bienale 2002 in Venedig mit einem Preis ausgezeichnet wurde. Die beteiligten Architekten aus Peking, Hongkong und Japan haben damit einen wichtigen Beitrag auf dem Weg zu zeitgenössischen Ausdrucksformen der Architektur in China und generell in Asien geleistet. Nach Jahrzehnten sozialistischer Planwirtschaft, als es weder Architekten noch Architektur gab, hat China in diesen wie in anderen Technik- oder Kunstbereichen einen gewaltigen Nachholbedarf.

Ausländische Architekten haben bei der historisch beispiellosen Modernisierung Chinas der letzten 20 Jahre von Anfang an eine Rolle gespielt, der zweite große Sprung nach vorn wäre ohne den Import von

Foreign Architects in China

Even though in recent years its economic growth has slowed down, the vast country of China with its 1.2 billion people is still the world's largest construction market. The process of urbanization, triggered by the ruling Communist party in 1978 with the economic opening up of the country and the subsequent development of a Socialist market economy, was primarily marked by its unique historic dimensions and unprecedented speed. Since 1980, the number of Chinese cities has trebled (three dozen of them have over one million inhabitants). Due to multiple unforeseen collateral effects of this boom, the country is now experiencing a gradual transition from excessive to intensive growth. What is interesting with regard to planning and construction is that China's accession to the World Trade Organization (WTO) promoted the trend towards the global marketplace. Large events which China has applied to host are responsible for the fact that the breath-taking dynamism of China's metropolises is keeping up momentum, but even here one can observe a gradual change from quantitative to qualitative development.

For the Olympic Games 2008 that are to be held in Beijing, the city will be subjected to a colossal urban restructuring and the World Expo of Leisure 2006 gives further important economic impulses, as does the coming World Exposition 2010 in Shanghai, the metropolis that has so far been regarded as a synonym for the Chinese construction boom. With these international events, China is positioning itself on the international architectural market. Formerly conservative Beijing especially – where a mere ten years ago high-rises still had to be built with pagoda-type roofs – today commissions representatives of the international architectural avant-garde (who a short while ago may still have smiled deprecatingly at the idea of building in China). Spectacular designs by Rem Koolhaas/OMA (headquarters of the Chinese state television CCTV); Herzog & de Meuron (Olympic Stadium); Paul Andreu (Opera House); PTW Architects, Sydney (Olympic Swimming Stadium) and Norman Foster (International Airport) are to give Beijing a modern face, and the People's Republic of China prestige, although at present it is not certain that the designs will actually be implemented.

Yet why, given the fact that it dominates the worldwide construction market, should China not strive for an important role in the international world of architecture? After having turned the entire world trade upside down, China has long since been playing in its own league class in almost every economic sector and can therefore only surpass itself. Another fact is that it is much easier to win the attention of the international media, and with it the international economic world, with architectural imports from abroad than with repeated record export figures. The skilfully staged architectural projects in Beijing play an important part in the Chinese strategy to direct international media attention to China as often as possible. So far, professional exchanges have been more or less unilateral, as Chinese architects have not been active internationally, while their western colleagues have worked successfully in China and been noticed by the Chinese media as well. An exception to the rule is the Beijing project "Commune of the Great Wall' which was awarded a prize at the Venice Architecture Biennale 2002. Its designers from Beijing, Hong Kong and Japan thus made an important contribution to contemporary architectural expression in China and in Asia as a whole. After decades of a Socialist planned economy – when there were neither architects nor architecture – in China there is now a huge backlog demand for architecture, technology and art.

Right from the beginning, over the past twenty years, foreign architects have had an important part in the unprecedented modernization of China. The country's second big leap forward would not have been possible without the import of foreign architectural skills and construction technology. The architects and builders

Architekten und Bautechnologie nicht denkbar gewesen. Sie kamen mit den Investoren aus den asiatischen Metropolen Hongkong, Singapur und Taiwan. Allerdings handelt es sich bei der Mehrzahl der rund 3.000 Hochhäuser, die der Bauboom Shanghai beschert hat, weniger um Werke einzelner Architekten als um Massenprodukte überwiegend Hongkonger Immobilien- und Bauunternehmen, die – wie in Asien üblich – über große eigene Architektenabteilungen verfügen. Nicht zufällig waren die ersten namhaften Architekten ausländische Chinesen wie I.M. Pei mit dem Fragrant Hill Hotel in Peking (1982) oder Dennis Lau & Ng Chun Man mit dem CITIC Plaza (1995)[1]. Mit der Öffnung der chinesischen Exportwirtschaft kamen dann auch Architekten aus dem Westen, zunächst im Gefolge der Investoren aus den USA und Hongkong, erst viel später aus Europa. Beispiele guter Hochhausarchitektur in Shanghai seit 1996 sind u.a. Xin Mao Tower von SOM, Chicago, World Financial Centre von KPF, New York oder Wan Xiang Plaza von Ingenhoven, Overdiek & Partner, Düsseldorf.

In den vergangenen zehn Jahren hat sich die Zahl der ausländischen Architekten auf dem chinesischen Markt vervielfacht, auch deutsche Architekten, Stadtplaner, Landschaftsplaner und Ingenieure haben auf vielfältige Art und Weise am Baugeschehen in China teilgenommen. Deutsche Architekten entdeckten den chinesischen Markt viel später als ihre Konkurrenten aus den USA, Kanada, Australien, Frankreich oder Großbritannien, aus Gründen fehlender Auslandserfahrung und weil die Wiedervereinigung seit 1990 einen komfortablen heimischen Bauboom bescherte. Neben den spektakulären Auftritten großer Büros wie gmp (von Gerkan, Marg und Partner) oder AS&P (Albert Speer & Partner GmbH), über die die Medien im Rahmen des allgemeinen Chinabooms berichten, ist das Betätigungsfeld mittlerweile viel breiter und umfasst einerseits den akademischen Austausch, Lehraufträge an chinesischen Hochschulen, Studienreisen usw., auf der anderen Seite Kooperationen mit jungen chinesischen Büros, die für die meisten kleineren Büros hier zu Lande oft die einzige Möglichkeit bieten, an Projekten oder Wettbewerben in China mitzuarbeiten.

Traditionell besitzt Technik aus Deutschland in China einen guten Ruf, Ingenieurwissen vor allem, während heute bei jungen chinesischen Architekten das Bauhaus hoch im Kurs steht. Erste fachliche Kontakte entstanden Mitte der 1980er-Jahre in der Kooperation der TH Darmstadt mit der Tongji Universität in Shanghai, die aus der dort 1907 gegründeten deutschen Medizinschule hervorging. Eine gewisse Vorreiterrolle unter den deutschen Architekten und Planern hatte das Büro AS&P – Albert Speer & Partner aus Frankfurt, das sich als internationaler Consultant versteht und seit Ende der 1960er-Jahre im Ausland plant und baut. Die Teilnahme an der Chinareise des damaligen Bundesbauministers Klaus Töpfer führte Prof. Albert Speer 1994 zum ersten Mal nach China. Damals war der Aufstieg Chinas zur globalen Wirtschaftsmacht, angestoßen durch die Hinwendung zur Marktwirtschaft nach Maos Tod 1976 unter Deng Xiaping, bereits in vollem Gang und das enorme Potenzial in dem Riesenland verheißungsvoll. In ökologisch nachhaltigen Planungskonzepten war die Marktlücke erkannt, die zum ersten Engagement des Büros in China im Jahre 1994 führte. Zehn Jahre später organisierte AS&P über eine Repräsentanz in Shanghai mit einem Geschäftsführer vor Ort eine große Zahl von Projekten überall in China, die zunehmend in einem Netzwerk mit chinesischen Partnern entworfen werden.

Bei gmp, den erfolgsreichsten deutschen Wettbewerbsarchitekten, waren es erwartungsgemäß Wettbewerbe, die den Einstieg nach China vermittelten. Auf die Deutsche Schule in Peking, das erste Bauvorhaben in China, das 2001 fertiggestellt war, folgte eine Serie von Projekten und die Gründung eines Büros in Peking mit einem eigenen Entwurfsteam vor Ort. Unter den internationalen Architekten ist gmp in Peking mit den meisten Arbeiten vertreten.

came together with the developers from the Asian metropolises of Hong Kong, Singapore and Taipeh. However, most of the roughly three thousand new high-rises the construction boom produced in Shanghai were not the creations of individual architects, but of Hong Kong property developers and contractors who, as is the custom in Asia, had their own large architectural departments. It was no coincidence that the first famous architects commissioned in China were expatriate Chinese, among them Ieo Ming Pei (Fragrant Hill Hotel, Beijing, 1982) and Dennis Lau & Ng Chun Man (CITIC Plaza, 1995).[1] The establishment of the Chinese export market then also brought western architects into the country, the first following investors from the United States and Hong Kong and, much later, from Europe. Among the examples of good high-rise architecture built in Shanghai since 1996 are the Xin Mao Tower by SOM, Chicago, the World Financial Centre by KPF, New York, and the Wan Xiang Plaza by Ingenhoven, Overdiek & Partner, Düsseldorf.

In the past decade, the number of foreign architects active in China has multiplied, among them German architects, urban and landscape designers who have participated in various ways in the construction industry of the country. The fact that German architects discovered China as a market much later than their competitors from the States Canada Australia, France or Great Britain was due to lack of experience acquired abroad and the domestic construction boom in Germany after reunification in 1990. Apart from the spectacular projects of large partnerships such as gmp (von Gerkan, Marg and Partners) or AS&P (Albert Speer & Partners Ltd.) reported by the media in Germany in connection with the general "run on China", the scope of activity has widened and now includes academic exchanges; teaching assignments at Chinese universities; study excursions, etc., as well as co-operations with young Chinese offices. For most smaller German architectural firms, the latter often represent the only inroad to working on projects or competition designs in China.

Traditionally, German technology – in particular mechanical engineering – has a good reputation in China, while today young Chinese architects have a high regard for the Bauhaus school. In the mid-1980s, first professional contacts were established between Darmstadt Technical University and Tongji University in Shanghai, the successor institution to the German medical school founded there in 1907. To some extent, Albert Speer & Partners, Frankfurt/Main – who see themselves as international architectural consultants and have been planning and building abroad since the late 1960s –, paved the way for subsequent activities in China by German architects and planners. When Klaus Töpfer, then Federal Minister of Building, went to China on an official visit in 1994, Professor Albert Speer was among his entourage. At that time, China's rise to global economic power, initiated by the government under Deng Xiaoping who, after Mao's death in 1976, had opted for a market economy, was already in full swing. The enormous potential of that vast populous country promised well. Speer & Partners recognized ecologically sustainable projects as a gap in the market and started working in China in 1994. Ten years on AS&P, via their Shanghai branch office with a local manager, have designed and co-ordinated a large number of projects all over China increasingly with a network of Chinese partners. As was to be expected, the office of gmp, the most successful German architects in competitions, won commissions in China via competition designs. Their first, the German School in Beijing, was completed in 2001, followed by a string of other projects and the establishment of a gmp branch office in Beijing with its own team of designers. Among international architects gmp has designed the greatest number of projects in Beijing.

At a time of economic decline, an increasing number of German architects are naturally infected with the fascination by China that is constantly fuelled by the media. Today primarily smaller offices are in one way or another involved in projects in the People's

Die Faszination, die von China ausgeht und durch die Medien ständig transportiert wird, erfasst in Zeiten anhaltender Rezession natürlich immer mehr deutsche Architekten, und heute sind es vor allem auch kleinere Büros, die auf die eine oder andere Art mit Projekten in China beschäftigt sind. Die Architekten vollziehen damit einen Trend in der Wirtschaft nach, wonach immer mehr mittelständische deutsche Firmen den „Sprung auf den Drachen" wagen, während für Unternehmen mit globaler Ausrichtung die Präsenz in China heute längst eine Überlebensfrage ist.

Mit dem erwarteten Wandel zu mehr Qualität in der Entwicklung bei nachlassender wirtschaftlicher Dynamik relativieren sich auch einige der Vorbehalte gegenüber dem chinesischen Modernisierungsmodell. An dessen Grundpfeilern, Parteidirigismus gepaart mit neoliberalem Wirtschaftsstil, wird sich indessen so schnell nichts ändern, hat sich diese historisch einmalige Form einer Entwicklungsdiktatur in der Aufbauphase doch als äußerst effizient erwiesen. In dem atemberaubenden Veränderungsdruck der großen Städte sind aber auch die Schattenseiten des Booms sichtbar geworden. Der exzessive Hochleistungs-Urbanismus, dessen Tempo darauf beruhte, daß Expansionspläne ungehindert von demokratischen Verfahren in Rekordzeit aufgestellt und dann von privaten Investoren im Hau-Ruck-Verfahren ohne Rücksicht auf lokale Interessen durchgesetzt wurden, oft von Zwangsumsiedlungen begleitet, stößt an Grenzen physischer Machbarkeit und sozialer Akzeptanz. Auch wenn es noch einige Jahre dauern wird, bis die kürzlich in der Verfassung verankerten Bürgerrechte in der städtebaulichen Praxis eine Rolle spielen, unausweichlich wird Planung auch in China allmählich die gesellschaftlichen Veränderungen, unter anderem der Bildung eines neuen Mittelstands, widerspiegeln und damit auch an Effizienz im Sinne einer nachhaltigen Entwicklung gewinnen.

Angesichts des erreichten Fortschritts fällt es China heute leichter, die Kehrseite des wirtschaftlichen Wachstums anzusprechen. Dem rasanten Wohlstand in den Küstenregionen, den schon immer von der Natur begünstigten Fisch- und Reistöpfen Chinas, stehen immer krassere Armutsregionen im Hinterland gegenüber, sowohl in den traditionellen Agrargebieten als auch in den fast vollständig zusammengebrochenen alten Industriestandorten. Aber auch in den Metropolen selbst ist die Kluft zwischen Arm und Reich tiefer geworden. Beschleunigt wurde dieser Prozess durch das Heer der auf rund 300 Millionen geschätzten Wanderarbeiter, ohne die der Bauboom in den Metropolen, unter den historisch einmaligen Bedingungen einer Infrastruktur der 1. Welt, aber dem Lohniveau der 3. Welt, undenkbar gewesen wäre.

In dem Maße, in dem sich ein Wandel zu mehr qualitativem Wachstum vollzieht, eröffnen sich angesichts der fast grenzenlosen Perspektiven und Potenziale, die das Riesenland bietet, Chancen und Betätigungsfelder für ausländische Partner. Ein Transfer von Know-how ist vor allem dort gefragt, wo es um Erfahrungen mit ökologischem, Energie und Ressourcen sparendem Planen und Bauen, stadträumlichen Zusammenhängen, Qualität im öffentlichen Raum, Wohnquartiersentwicklung, Landschaftsplanung usw. geht. Europäische Beiträge sind dabei stärker gefragt als amerikanische, denn bei aller Imitationsfreude halten es die Chinesen doch eher mit den historisch älteren Vorbildern. China ist längst selbst Hochtechnologie-Standort und hat mit der Weltraumtechnik bewiesen, dass es über genügend Potenzial, Ehrgeiz und Talente verfügt, um seine Probleme selbst zu lösen. Indessen, China wäre nicht das einzige hoch entwickelte Land, das seine urbanen Probleme nicht in den Griff bekommt.

Bisher umfassen die Tätigkeitsbereiche ausländischer Architekten und Planer in der Regel städtebauliche Planungen, Entwicklung und Bau neuer Wohnquartiere, Industrieparks und natürlich alle Arten von öffentlichen oder gewerblichen Bauten. Vereinzelt kommt es zu Projekten außerhalb der großen Metropolen, etwa im

Republic. In this they follow the general trend in business and industry with ever greater numbers of medium-sized German firms hazarding the 'leap onto the dragon's back', while for large multinational corporations business in China has long since been a question of survival.

The expected shift from quantity to better quality due to slackening economic development also means that some reservations about the Chinese modernization model have been relativized. However, the main pillars of China's national economy – i.e. state control coupled with a kind of neo-liberalism – will not be demolished for some time as this historically unique form of dictated development proved most efficient at the initial stages. Yet the dark side of the economic boom, as a side-effect of the present breathtaking process of change, has also become apparent in the large cities. Excessive high-performance urbanism, and urban extensions implemented with record speed were only possible, because they were unfettered by democratic decision-making, erected at breakneck speed by private developers irrespective of local interests and accompanied by forced displacements – all this to the limits of physical feasibility and social acceptance. Even though it will take some years for the civic rights recently included in the constitution to affect urbanist practice, planning in China will inevitably reflect social changes such as the rise of a new middle class and thus also become more efficient in terms of sustainable development.

In view of the progress already achieved, China now admits more easily that economic growth has its drawbacks. The fast-growing wealth of the coastal regions blessed by nature – since millennia China's fish and rice pots – is countered by ever poorer hinterland regions, both in the traditional agrarian and the almost completely abandoned industrial areas. Even in the large cities, the gulf between rich and poor has widened. This process was accelerated by the multitude of itinerant workers – an estimated 300 million – without whom China's metropolitan construction boom (First-World infrastructures at Third-World wage levels) would have been inconceivable.

As the change towards more qualitative growth gains momentum, the almost infinite perspectives and potentials offered by this vast land will also open more and more opportunities and fields of activity to foreign partners. The transfer of skills and knowledge is in particular demand in the fields of ecological, energy-efficient and resource-saving planning and building; urban spatial relationships; high-quality public spaces; housing; landscape architecture, etc. European contributions are in greater demand than American ones as the Chinese – with their pleasure in copying – prefer older historic models. China has itself been a high-tech location for some time and has proved with its space technology that it has sufficient resources, potential, ambition and talent to solve its own problems. However, China would not be the only highly developed country not to come to grips with its urban problems.

So far, the fields of activity of foreign architects and urban planners have generally included urbanist projects, housing, industrial estates and, of course, all types of public or commercial buildings. In a few instances they have designed projects outside the large urban centres, for example leisure and tourist facilities, for which AS&P in particular have been able to use their international experience in the field. Among AS&P's local partners are young Chinese architects who studied in Germany and gained sufficient experience abroad before returning to China and establishing their own offices. Dong Wu with his Shanghai office, artform, for example, creates projects of a different type, i.e. careful urban redevelopments and conversions and monument preservation projects in small towns and medium-sized cities where foreign architects would come up against insurmountable cultural barriers.

Freizeit- und Tourismusbereich, wo beispielsweise AS&P eigene internationale Erfahrungen auf dem Gebiet einbringen konnte. Zum Netzwerk des Büros gehören mittlerweile junge chinesische Architekten, die in Deutschland studiert und dort genügend Erfahrung gesammelt haben, bevor sie zurück in China ein eigenes Büro gründeten. Zum Beispiel betreibt Dong Wu mit seinem Shanghaier Büro artform Projekte ganz anderer Art, die mit behutsamem Stadtumbau und Denkmalschutz in mittleren und kleinere Städten zu tun haben und in denen ausländische Architekten an unüberwindbare kulturelle Grenzen stoßen würden.

Stadtplanerische Aufgaben

Stadtplanung ist im sozialistischen China eine staatliche Angelegenheit. China verfügt über ein entwickeltes Planungssystem, das auf allen Ebenen bis hin zur einheitlichen Plangrafik im ganzen Land durchorganisiert ist. Aus dem Zusammenspiel kommunaler und regionaler Planungsbehörden mit den privatisierten, de facto aber halbstaatlichen Planungsinstituten entstand unter dem allgegenwärtigen Einfluss der kommunistischen Partei jene seltsame Melange aus Beaux Art und asiatischer Postmoderne, die Chinas Städte heute prägt und ihre Entsprechung in der neo-klassischen Anlage und Architektur der Wohnsiedlungen hat, die wiederum ausschließlich von privaten Investoren gebaut und vermarktet werden. Die Expansion der Städte führt zu einem radikalen Wandel der chinesischen Stadtstruktur, die den Verlust der traditionell engen Verflechtung von Wohnen und Arbeiten und damit die funktionale Trennung in Wohnen und Arbeiten zur Folge hat – mit den unvermeidlichen Verkehrsströmen, unter denen die chinesischen Großstädte immer mehr leiden. Die Masterpläne von Peking, Shanghai und der anderen Metropolen folgen fast einheitlich dem seit den 1960er-Jahren universellen Muster weit gespannter Straßenraster mit breit angelegten Erschließungskorridoren, die rasche Expansion und rationale Stadttechnik gewährleisten. Es sind meist einfache Pläne, die auf Wachstumsringen basieren, mit einem System aus Ringstraßen, Entwicklungsachsen, Grüngürteln zur Gliederung, Industriezonen, Satellitenstädten usw., und die in erster Linie dazu dienen, dem Stadtwachstum in einem bisher nie gekannten Tempo die nötige öffentliche Infrastruktur bereitzustellen, damit Investitionen durch privates Kapital möglichst reibungslos erfolgen. Den darin ausgewiesenen Wohn- und Industriegebieten war oftmals wenig mehr als ein grobes Straßenraster mit Nutzungszonierung vorgegeben. Eine zentrale Rolle in der Stadtentwicklung spielten seit Mitte 1980 die neuen Sonderwirtschaftszonen und später die Hightech-Parks, mit denen ausländische Investitionen in die moderne Industrieproduktion angelockt wurden, auf denen der gesamte wirtschaftliche Aufschwung Chinas in der Folgezeit beruhte. In technischer Hinsicht hat sich diese Planungsstrategie als äußerst effizient und robust erwiesen, Straßenbau und Stadttechnik haben mit dem enormen Flächenwachstum gerade in den riesigen Industriezonen Schritt zu halten vermocht, der beachtliche Infrastrukturaufbau, weil selbstverständlich oder weit gehend unsichtbar, wird bisher wenig gewürdigt.

Die weit gehend Marktmechanismen überlassene Stadtentwicklung folgt nordamerikanischen Vorbildern: auf der einen Seite immer höher verdichtete Stadtzentren nach dem Vorbild der Central Business Districts (CBD) und auf der anderen Seite fortschreitende Suburbanisierung, Hochhauswohnquartiere am Stadtrand bis hin zu Villengebieten in der ländlichen Umgebung, und schließlich die modernen Industrieparks, die aufgrund der Bodenpreise an die Peripherie abwandern. Neben der Hochhaussilhouette prägen die gewaltigen Verkehrsbauwerke das Bild der großen Städte. Die expandierende, streng nach Funktionen getrennte Stadtstruktur erzwingt Mobilität in fast allen alltäglichen Lebensbereichen, mit dem konventionell-modernen Stadtmodell hat sich China natürlich auch dessen Verkehrsprobleme eingehandelt. Nach der Eigentumswohnung steht das Auto auf der Wunschliste junger Familien in den Wohn-

Urban Planning Tasks

In Socialist China, urban planning is the domain of the state. The country has a highly developed, unified multi-level national planning system that is well organized and regulated right down to the harmonized style of graphic rendering. Communal and regional planning departments working together with privatized, yet in fact semi-state planning firms (under the all-pervading influence of the Communist Party) have produced that curious melange of Beaux-Arts and Asian Postmodernism that marks China's cities today and is matched by the neo-classical layouts and architectural designs of housing estates funded and marketed exclusively by private developers.

Urban extensions cause fundamental changes in the traditional structure of China's cities, i.e. the loss of the closeness, or the separation, of working and living and the concurrent inevitable heavy traffic which many Chinese cities are increasingly suffering from. The masterplans for Beijing, Shanghai and other large cities are based on a straightforward system of ring roads, development axes, green belts as organizing elements, industrial zones, satellite towns, etc.. They are designed to provide the necessary public infrastructures to promote urban growth at an unprecedented speed and to make private capital investments in building as easy and attractive as possible. The zoning of residential and industrial areas has often provided little more than a rough street grid and assignment of uses to certain areas. As of the mid-1980s, the new privileged business and industrial districts and after that the high-tech parks (created to attract foreign investments in China's modern industrial production) have played a central role in paving the way for the country's entire subsequent economic upswing. Technically, this planning strategy has proved highly efficient and robust. The construction of roads and municipal service facilities has kept pace with the enormous urban expansion especially of the huge new industrial districts. This remarkable infrastructural achievement has received little attention so far as it seems self-evident and is for the most part invisible.

China's current urbanization is basically left to market mechanisms and follows the North-American pattern, on the one hand with increasingly dense central business and commercial districts and on the other with sprawling suburbs; high-rise quarters at the periphery; high-class residential estates in close-by rural environments and, finally, modern industrial districts outside the city where building land is cheaper. Apart from the high-rise skylines, the large cities are characterized by their enormous traffic structures. The expanding urban fabric, strictly divided into separate functional zones, demands mobility in almost every area of daily life so that China has not only adopted the conventional modern urban model, but has inevitably also acquired its traffic problems. On the list of desirables of young Chinese families, a car figures second after the owner-occupied flat, while motorization is massively promoted by the state which also pushes automobile production. The question will not only be what this will mean for global CO_2 emissions, but also whether the Chinese road construction effort will be able to keep up with the pace of urban motorization. While western countries build streets reserved for bicycles, China bans cycles – the traditional mass vehicle – from the inner cities of Beijing and Shanghai to make way for the car, the new status symbol. Of course, new satellite cities are provided with rail links, but otherwise the planning of urban extensions pays little attention to local/suburban public transport. Motor traffic corridors have over-wide lanes which, depending on changing demand, can be adapted to include railway lines or bus lanes.

On a marginal note, even public green areas are used according to the principle of maximum efficiency. Landscaped green spaces, cared for by gardeners, invariably accompany the large new traffic arteries where it is most visible. This is a kind of 'Potemkin

vororten, gleichzeitig wird die Motorisierung durch die staatlich forcierte Automobilproduktion massiv vorangetrieben. Die Frage wird neben den Folgen für den globalen CO_2-Ausstoß sein, ob der Straßenbau mit dem Tempo der Motorisierung in den Städten Schritt halten kann. Es sieht so aus, als würde China alle negativen Erfahrungen mit dem Individualverkehr in Städten wiederholen. Während man im Westen Fahrradstraßen einrichtet, werden in China Fahrräder, das traditionelle Fortbewegungsmittel der Massen, aus Innenstadtstraßen in Peking und Shanghai verbannt, um Platz für das Auto, dem neuen Statussymbol, zu machen. Gleichzeitig werden in den chinesischen Metropolen moderne öffentliche Nahverkehrssysteme wie U- und S-Bahnen auf- und ausgebaut. Während neue Satellitenstädte selbstverständlich eine Schienenanbindung haben, ist die Stadterweiterung ansonsten kaum am öffentlichen Nahverkehr ausgerichtet. Erschließungskorridore mit überbreiten Trassen sollen eine spätere Anpassung an den Verkehrsbedarf in Form von Bahnlinien oder Busspuren gewährleisten.

Am Rand sei erwähnt, wie selbst öffentliches Grün unter dem Prinzip größtmöglicher Effizienz eingesetzt wird: Gestaltetes und gärtnerisch intensiv gepflegtes Grün wird stets entlang der großen neuen Stadtachsen angelegt, wo es den größten sichtbaren Effekt hat, Potemkinscher Landschaftsbau gewissermaßen, in dem der dekorative Wert über der sozialen Funktion steht. Flüsse und Wasserläufe als Strukturelemente einer Landschaft einzusetzen ist hingegen relativ neu.

Ausländer spielen auf der Ebene der Stadtplanung so gut wie keine Rolle, sieht man einmal ab von den städtebaulichen Entwürfen für einige Satellitenstädte mit internationalem Prestige oder Priorität, die aber in der Gesamtheit des Planungsgeschehens in Chinas Städten kaum ins Gewicht fallen. Dieses vollzieht sich in einem für Außenstehende sowieso kaum nachvollziehbaren Beziehungsgeflecht zwischen Partei, Stadtverwaltung und Investoren, das weder öffentlich ist noch einer Kontrolle außerhalb der Behörden unterliegt, da solche Institutionen bisher fehlen. Die zwischen Partei und Verwaltung eng verflochtenen Entscheidungsstrukturen begünstigen natürlich Fehlplanungen. An der städtebaulichen Planung beteiligt werden häufig die zwar privatisierten, de facto aber immer noch halbstaatlichen Planungs- oder Entwurfsinstitute, die nach wie vor allein zur Aufstellung von Bebauungsplänen nach dem nicht unkomplizierten chinesischen Planungsrecht berechtigt sind. Gleiches gilt auch für die Bauausführung im Hochbau. Eine Besonderheit sind die Entwurfsinstitute der großen Universitäten wie Tsinghua in Peking und Tongji in Shanghai, die selbstständig auf dem Markt auftreten und bis auf die formalen Bebauungspläne die gleichen Leistungen vom Städtebau bis zum Hochbau anbieten wie die ehemals staatlichen Institute. Aufgrund ihrer kommerziellen Betätigung sind sie finanziell bestens ausgestattet. Wegen der eingeschränkten Tätigkeitsfelder und der Konkurrenz der halbstaatlichen und universitären Institute haben es die freien Planungs- und Architekturbüros, die seit Mitte 1990 offiziell in China wieder zugelassen sind, natürlich schwer und sind daher noch wenig entwickelt.

Mit der Veranstaltung internationaler Wettbewerbe bei wichtigen Projekten kam in den letzten Jahren erstmals Bewegung in die Städtebaudiskussion in China. Man erhofft sich durch die Beteiligung von Ausländern einen Erfahrungsaustausch, der es den chinesischen Teilnehmern, zumeist den halbstaatlichen Planungsinstituten und den Universitätsinstituten ermöglichen soll, auch auf diesem Gebiet Anschluss an die internationale Entwicklung zu finden. Die anfänglich schroffen Gegensätze zwischen den Entwürfen der Ausländer und denen der Chinesen, deren Architektenausbildung immer noch stark der Beaux-Art-Tradition verhaftet ist, haben sich in der Zwischenzeit angeglichen. Grob betrachtet sind die chinesischen Städtebauentwürfe sachlich-moderner geworden, aus den Entwürfen sind die großen Achsen, Symmetrien und neoklassisches Dekor weit gehend verschwunden, während die Aus-

landscape' in which decorative value is more important than social usefulness. Using streams and bodies of water to structure a green area, is relatively new.

Foreigners have practically no part in urban planning projects, the few exceptions being designs for a small number of satellite towns with international prestige or priority projects which, compared to the entire planning volume in Chinese cities, are negligible. Urban planning happens in a complex web of relations and dependencies – impossible for foreigners to penetrate – between party, city administration and developers and is neither open to public review nor controlled by public inspectorates (which do not yet exist). Of course, the decision-making procedures within this closely entwined mesh of party and administration officials favour deficient planning. The privatized, but in fact still semi-state planning and/or design firms are the only ones entitled (according to the quite complicated Chinese building laws) to develop masterplans and zoning maps. The same applies to construction. Design institutes of large universities like Tsinghua in Beijing and Tongji in Shanghai act as independent design offices and offer the same urban and architectural design services (except for official zoning plans) as the formerly state-run planning departments. As they are profit-oriented, they are financially well-equipped. As a result of the limited fields of activity open to them, and due to competition from semi-public firms and university design institutes, the independent planning and architectural offices – since the mid-1990s officially allowed to operate in China – are having a tough time and are therefore still 'underdeveloped'. In recent years for the first time, triggered by international competitions for important architectural projects, the urban design debate has gained momentum in China. Involving foreigners and exchanging experiences with them will, it is hoped, enable Chinese contributors – most of them semi-public and university planning institutes – to catch up with international developments. The initial extreme differences between designs by foreign architects and those by their Chinese counterparts – whose architectural education is still deeply rooted in the Beaux-Arts tradition, have since become less marked. Generally speaking, the Chinese urban designs have become more functional and modern with almost none of the great axes, symmetries and neo-classical décors of the past, while foreign architects have learnt to adapt their designs to specific Chinese preferences such as theme architecture and formality. Due to the extremely short competition periods, there is no time anyway for the thoroughness of detailed planning customary in Europe, and competition projects cannot escape the Chinese tendency to symbolic formal expression. The examples clearly show that the designs submitted for competitions unavoidably replicate certain patterns. In many cases, German offices won through in competitions with architects from other European countries, the United States, Australia, Japan or Hong Kong. AS&P gained the commission for building the International Automobile City in Shanghai-Anting and the office of gmp that for the new harbour city of Luchaogang via international design competitions. Thus two of the new Chinese satellite towns have been designed (and will be partly built) by German architectural partnerships. Both AS&P and gmp are among the reputable foreign firms who, together with Chinese colleagues, are regularly invited to participate in competitions for projects in China. Other German offices are working on urban development projects. The successful German players have thus given the Chinese a better understanding of German competition culture and of European urban design.

As shown by the projects presented in this book, there is a distinct continental-European urban design of a rational austerity that seems to match Confucianism, but is not favoured everywhere in China. However, gmp's design for Luchao proves that formal austerity is possible even in a large geometric building if it represents a formal symbol, in this case a drop of liquid. The fact that there is yet another kind of modernism in China, i.e. from the time when Maoist China extended

länder gelernt haben, in ihren Entwürfen auf spezifisch chinesische Bedürfnisse wie der Vorliebe für das bild- und formelhafte Rücksicht zu nehmen. Unter dem enormen Tempo, in dem die Wettbewerbe durchgeführt werden, bleibt für die in Europa übliche Entwurfstiefe sowieso keine Zeit und die Wettbewerbsproduktion kann sich dem chinesischen Hang zu einer einprägsamen, symbolhaften Formensprache nicht entziehen. Dabei bleibt nicht aus, wie anhand der Beispiele unschwer zu erkennen ist, dass die verschiedenen Wettbewerbsentwürfe gewisse Muster replizieren.

In vielen Fällen konnten sich dabei auch deutsche Büros bei Wettbewerben gegen Konkurrenten aus europäischen Ländern, den USA, Australien, Japan oder Hongkong durchsetzen. AS&P – Albert Speer & Partner hat den Planungsauftrag für die Internationale Automobilstadt in Shanghai-Anting ebenso über den internationalen Wettbewerb gewonnen wie gmp für die neue Hafenstadt Lingang. Damit werden zwei der neun Satellitenstädte um Shanghai von Deutschen entworfen und zum Teil auch gebaut. Beide Büros gehören zu den renommierten Ausländern in China, die regelmäßig zu Wettbewerben mit internationaler und chinesischer Beteiligung eingeladen werden. Andere deutsche Büros sind mit städtebaulichen Projekten beschäftigt. Die erfolgreichen Protagonisten haben den Chinesen damit sowohl deutsche Wettbewerbskultur als auch europäischen Städtebau näher gebracht.

Wie die Beiträge in diesem Buch zeigen, gibt es einen unverkennbar mitteleuropäischen Städtebau, der durch rationale Strenge fast konfuzianisch daherkommt, aber nicht überall in China ankommt. Auf der anderen Seite zeigt der Entwurf von gmp für Lingang, dass formale Strenge auch in einer geometrischen Großform möglich ist, wenn darin eine symbolhafte Form, in diesem Fall der Tropfen, verkörpert wird. Dass China noch eine ganz andere Moderne aus der Zeit der Stadterweiterung für die Schwerindustrie im maoistischen China besitzt, etwa der Satellitenstadt Minhang in Shanghai, die nach 1959 ganz im Zeichen des Funktionalismus entstand und auf sowjetische Einflüsse zurückgeht – sie ist bei uns durch Veröffentlichungen möglicherweise bekannter als in China. Wettbewerbsentwürfe von AS&P für Jiading (Juyuan Water Parks), einer Industriestadt jener Epoche bei Shanghai, knüpfen an die Tradition lang gestreckter kubischer Zeilen mit horizontalen Fensterbändern ebenso an wie Otto Steidles Wohnquartier „Beijing Image".

Immobilienmarkt

Neben den produktiven Investitionen ist der Immobilienmarkt zum höchst profitablen Betätigungsfeld geworden, der über die Vergabe von Nutzungsrechten – in der Volksrepublik gibt es Privateigentum an Gebäuden, an Grund und Boden aber nur Nutzungsrechte – effektiv gesteuert wird. Zumal Privatunternehmer und kommunistische Partei meist eng miteinander verflochten sind, garantiert dies ein rasantes Entwicklungstempo ohne Widerstände oder Kontrolle und den Privatunternehmern so enorme Gewinne. Die weltweite Immobilienflaute lässt viele deshalb begierig nach China blicken. Auch auf diesem Markt ist man um Internationalisierung bemüht, wie die erste große Immobilienmesse in China, die Expo Real in Shanghai 2004 zeigte. Seit 2004 muss die Vergabe von Nutzungsrechten zwar im öffentlichen Bieterverfahren erfolgen, aber der komplizierte, bisher nur vage gefasste rechtliche Rahmen macht den Immobilienmarkt anfällig für alle Arten von wilder Spekulation und Korruption, in dem nichts ohne Beziehungen geht. Dieses Verfahren steht einem breiten Engagement nicht-chinesischer ausländischer Investoren entgegen.

Wohnungsbauprojekte

Einer der interessantesten Bereiche, in denen die Übertragbarkeit europäischer Städtebaumuster an kulturelle Grenzen stößt, betrifft die in Rekordtempo um die Großstädte wachsenden Wohnsiedlungen und

its cities with heavy-industrial zones such as Shanghai's satellite town of Minhang which was built in 1959 still utterly faithful to functionalist design and Soviet influences. Through publications Minhang is possibly better known in the West than in China itself. AS&P's competition projects for Juyuan Water Parks, another industrial city of around 1960 near Shanghai, follows the tradition of both ribbon development with window bands and Otto Steidle's residential quarter, 'Beijing Image'.

The Property Market

Apart from investments in industrial production, the Chinese property market has become a highly profitable field of activity that can be efficiently controlled (the People's Republic allows private ownership of buildings, but only the usufruct of land). Most Chinese private entrepreneurs have close connections with and depend on the Communist Party. This guarantees speedy progress with developments without resistance or restrictions -- and enormous profits for private companies. Given the worldwide lull in the property market, many covetously look to China for relief. In this market, too, property dealers/developers strive for globalization, which was proved by the first large property fair in China, the Expo Real in Shanghai 2004. As of 2004, usufruct licences must be granted via public tendering procedures, but the complicated legal framework (as yet only vaguely formulated) makes the property market susceptible to all kinds of wild speculations and corruption. Nothing works without 'pulling strings'. This counteracts any non-Chinese foreign investments on a larger scale.

Housing Projects

One of the most interesting developments, in which the transfer of European urban design patterns comes up against cultural barriers, is the mushrooming – in record time – of new housing estates and satellite towns around the large cities. One essential driving factor behind the 'building frenzy' in China's, and for that matter Asia's, metropolises is the enormous demand for owner-occupied flats with modern amenities from the emerging middle class, especially from high-income young families, who wish to escape from cramped, dilapidated living conditions in the old over-populated urban districts. The razing of entire old residential neighbourhoods in Shanghai and Beijing to make way for new office and commercial buildings is also part of China's current social reality, as large groups of citizens are forcefully removed to new housing estates on the urban periphery without public transport connections, shopping facilities or job opportunities.

Despite the enormous changes in Chinese society over the past century – from the empire to the Socialist republic –, most especially as of 1990 under mounting pressure for transformation in every area and aspect of life, the old basic residential structures have demonstrated a surprisingly stubborn resistance. Though the traditional identity of living and working quarters has been lost in the modern urban fabric, the cellular spatial organization of these walled basic urban units is still reflected by the new residential developments. For the most part, this is due to the fact that housing blocks/ estates are built by individual developers to the same pattern, by covering sites, and sometimes entire districts, with independent and protected estates turned in upon themselves, so to speak. In the chaotic situation of rapidly redeveloping old industrial and new agricultural wastes, the pattern of these largely autonomous walled and gated communities offers investors certain advantages, and residents a certain sense of identity, security and basic utilities/amenities, including green spaces. When, a few years on, the urban environment has 'stabilized', the gated communities may open up so that interconnected urban areas may develop from ghetto-type structures.

Satellitenstädte. Ein wesentlicher Motor der Bauwut in den Großstädten Chinas wie überall in Asien ist die enorme Nachfrage des aufstrebenden Mittelstandes, vor allem junger einkommensstarker Familien, nach Eigentumswohnungen mit modernem Komfort, um den beengten, zum Teil schlimmen Wohnverhältnissen in den alten überbelegten Stadtquartieren zu entkommen. Zur sozialen Wirklichkeit gehört auch, dass mit dem Abbruch ganzer Wohnviertel in den alten Vierteln von Shanghai und Peking zu Gunsten von Büro- und Geschäftshäusern große Bevölkerungsteile gegen ihren Willen in Neubauquartiere an den Stadtrand verfrachtet wurden, ohne Verkehrsanbindung, Arbeits- und Einkaufsmöglichkeiten. Trotz der gewaltigen gesellschaftlichen Umbrüche der letzten hundert Jahre, vom Kaiserreich über die sozialistische Republik in die Marktwirtschaft, vor allem aber dem seit 1990 alle Lebensbereiche erfassenden Veränderungsdruck, haben die Wohnviertel in ihrer Grundstruktur ein erstaunliches Beharrungsvermögen bewiesen. Die überkommene Identität von Wohn- und Arbeitsort der traditionellen Wohnviertel ist zwar in der modernen Stadtstruktur verloren gegangen, die räumlichen Grundprinzipien jener in sich abgeschlossenen, von Mauern umgebenen traditionellen chinesischen Stadtzellen spiegeln sich jedoch auch in den modernen Neubauquartieren wider. Dies hat größtenteils damit zu tun, dass der Wohnungsbau durch einzelne Investoren nach dem gleichen Muster entsteht, und zwar in der Addition selbstständiger, introvertierter Einheiten, die bisweilen ganze Quartiere umfassen. Unter dem rasanten Tempo der Stadterweiterung in einem meist chaotischen Umfeld aus alten Industrie- und neuen Landwirtschaftsbrachen bietet dieses Muster der mit Mauer und Tor versehenen, in sich weit gehend autonomen Wohnquartiere dem Investor praktische Vorteile und den Bewohnern eine gewisse Identität, Sicherheit und eine Grundversorgung, zu der auch eine Grünfläche gehört. Stabilisiert sich das Wohnumfeld nach einigen Jahren, kann es durchaus sein, daß eine Öffnung nach außen eintritt und aus den ghettoähnlichen Gebilden allmählich zusammenhängende Stadträume entstehen. Mit Beginn des freien Wohnungsmarktes etwa um 1990 setzte sich diese Form der insulären, kommerziellen Wohnungsbauprojekte unter dem Begriff Micro Residential Districts MRD als chinesische Variante der amerikanischen Gated Communities überall durch. Seither ist der Wohnungs- und Immobilienmarkt durch die staatliche Förderung und großzügige Firmendarlehen zu einem wahren Eldorado für Investoren geworden. Verschiedene Autoren[2] weisen aber auch auf die Segregationstendenzen hin, die der freie Wohnungsmarkt für die soziale Topografie der Städte mit sich bringt. Auf der einen Seite formiert sich die Wohnbevölkerung in den neuen Quartieren streng nach Einkommen, wie das bei den amerikanischen Gated Communities der Fall ist, während auf der anderen Seite die unteren Einkommen auf dem privaten Wohnungsmarkt außen vor bleiben und entweder in die innerstädtischen Slums oder wie die Wanderarbeiter, das moderne Subproletariat, in Slums oder Squatter abgedrängt werden. Vieles deutet darauf hin, dass das Phänomen von Luxus und Armut, charakteristisch für die modernen Megastädte, aber auch für das alte Shanghai Anfang des 20. Jahrhunderts, zum Erscheinungsbild der chinesischen Großstädte gehören wird.

Neben der Zellenstruktur wird in den modernen Wohneinheiten auch noch ein anderes Grundprinzip chinesischen Wohnens streng bewahrt, nämlich die konsequente Südausrichtung der Wohnungen, was die alten Stadtviertel gleichsam magnetisch ausgerichtet erscheinen lässt, ähnlich dem europäischen Zeilenbau der 1920er-Jahre oder modernen Solarsiedlungen. Die typische Anlage besteht aus einer Nord-Süd-Achse, einem weiteren traditionellen chinesischen Raumelement, von der aus möglichst viele südorientierte Wohnungen erschlossen werden. Eine Studie des Städtebau-Institutes der Universität Stuttgart hat anhand der Wohnprojekte in Peking Anfang 2004 die damit zusammenhängenden mythologischen, bauphysikalischen und nachfragespezifischen Aspekte dargestellt[3]. Die Orientierung zur Sonne, auf der die Bautradition in ganz Ost-

From around 1990, from the beginnings of the free property market, this form of profit-oriented 'insular' housing projects became widespread and known as 'micro-residential districts (MRD)' – the Chinese versions of the US 'gated communities'. Since then, due to government subsidies and generous corporate funding, the housing construction and property market has become a developers' paradise. However, a number of authors[2] have pointed out that segregatory tendencies emerge in the social urban topography in the wake of the free residential property market. On the one hand, as in American gated communities, there is strict segregation between different income groups, while on the other hand people with lower incomes are excluded from the free housing market and are relegated to inner-city slums or, like the migrant workers (today's subproletariat) to suburban slums and squatter settlements. Many signs lead to the assumption that the phenomena of luxury and poverty, characteristic of the contemporary mega-city, but also of the old Shanghai of around 1900, will remain part of the image of China's large cities.

Apart from the cell structure, the modern residential units have preserved another basic feature of Chinese living quarters, i.e. their consistent south-orientation, as if they were all drawn that way by a magnet, similar to the European ribbon developments of the 1920s or modern solar-heated blocks. The typical housing layout has a north-south axis – another traditional Chinese space-shaping element which gives access to as many south-facing flats as possible. Early in 2004, The Urban Design Institute of Stuttgart Technical University published its study of Beijing's housing projects, including aspects of mythology, physics of construction and demand.[3] Solar orientation, a basic factor of building traditions all over eastern and central Asia also reflected by geomantic science or Feng-shui, probably originated with the Mongolian nomads who in winter opened their yurtas to the warmth of the sun and in summer protected them from its heat with simple means. The energetically as well as mythologically correct orientation therefore applied to the entrance, so that one enters the house from the south. It is a well-known fact that China's living and food culture was determined by the lack of heating fuels. Under Mao Zedong (Mao Tse-tung), heating in winter was entirely prohibited south of the Yangtse and even today the rule is still that every flat must have at least two hours of warming winter sun per day. Apartments without this are hard to sell and the market has been conditioned to avoid producing them, as heat insulation on west and east facades (that are most affected by outward temperatures) is still largely unknown in China. This energetically advantageous form of building has lost much of its efficiency due to the change from brick masonry to concrete, coupled with large windows and facade structures with negative effect on interior climates. Due to the growing demand for comfortable interior temperatures, air-conditioning systems are used everywhere from Beijing to Shanghai.

The European model of the perimeter street block has also remained largely unknown in China and investors still persistently stick to the traditional rules, while borrowing from every conceivable architectural period and style. To European architects who experienced the 1960s' change of paradigm from ribbon to street block development, the lack of urban spatial organization and the endless monotony of such residential projects therefore present special challenges. The three so far designed and built in China by German architects represent different approaches. With their Xinzhao Residential Area in Beijing, gmp have succeeded in creating a street block 'courtyard' surrounded by perimeter blocks and a high-rise, while Otto Steidle created patios by interconnecting the south-facing apartment blocks of his Beijing Image estate with transverse building sections. In this respect, the urban project of Anting New Town – marketed as 'German town' – also offers a unique field of experimentation. It is being built next to the International Automobile City of Shanghai-Anting and was explicitly designed as an example of German urban planning and housing. In addition, there

und Mittelasien beruht und sich in der Geomantik oder im Feng-shui widerspiegelt, geht im Ursprung vermutlich auf die Jurte der mongolischen Nomaden zurück – die Öffnung zur wärmenden Sonne im Winter, im Sommer mit einfachen Mitteln den Schutz vor der hoch stehenden Sonne. Zur energetisch wie mythologisch korrekten Ausrichtung gehört daher auch die Lage des Eingangs, sodass man das Haus von Süden betritt.

Bekanntlich war Chinas Wohn- wie Kochkultur vom Mangel an Heizmaterial bestimmt. Südlich des Jangtse war das Heizen im Winter unter Mao Tse-tung gänzlich verboten und noch heute gilt die Regel, dass jede Wohnung mindestens zwei Stunden wärmende Wintersonne erhält. Wohnungen, die davon abweichen, gelten als schwer verkäuflich und werden auf dem so konditionierten Markt daher auch kaum gebaut. Denn die besonders intensiver Strahlung ausgesetzten West- und Ostfassaden erfordern Dämmung und Sonnenschutz, beides ist in China bisher weit gehend unbekannt. Indessen hat diese energetisch günstige Bauform, insoweit auch ein Beispiel für nachhaltigen Wohnungsbau traditioneller Art, in ihrer modernen Ausformung durch Materialwechsel von Ziegel zu Beton, großen Fensteröffnungen und bauklimatisch ungünstiger Fassadengestaltung viel an Effizienz verloren. Von Peking bis Shanghai sind durch den gestiegenen Komfortanspruch heute überall Klimageräte im Gebrauch.

Das europäische Modell der Blockrandbebauung ist in China daher weit gehend unbekannt geblieben, und obwohl die neuen Wohnquartiere stilistische Anleihen an alle nur denkbaren Bauepochen und -formen aufweisen – an den traditionellen Regeln hält der Investorenmarkt ehern fest. Europäische Architekten, die den Paradigmenwechsel von der Zeile zum Block in den 1960er-Jahren noch miterlebt haben, fühlen sich durch die fehlende städtebauliche Raumbildung und die grenzenlose Monotonie solcher Quartiere denn auch in besonderer Weise herausgefordert. Die drei bisher in China von deutschen Architekten gebauten Wohnquartiere zeigen unterschiedliche Lösungsansätze. gmp ist es mit dem „Xinzhao Residential Area“ in Peking gelungen, mittels Zeilen und Hochhaus einen Blockinnenraum herzustellen, während das Wohnquartier „Beijing Image“ von Otto Steidle südgerichtete Zeilen durch Querriegel so miteinander verbindet, daß Binnenräume entstehen. Ein in dieser Hinsicht bisher einmaliges Experimentierfeld bietet auch die neue Stadt „Anting New Town“. Als „German Town“ vermarktet, entsteht sie in direkter Nachbarschaft der Internationalen Automobilstadt in Shanghai-Anting und soll explizit deutschen Städte- und Wohnungsbau demonstrieren. Außerdem ist auch noch ein holländisches und ein italienisches Stadtquartier in Shanghai geplant. Der postmodern anmutende Stadtgrundriss von „Anting New Town“ basiert im Prinzip auf einer klassischen Blockrandbebauung, die zwar an chinesische Baurichtlinien soweit angepasst wurde, aber von der üblichen Südausrichtung bei rund einem Drittel der Wohnungen abweicht, was unter den Investoren und Auftraggebern lange Zeit umstritten war. An dem Projekt waren neben AS&P – Albert Speer & Partner, die auch den Masterplan erstellten, vier weitere deutsche Büros mit Entwürfen für die Wohnungsbauten und die Stadtmitte beteiligt: ABB Architekten, Frankfurt, Auer & Weber, München, Braun & Schlockermann und Partner, Frankfurt, gmp – von Gerkan Marg & Partner, Hamburg sowie die Landschaftsplaner Wittig & Rietig, Weimar.

Mittels Außendämmung der Gebäude, Isolierglasfenster und Sonnenschutz soll ein komfortables Wohnen auch bei West- und/oder Ostausrichtung gewährleistet werden. Es bleibt abzuwarten, ob die fertigen Wohnungen eher von den Ausländern aus der Automobilstadt angenommen werden, wie der Investor vermutet, oder ob chinesische Familien mit fortschreitender Verwestlichung des Lebensstils die Qualitäten des Durchwohnens mit Morgen- und Abendsonne schätzen lernen. Im Massenwohnungsbau jedenfalls wird sich diese Wohnform bei allgemein zu niedrigen Energiekosten – Shanghai bildet hier eine Ausnahme – und deutlich teuren

are plans to build a Dutch and an Italian quarter in Shanghai. The postmodernist masterplan for Anting New Town, principally based on the classical perimeter street block, though largely adapted to Chinese building guidelines, deviated from the usual south orientation for about a third of the residential units, a point which for a long time was a bone of contention among developers and clients. Apart from AS&P – who authored the masterplan – four other German architectural partnerships contributed designs for residential buildings and the city centre, i.e. ABB Architects, Frankfurt/Main; Auer & Weber, Munich; Braun & Schlockermann and Partners, Frankfurt/Main, and von Gerkan Marg & Partners, Hamburg, together with the landscape planners of Wittig & Rietig, Weimar.

Heat insulation of the facades, double-glazing and sun shading systems are to guarantee comfortable interior temperatures even in east- or west-facing flats. Whether these will be more acceptable to the foreigners from the Automobile City – as the developer assumes – or to Chinese families who are increasingly adopting a western lifestyle and are therefore learning to appreciate the morning or evening sun, remains to be seen. Given that energy costs are generally too low (Shanghai being the exception) and costly heat insulation leads to considerably higher buying prices or rents, this new type of dwelling will not win through that quickly, at least not in mass housing. One design solution – the combination of linear and point blocks – preserves the traditional south orientation and is a variation of the perimeter street block with inner and outer open areas. It was tested in a number of competition designs by AS&P for sites in northern and southern China and thought feasible.

Environmental Problems

There is almost no other area, in which the Chinese hinder themselves in their project of modernization more than in environmental protection. Since the country's industrialization, the destruction and pollution of the environment have been glaringly obvious and are, of course, well known to present planners and politicians. Half a dozen Chinese cities with over a million inhabitants rank highest on the list of most polluted agglomerations. Over the past decade, though, air pollution has been markedly reduced as many large heavy-industrial plants were closed down. There have already been some water purification initiatives and China now has progressive environmental laws which even demand proof of environmental compatibility of every large building project. Yet the inherited structural problems are so serious that they can only be solved in the long term. They include the precarious hydroecology of the fertile delta land in the old locations of heavy industry such as Shanghai, where large agricultural areas are highly polluted with unidentified chemicals and heavy metal residues from industry. Under the primacy of economic growth, which constantly produces more causes of pollution than it eliminates, the chances of a sustainable improvement in environmental quality are slim. The country's enormous demand for energy, steel and concrete and the rapid increase in motor traffic volumes threaten to undo the improvements in air quality already achieved.

From the beginning of AS&P's activities in China, environmental aspects have played an essential role, and with every project, the office has endeavoured to promote environmentally sustainable planning concepts. As early as in 1997, in co-operation with the German engineering firms Fichtner (Stuttgart), RRI (Rhein-Ruhr Ingenieurgesellschaft) and Shanghai municipality, AS&P developed an ecologically motivated model project (Yangpu/Dinghai), including practical refuse material and energy recycling systems. One year later, the office won an international urban design competition for Jiangbei Town (an inner-city extension of notoriously air-polluted Chongqing) with a plan which complied faithfully with the aims of Agenda 21. On account of

Wohnungen aufgrund aufwändiger Dämmung jedenfalls nicht so schnell durchsetzen. Eine Lösung, die die Südorientierung beibehält und eine Art Blockform mit Innen- und Außenraum bildet, liegt in der Kombination von Zeilen und Punkthäusern. Sie wurde bei verschiedenen Wettbewerbsbeiträgen von AS&P in Nord- und Südchina getestet und als praktikabel empfunden.

Umweltproblematik

In kaum einem anderen Bereich steht sich die chinesische Modernisierung bei all ihren Leistungen derart selbst im Weg wie bei der Umweltproblematik. Seit der industriellen Entwicklung Chinas sind die Probleme der Umweltverschmutzung unübersehbar und Planern und Politkern selbstverständlich vertraut. Auf der Rangliste der am meisten verschmutzten Städte steht nach wie vor ein halbes Dutzend chinesischer Millionenstädte ganz vorn. Die Luftverschmutzung in den Großstädten ist in den letzten zehn Jahren durch die Stilllegung der Schwerindustrie deutlich verbessert worden. Es gibt Ansätze im Gewässerschutz und China verfügt inzwischen über ein fortschrittliches Umweltrecht, das sogar Umweltverträglichkeitsstudien bei größeren Maßnahmen verlangt. Aber die ererbten Strukturmängel sind derart gravierend, dass sie nur langfristig gelöst werden können. Dazu gehört in den alten Schwerindustriestandorten wie Shanghai die prekäre Gewässerökologie der fruchtbaren Deltagebiete, in denen ein großer Teil der landwirtschaftlichen Anbauflächen durch ungeklärte, chemieverseuchte Abwässer und schwermetallangereicherte Böden enorm belastet ist. Die Aussichten auf eine nachhaltige Verbesserung der Umweltqualität sind begrenzt unter dem herrschenden Primat des wirtschaftlichen Wachstums, das beständig mehr neue Umweltbelastungen schafft als alte löst. Der enorme Bedarf an Energie, Stahl und Beton und die rasante Zunahme des Straßenverkehrs droht die erreichten Verbesserungen der Luftqualität wieder rückgängig zu machen.

Umweltfragen waren deshalb für AS&P seit Anbeginn des Engagements in China ein konstantes Anliegen und das Büro hat sich bei allen Arbeiten stets um die Förderung nachhaltiger Planungskonzepte bemüht. Bereits 1997 wurde zusammen mit den zwei deutschen Ingenieurbüros Fichtner, Stuttgart, und RRI (Rhein-Ruhr Ingenieurgesellschaft) sowie der Stadt Shanghai ein ökologisch motiviertes Modellprojekt (Yangpu/Dinghai) bis hin zu konkreten Wertstoff- und Energiekreisläufen praxisnah entwickelt. Ein Jahr später wurde im notorisch luftverschmutzten Chongqing ein internationaler städtebaulicher Wettbewerb für die Innenstadterweiterung (Jiangbei Town) mit einem Konzept gewonnen, das konsequent den Zielen der Agenda 21 verpflichtet war. Auf diesen Erfahrungen aufbauend und als Beitrag zur deutsch-chinesischen Umweltkonferenz in Peking im Jahr 2000 wurde AS&P von der Zhangjiang High-Tech Park Development Corporation, dem Bundesministerium für wirtschaftliche Zusammenarbeit (BMZ) und der Deutschen Gesellschaft für Technische Zusammenarbeit (GTZ) beauftragt, in Kooperation mit chinesischen Partnern ein Planungskonzept zur nachhaltigen Entwicklung des Hightech-Parks im Stadtteil Pudong zu entwickeln. Auch bei dem im Jahr 2002 entwickelten Konzept für die Große Achse in Peking spielten ökologische Überlegungen wie Frischluftschneisen, Energie sparende Bauweisen bis hin zu einer modernen urbanen Landwirtschaft eine wichtige konzeptionelle Rolle. Seit 2002 arbeitet ein ehemaliger Mitarbeiter im nationalen Umweltinstitut in Peking mit.

Trotz viel deklamatorischer Unterstützung scheitern fast alle Vorschläge bisher an den fehlenden organisatorischen und institutionellen Voraussetzungen. Zwar sind die theoretischen Grundprinzipien einer nachhaltigen Stadtentwicklung wie in der Agenda 21 in China nicht gänzlich unbekannt, es fehlt aber an einer übergreifenden, horizontalen Kooperation aller relevanten Verwaltungsstellen (Planung, Verkehr, Finanzen) und sonstigen Trägern öffentlicher Aufgaben (Wasser, Abwasser, Energieerzeugung etc.). Effizientes Umweltma-

this experience, in 2000 AS&P were commissioned by Zhangjiang High-Tech Park Development Corporation, the German Federal Ministry for Economic Co-operation (BMZ) and the German Society for Technical Co-operation (GTZ) to design the sustainable High-Tech Park in the district of Pudong as a contribution to the German-Chinese Environmental Conference in Beijing. Ecological factors such as fresh-air corridors, energy-saving constructions and a modern urban agriculture also determined AS&P's 2002 design for Beijing's Great Axis. Since 2002 a former AS&P employee has been working in China's national environmental agency in Beijing.

Despite much 'declamatory support', almost all proposals for ecological architecture have miscarried because of the lack of organizational and institutional frameworks. While the basic theory of sustainable urban development as formulated in Agenda 21 is not altogether unknown in China, there is no overall 'horizontal' co-operation between all those involved, i.e. public departments (planning, traffic, finance) and other public suppliers and services (water, sewerage, energy, etc.). In these institutions with hierarchical power structures, efficient environmental management is not yet the order of the day and regularly fails because of compartmental attitudes. In addition, so far only a few authorities charge for environmentally relevant supplies and services such as fresh water, sewerage and waste disposal so that funding the necessary systems is difficult. In most cases, the creation of integrated infrastructures which make efficient use of available resources – e.g. integrated water supplies and sewerage; combined production of energy for heating and cooling and other components of resource-saving sustainable urban development – miscarries because of the inevitably protracted processes needed to develop and optimize such systems. In most cases there is enough technological potential, but as long as the extremely low energy costs do not provide the incentive to save energy, no developer will risk using decentralized, unconventional media systems. The government does not provide the incentives either and is reluctant to initiate or subsidize ecological pilot projects. Unlike the very large cities, the medium-large cities (medium by Chinese standards) offer better conditions for sustainable urban development. A number of have used gas instead of coal, district heating and 'clean' industrial production for some time and – like Weihai in Shandong, or Nanning in Guanxi Province, to name two geographically extreme examples – consistently pursue ecological aims.

In the mega-cities, however, the energy crisis becomes worse every summer when air-conditioning units in uninsulated buildings raise energy consumption to extreme peaks. The speed of development inevitably produces a loss of quality. So far anyway, it has not figured as a target in a highly speculative booming and insatiable market which has bought and sold almost anything, not least because there are no fixed quality standards whatsoever. Defective structures are the result of a construction practice based on unskilled labour and hand-crafting. One heritage of the former Socialist planned economy is the lack of skilled craftsmen in almost every building trade. The construction boom and a workforce made up of impoverished small farmers from urban surroundings and migrant workers from traditionally poor central Chinese provinces mutually condition each other. In no other city in the world has it been possible to build as cheaply as in Shanghai, Guangzhou, Shenzen or Beijing – but with correspondingly poor results. The dereliction of many buildings starts almost as soon as they have been completed; maintenance costs are prohibitive. The biggest problem, however, is the huge energy consumption of new buildings in China. Heat insulation and sun-shading are largely unknown. German architects have had to contend with this fact. Gmp, for example, had to fight for a long time for exterior sun-shading on a high-rise in Guangzhou, and AS&P only managed after lengthy discussions to convince the client and administrator of the Zhangjiang High-Tech Park in Shanghai to have the new administra-

nagement ist in den durch hierarchische Machtstrukturen geprägten Institutionen strukturell noch nicht gegeben und scheitert regelmäßig am Ressortdenken. Weiterhin ist die Erhebung von Gebühren für umweltrelevante Medien (Wasser, Abwasser, Müll) bisher nur in Ansätzen vorhanden, was die Finanzierung entsprechender Systeme erschwert. Der Aufbau vernetzter Infrastrukturen mit effizienterem Ressourceneinsatz, z.B. integrierter Wasserver- und -entsorgung, kombinierte Kraft-/Wärme- und Kälteerzeugung sowie anderen Komponenten einer Ressourcen schonenden, nachhaltigen Stadtentwicklung, scheitern meist an der unweigerlich langwierigen Entwicklungs- und Ausreifungszeit solcher Systeme. Die technologischen Möglichkeiten sind meist vorhanden, aber solange die viel zu niedrigen Energiekosten jeden Anreiz zum sparsamen Verbrauch nehmen, geht natürlich auch kein Investor das Wagnis dezentraler unkonventioneller Versorgungstechnik ein. Andererseits schafft der Staat selbst dazu bisher wenig Anreize und hält sich mit öffentlich geförderten Modellvorhaben zurück. Im Gegensatz zu den Metropolen sind die Voraussetzungen für eine nachhaltige Stadtentwicklung in den nach chinesischen Maßstäben kleineren Großstädten günstiger. Es gibt eine Reihe solcher Städte, die schon seit längerem auf Gas anstatt Kohle, auf Fernheizung und saubere Industrien umgestellt haben und die wie Weihai (Shandong) oder Nanning (Guanxi), um zwei geografisch extreme Beispiele zu nennen, konsequent an ökologischen Zielen ausgerichtete Leitbilder verfolgen.

In den Metropolen hingegen verschärft sich die Energiekrise in jedem Sommer, wenn der Stromverbrauch durch die Klimageräte in den ungedämmten Gebäuden in die Höhe schnellt. In dem rasanten Entwicklungstempo kommt Qualität zwangsläufig zu kurz. Sie war bisher auch kaum eine Zielgröße in dem hochspekulativen Boom, wo ein unersättlicher Markt fast alles absorbierte, nicht zuletzt weil Qualitätsstandards völlig fehlten. Baumängel sind die Folge einer Bautechnologie, die auf dem Einsatz vorwiegend ungelernter Arbeitskräfte und Handarbeit beruht. Ein Erbe der sozialistischen Planwirtschaft ist heute das Fehlen ausgebildeter Handwerker in fast allen Bauberufen. Bauboom und billige Arbeitskräfte durch den nie versiegenden Zustrom verarmter Bauern aus dem Umland und Wanderarbeitern aus dem traditionell armen Zentralchina bedingen sich gegenseitig. In keiner Metropole der Welt konnte jemals so billig gebaut werden wie in Shanghai, Guangzhou, Shenzen oder Peking. Das Ergebnis ist natürlich entsprechend. Bei vielen Gebäuden setzt der Verfall schon bei Fertigstellung ein, der Unterhaltungsaufwand ist enorm. Mit am problematischsten ist sicherlich der Energieverbrauch von Neubauten in China. Dämmung oder Sonnenschutz sind weit gehend unbekannt. Die deutschen Architekten haben damit ihre eigene Erfahrung gemacht. So kämpfte gmp lange für einen außen liegenden Sonnenschutz bei einem Hochhaus in Guangzhou. AS&P konnte erst nach langwieriger Überzeugungsarbeit den Bauherrn, immerhin die Verwaltung des Zhangjiang High-Tech Parks in Shanghai, zu einer Doppelglasfassade für die neuen Verwaltungstürme bewegen, bisher war das in Shanghai erst Norman Foster gelungen.

Chancen und Risiken

Nach wie vor werden in den meisten Fällen die Entwürfe ausländischer Architekten von chinesischen Büros realisiert und dabei auf das technisch wie gestalterisch machbare reduziert und oft entstellt. Als Erbe jahrzehntelanger sozialistischer Planwirtschaft sind Ausführungsplanung und Bauleitung noch immer das Privileg der aus den ehemals staatlichen Kombinaten hervorgegangen Planungs- und Entwurfsinstitute, denen die staatliche Lizenz das Monopol sichert. Architekten wurden wie andere selbstständige Berufe Opfer der anti-städtischen kommunistischen Politik nach 1949. Seit Mitte 1990 überhaupt erst wieder zugelassen, sind freie Büros in China genauso wie ihre ausländischen Kollegen beim Bauen auf die lizenzierten Institute

tion towers fitted with a double-glazed facade. Before that, Norman Foster had been the only one to succeed in doing so in Shanghai.

Opportunities and Risks

Now as then, most designs by foreign architects are implemented by Chinese offices which reduce them to their technically and aesthetically feasible minimum, and often disfigure them. As the heirs to the decades-old Socialist planned economy and state planning collective combines, the present planning and design institutes still hold the monopoly on state-licences for final planning and site management. Like other free professionals, architects became the victims of anti-urban Communist policies after 1949. Independent architectural practices were again permitted in China only in the mid-1990s and, just like their foreign colleagues, depend on the licensed planning institutes. This means that independent Chinese architects are severely hampered in their professional development; as a result there are relatively few of them. Joint ventures with Chinese partners are the only chance for foreign architects to influence the implementation of their designs, but do not always guarantee the desired quality of execution. Designs by OMA and Herzog & de Meuron especially were expected to bring a breakthrough in technological transfer, in particular as these designs require special engineering knowledge which is beyond the present skills of the Chinese construction industry. The transfer of western know-how might help to accelerate the liberalization of markets, which China has committed itself to by becoming a member of the WTO, and to create the framework for foreign architects and engineers establishing offices in China (copyright and warranty laws, list of fees).

Foreign architects have clearly been assigned the role of suppliers of ideas and are commissioned with their implementation only in exceptional cases. It is one of the rules of the Chinese market game that – given the uncertainties accompanying the country's frenzied construction efforts, i.e. missing quality standards and close competition – the activities of prominent foreigners in China must primarily lend Chinese projects prestige and exclusiveness. Good marketing demands unusual designs; and these represent the media attraction of China's architectural policy. Once the foreigners have done their PR-functional duty, the Chinese build the projects quite differently as Rem Koolhaas, Herzog & de Meuron or Zaha Hadid experienced with their designs for Beijing. Munich architect Gunter Henn suffered a similar fate with his spectacular design for the Beijing Automotive Expo. Yet since then, there has been mounting opposition inside China against Beijing's architectural policy, which in recent years has preferred foreign star architects for almost every large project. Chinese critics oppose the lavish extravagance of foreign designs which, as in the case of the Beijing Olympic Stadium, made omissions and modifications necessary for cost reasons, especially as the IOC had demanded financial viability as early as in 2003. As the criticism comes from academic circles, it is probably the outcome of a concerted action aiming to remove the shining foreign design examples staged in the media without loss of face for the government. Even younger Chinese architects are increasingly frustrated by foreigners being given preference, not least because they themselves only receive a fraction of the fees granted to foreigners, and because the usual fees in China do not allow them to produce real quality.

For a long time, everything foreign was regarded as superior to anything Chinese. This, of course, also benefited foreign architects. Until recently any project not presented by a western foreigner was thought to have no chance of success. The general uncertainty which came with the radical changes in the country, was aggravated by the fear of grave consequences from wrong decisions taken by an almighty planning bureaucracy unchecked by democratic processes.

angewiesen. Dadurch wird die chinesische Architektenschaft in ihrer Entwicklung natürlich stark behindert, mit der Folge, dass es relativ wenig selbstständige Büros gibt. Joint Ventures mit geeigneten chinesischen Partnern sind der einzige Weg für Architekten, Einfluss auf die Realisierung zu nehmen, garantieren aber nicht immer die gewünschte Qualität. Gerade von den Entwürfen von OMA und Herzog & de Meuron wurde ein Durchbruch im Technologietransfer erwartet, zumal diese Entwürfe ein ingenieurtechnisches Know-how in der Planung und Ausführung erfordern, das die heutigen Fähigkeiten der chinesischen Bauindustrie übersteigt. Dieser Austausch könnte dazu führen, daß die Liberalisierung der Märkte, zu der sich China durch die WTO-Mitgliedschaft verpflichtet hat, schneller vorankommt und die dafür nötigen Voraussetzung für die Niederlassung ausländischer Architekten und Ingenieure (Urheberrecht, Gewährleistung, Honorarordnung) geschaffen werden.

Unverkennbar haben die ausländischen Architekten die Rolle von Ideenlieferanten, werden aber in den seltensten Fällen mit der Ausführung betraut. Es gehört zu den Spielregeln des chinesischen Marktes, dass unter den Ungewissheiten, die das rasende Bautempo mit sich bringt – fehlende Qualitätsstandards und riesige Konkurrenz – das Engagement prominenter Ausländer in erster Linie dazu da ist, entsprechenden Projekten Exklusivität und Prestige zu verleihen. Zum Marketing gehört, dass oft besonders ausgefallene Entwürfe gefragt sind, was ja den medialen Reiz dieser Architekturpolitik in China ausmacht. Haben die Ausländer ihre PR-Funktion erfüllt, wird sowieso ganz anders gebaut, wie Rem Koolhaas, Herzog & de Meuron oder Zaha Hadid mit ihren Pekinger Entwürfen feststellen mussten. Ein ähnliches Schicksal erlitt der Münchner Architekt Gunter Henn mit seinem spektakulären Entwurf für die Peking Automotive Expo. Denn mittlerweile formiert sich im Land Widerstand gegen die Pekinger Architekturpolitik, die bei nahezu allen Großprojekten in jüngster Zeit ausländische Stararchitekten bevorzugt hat. Kritisiert wird die verschwenderische Extravaganz der Entwürfe, sodass bei der Realisierung des Pekinger Olympiastadions aus Kostengründen Abstriche gemacht werden, zumal das IOC bereits 2003 die Einhaltung von Wirtschaftlichkeit angemahnt hat. Da die Kritik aus akademischen Kreisen kommt, handelt es sich vermutlich um eine abgestimmte Aktion mit dem Zweck, die „Weißen Elefanten", also die medial inszenierten Vorzeigeentwürfe aus dem Ausland, ohne Gesichtverlust für den Staat wieder aus dem Verkehr zu ziehen. Aber auch bei den jüngeren chinesischen Architekten wächst der Frust über die Bevorzugung der Ausländer, nicht zuletzt weil sie bei Wettbewerben regelmäßig nur einen Bruchteil des Honorars der Ausländer erhalten und auch sonst die in China üblichen Honorare keine qualitätsvolle Bearbeitung erlauben.

Lange Zeit galt in China alles als überlegen, wenn es nur aus dem Ausland kam. Davon haben natürlich auch die Architekten profitiert. Bis vor kurzem war ein größeres Projekt so gut wie chancenlos, wenn es nicht von einem westlichen Ausländer präsentiert wurde. Zur allgemeinen Unsicherheit, die der rasante Wandel mit sich bringt, kommt das Risiko gewaltiger Fehlentscheidungen einer allmächtigen Planungsbürokratie ohne demokratische Kontrolle, wovor man sich durch die Beteiligung international erfahrener Ausländer zu schützen glaubt. Erwartungsgemäß werden weiterhin ausländische Architekten auf den chinesischen Markt drängen, die Konkurrenz wird sicherlich härter werden. Für deutsche Architekten könnte ein Wettbewerbsvorteil sein, dass Deutschland von allen Industriestaaten den Architekturimport am weitesten liberalisiert hat, ganz im Sinn der internationalen Arbeitsteilung, denn schließlich profitieren Exportländer wie Deutschland oder China am meisten von der Globalisierung.

Die Geschäftsbedingungen in China sind mit erheblichen wirtschaftlichen Risiken verbunden und alles andere als komfortabel. Jedenfalls war das Engagement für die dort schon länger tätigen Büros finanziell

Contributions by internationally experienced foreign architects were thought to provide protection against such risks. It is to be expected that foreign architects will continue to seek commissions in China and that the competition will intensify. The fact that of all industrialized countries Germany has liberalized architectural exports to the greatest extent, might give German architects the competitive edge, in line with the international division of labour for – after all – exporting countries like Germany or China benefit most from globalization.

Doing business in China involves considerable financial risks as general trade conditions are anything but promotive. In any case, the offices which have been active there for some time, have hardly made any profit, but in view of the experiences German exporters had had much earlier with Chinese partners this was to be expected. Yet this did not and does not prevent architects venturing out into the largest construction market of the world. The lack of domestic commissions no doubt contributes to the readiness of non-Chinese architects to contribute to this foreign business venture. By becoming a member of the WTO, China has committed itself to liberalization. It will take some years, though, for the Chinese to create the legal and other conditions for foreign architects to establish their own offices in the country (copyright, warranty, liability insurance, standard fees, etc.). Until then, joint ventures with Chinese partners will remain the right 'inroad', as not only language, but also cultural barriers form the almost insurmountable barriers to professional activities for all those who do not go to live in the country for several years.

Even though there are tremendous opportunities for German offices in China, it is not that easy to follow the cry, 'Auf nach China!' (Let's go to China!), as the title of a German magazine article on China recently read. Anybody who, over the past four years, has had a part in the breakneck development of Shanghai, this field of experimentation with dozens of competitions, will remember that we can always only make small contributions towards solving the huge problems of the Middle Kingdom. Such contributions are mostly restricted to the large cities, which will face enormous planning tasks once the estimated increase in China's urban population by about 500 million (today's population of EU countries) comes true. This population growth is expected to take place primarily in the cities of the Yangtse delta (Shanghai, Nanjing) and along the Pearl River (Guangzhou, Hong Kong, Shenzen) – of all places in the most fertile areas. Increasing metropolitan density will be accompanied by more air, soil and water pollution, which will require considerable improvements in environmental management. If there is any specific German know-how, then in the technological field where China has the greatest backlog demand. In general this includes improved facade components; HVAC; new integrated public supplies and services in the cities and combined heat and power systems which generally require co-operation with engineering firms and practical experience.

This book – the first attempt at a full documentation of the work of German architects in China – demonstrates graphically that they benefited from it themselves and represents a first comprehensive report on their 'Chinese experience'.

bisher kaum profitabel, was aber aufgrund der schlechten Erfahrungen, die die deutsche Exportindustrie schon wesentlich früher mit dem Chinageschäft gemacht hat, zu erwarten war. Weder damals noch heute hat man sich dadurch vom Engagement auf dem größten Baumarkt der Welt abschrecken lassen. Zweifellos wird die schlechte Auftragslage im Inland zum Interesse wie zur Risikobereitschaft am Auslandsgeschäft beitragen. Durch seine Mitgliedschaft in der Welthandelsorganisation WTO hat sich China zur Liberalisierung verpflichtet. Es wird jedoch noch einige Jahre dauern, bis die Voraussetzungen für die Gründung eigener Niederlassungen (Urheberrecht, Gewährleistung, Haftpflichtversicherung, Honorarordnung usw.) geschaffen sind. Joint Ventures mit chinesischen Partner bleiben der geeignete Weg, denn die kulturellen, nicht nur sprachlichen Hürden bilden ein fast unüberwindliches Hindernis für ein Engagement in China für jeden, der nicht mehrere Jahre im Land verbringt. Auch wenn sich in China enorme Chancen für deutsche Büros bieten, ganz so einfach ist es mit dem „Auf nach China" – wie kürzlich eine Zeitschrift einen Chinaartikel überschrieb – sicherlich nicht. Wer am furiosen Geschehen in den letzten vier Jahren in Shanghai teilgenommen hat, dem weltweit einmaligen urbanen Experimentierfeld mit Dutzenden von Wettbewerben, besinnt sich darauf, dass wir stets nur einen partiellen Beitrag zu den riesigen Problemstellungen im Reich der Mitte leisten können. Dieser beschränkt sich zumeist auf die großen Städte, denn dort stehen noch gewaltige planerische Aufgaben an, wenn die Prognosen eintreffen, nach denen China eine weitere Zunahme der Stadtbevölkerung von rund 500 Millionen, der heutigen EU-Bevölkerung, bevorsteht, zumal das Wachstum hauptsächlich in den Deltametropolen am Jangtse (Shanghai, Nanjing) und am Pearl River (Guangzhou, Hong Kong, Shenzen), ausgerechnet den fruchtbarsten Landesteilen, stattfinden wird.

Die Belastungen von Boden, Wasser und Luft werden mit zunehmender Verdichtung in den Metropolen weiter wachsen und ein deutlich besseres Umweltmanagement erfordern. Wenn es ein spezifisch deutsches Know-how gibt, so liegen die Zukunftschancen deutscher Büros sicherlich in den technologischen Bereichen, in denen China den größten Nachholbedarf hat. Generell sind das: beim Bauen verbesserte Komponenten für die Gebäudehüllen und die Gebäudetechnik und in der Stadtentwicklung neue integrierte Systeme der Ver- und Entsorgung, Kraft-/Wärme-Kopplung, die in aller Regel die Kooperation mit Ingenieurbüros und Praxisbezug erfordern.

Die vorliegende Dokumentation der Arbeiten deutscher Büros in China, die mit diesem Buch erstmals versucht wird, zeigt anschaulich, dass das Engagement für die Beteiligten ein Gewinn war und stellt damit zum ersten Mal einen Erfahrungsbericht zu diesem Thema zusammen.

Autor

Jürgen Frauenfeld, Architekt und Stadtplaner. 1974–1983 Partner bei AS&P – Albert Speer & Partner GmbH. Seit 1983 eigenes Planungsbüro in Frankfurt am Main. Gastdozent Technische Hochschule Darmstadt, Universität Frankfurt – Institut für Wirtschafts- und Sozialgeografie, Universität Stuttgart, Städtebau-Institut. Vorträge und Beratertätigkeit in China, Nigeria, Mexiko, Brasilien und Saudi Arabien.

About the Author

Jürgen Frauenfeld, architect and urban planner. From 1974–1983 partner with AS&P – Albert Speer & Partner GmbH (Ltd.). Established his own planning firm in Frankfurt/Main in 1983. Visiting lecturer at Darmstadt Technical University and Frankfurt University's Institute for Economic and Social Geography as well as the Urban Design Institute of Stuttgart University. Lectures and consultancy work in China, Nigeria, Mexico, Brazil and Saudi Arabia.

Quellenhinweise / Literature

1 Layla Dawson: Der große Sprung nach vorn, in: Baumeister 1/04
2 Eduard Kögel: Von der Nachbarschaft zur Gated Community, Planungsprinzipien der Stadt in der V.R. China, in: TRIALOG 81, 2/2004
3 Eckhart Ribbeck, Elmar Groß, Xiaowei Huo: Investoren-Städtebau in Peking, Schöner Wohnen, in: db deutsche bauzeitung 8/2004

PROJEKTE
PROJECTS

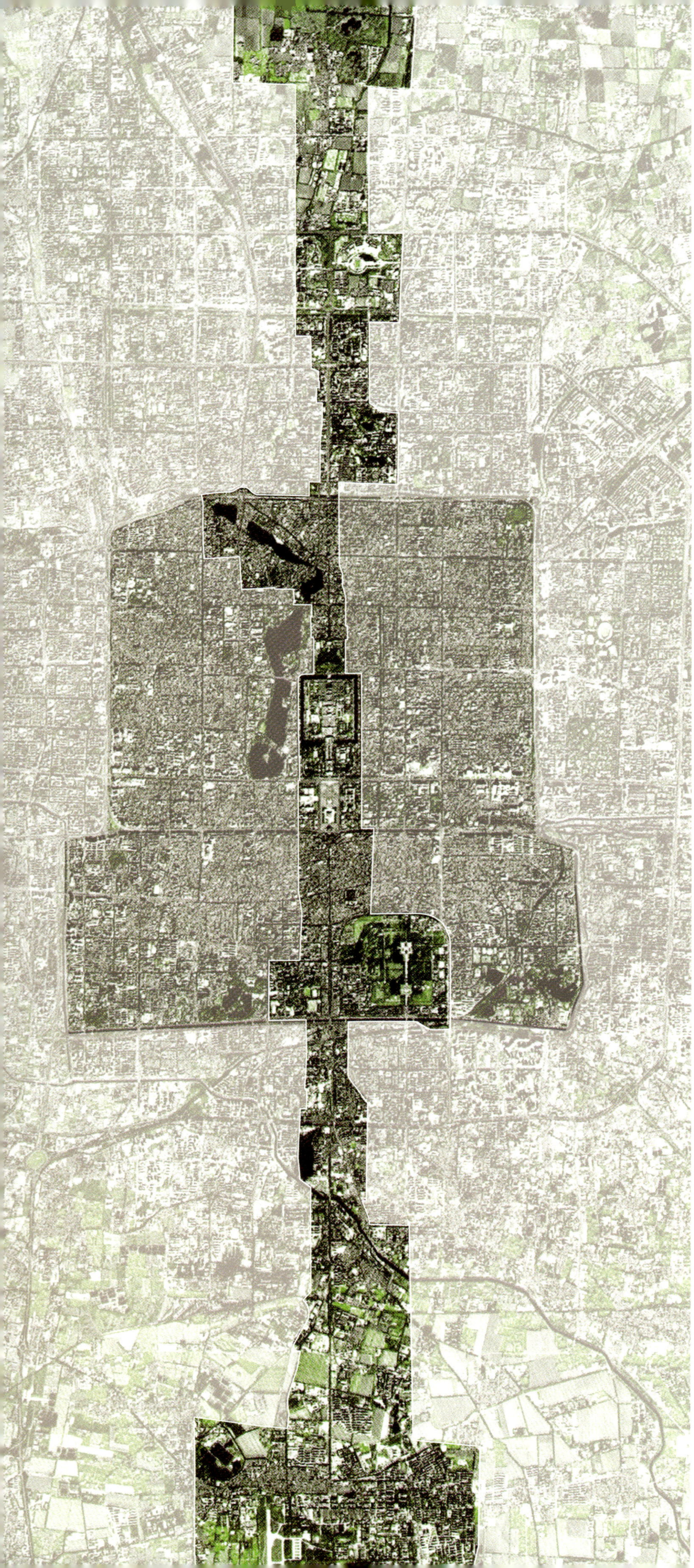

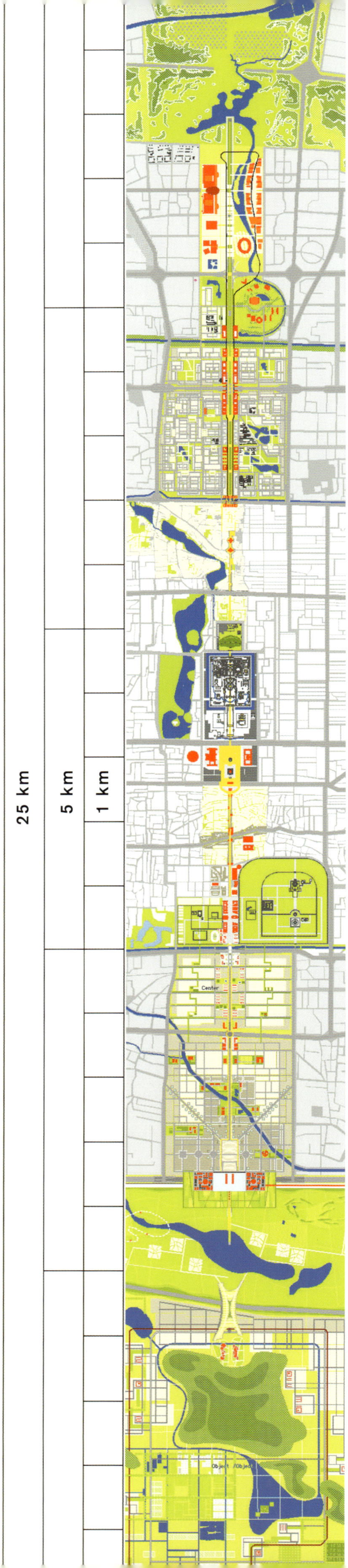
25 km
5 km
1 km
Center

AS&P – ALBERT SPEER & PARTNER, FRANKFURT AM MAIN

KONZEPT FÜR DIE ZENTRALE ACHSE IN PEKING

PROPOSAL FOR THE CENTRAL AXIS OF BEIJING

Visionen für die moderne Megacity aus den Theorien der traditionellen chinesischen Stadtplanung

Visions for the modern megacity, based on traditional Chinese urban planning rules

Im Oktober 2002 erhielt AS&P – Albert Speer & Partner einen außergewöhnlichen Auftrag: Die Beijing Municipal Planning Commission bat drei internationale und vier chinesische Planungsbüros in einem Gutachterverfahren um Visionen zur langfristigen städtebaulichen Entwicklung der zentralen Nord-Süd-Achse in Peking. Die Zentrale Achse in Peking bietet einen beispielhaften Querschnitt durch Probleme und Fragestellungen, mit denen die historische Stadt auf dem Weg zur modernen Megacity konfrontiert ist: Widersprüche zwischen Bewahrung und Erneuerung, Probleme der Versorgung, Infrastruktur, Ökonomie und Ökologie. Einen Schlüssel für die Lösung fand AS&P in den 2000 Jahre alten Theorien des chinesischen Städtebaus. Dessen Prinzipien Ganzheitlichkeit, Proportionalität, Modularität, Ökologie und Harmonie lassen sich auf die moderne Stadt im 21. Jahrhundert übertragen.

Die zentrale Achse ist eines der wichtigsten Symbole der kulturellen und nationalen Identität Chinas. Direkt an oder auf der Achse finden sich die bedeutendsten religiösen und politischen Gebäude Pekings, wie die „Verbotene Stadt", das Mao-Mausoleum oder der Platz des himmlischen Friedens. Dies gilt jedoch nur für den etwa acht Kilometer langen „historischen" Teil innerhalb der ehemaligen Stadtmauern. Die „neuen" Teile der Achse, die in den vergangenen Jahrzehnten nördlich und südlich der Altstadt entstanden sind, erscheinen gesichtslos und ohne besondere Bedeutung. Zwar wird mit der Ausrichtung der Olympischen Spiele 2008 ein wichtiger neuer Schwerpunkt im Norden der Achse geschaffen. Der Süden der Stadt dagegen wartet noch auf einen vergleichbaren Impuls.

In October 2002, AS&P – Albert Speer & Partner received an unusual commission: Beijing Municipal Planning Commission invited the firm – among three foreign and four Chinese planning offices – to propose ideas for the long-term architectural redevelopment of the city's central north-south urban 'axis'. This area represents a cross-section of the problems and challenges the historic city faces on its way towards becoming a modern megalopolis with its contradiction between preservation and renewal; problems of municipal and other supplies, infrastructure, economy and ecology. AS&P found one of the keys to these problems in 2000-year-old Chinese rules of urban design, which were based on the principles of holistic theory, proportionality, modularity, ecology and harmony. These can be applied to the city of the 21st century.

The Central Axis is one of the most important symbols of China's cultural and national identity. Its approximately 8-kilometre central 'historic' section within the former city walls is lined with, or incorporates, Beijing's major religious and political buildings like the Forbidden City, the Mao Mausoleum and Tianan-men Square (Square of Heavenly Peace). The 'new' sections of this central urban strip however, south and north of the old city, which have been developed over the past decades, appear anonymous and insignificant. While the constructions for the Olympic Games of 2008 will create an important new centre north of the historic city, the south is still waiting for similar impulses.

Das chinesische Zeichen „Zhong" hat beim Entwurf für die Zentrale Achse als Leitmotiv gedient. In ihm spiegeln sich die Grundprinzipien der chinesischen Stadtplanung: der orthogonale Stadtgrundriss und die zentrale Achse.

The Chinese character for 'zhong' served as the guiding motif for the Central Axis design. It reflects the basic principles of Chinese urban design: the orthogonal layout and the central axis.

这样就使城市和中轴线与国际机场、附近大城市以及巨型都市如天津或上海紧密连接(10分钟到市中心，15分钟到奥林匹克公园，15分钟到国际机场，180分钟到上海)。将来的游客将面对全新的城市入口：在中轴线上的“未来之门“。

> This will ensure an extremely close link of the city and the Central Axis with the international airport, the megacities located nearby, and other metropolises such as Tianjin or Shanghai (*10 min to the center, 15 min to the Olympic Green, 15 min. to the airport, 180 min. to Shanghai*). Future visitors will be greeted by a completely new access to the city - the "gateway to the future", directly situated on the Central Axis.

PROJEKT: Konzept für die Zentrale Achse in Peking
ARCHITEKTEN / PLANER: AS&P – Albert Speer & Partner GmbH, Frankfurt am Main / Shanghai

Die Analyse der überregionalen und innerstädtischen Verkehrsinfrastruktur brachte die Idee, dem Süden Pekings eine völlig neue Bedeutung zu geben: hier, am 4. Ring wäre der ideale Standort für einen großzügigen neuen Hauptbahnhof, eine „New Central Station". Der neue Hauptbahnhof könnte als „Flughafen für Züge" Bindeglied zwischen einem modernen, effizienten Schnellbahnsystem und dem öffentlichen Verkehrsnetz der Stadt funktionieren und wäre ein idealer Zielbahnhof für den Transrapid zwischen Shanghai und Peking. Die „New Central Station" wäre das neue Entree der chinesischen Hauptstadt auf der Zentralen Achse und das Eingangstor zu einem neuen Stadtteil. Auf einer Fläche von 10 Quadratkilometern könnte eine vielfältige Mischung aus Handel, Dienstleistung, Shopping und Wohnen entstehen – ein „Bahnhofsviertel des 21. Jahrhunderts".

The review of existing supraregional and inner-city traffic infrastructures led to the idea of giving Beijing's south completely new significance. Here the 4th ring road would be the perfect location for a large 'New Central Station' – a railway terminal and interchange between China's efficient modern express railway network and the public urban transport system. The 'New Central Station' would be the ideal terminal location for the transrapid Beijing–Shanghai and would form the new gateway to the capital city's Central Axis as well as to a new urban neighbourhood. A rich mixture of business, service, retail and residential functions could be created on an area of 10 km^2 around the station.

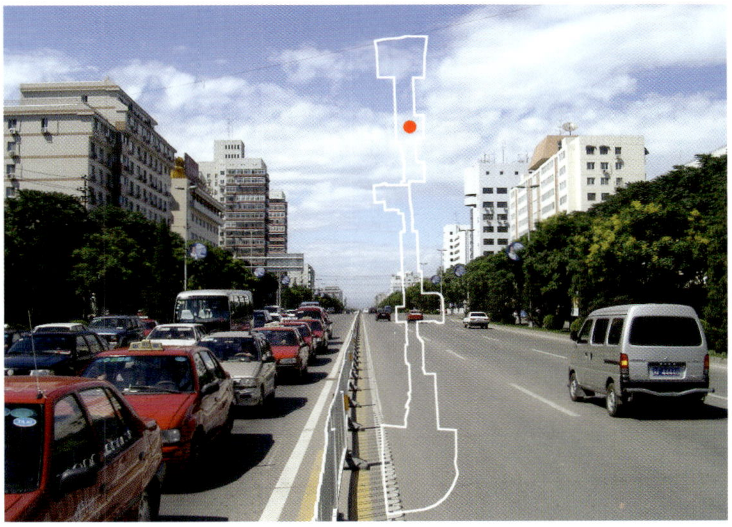

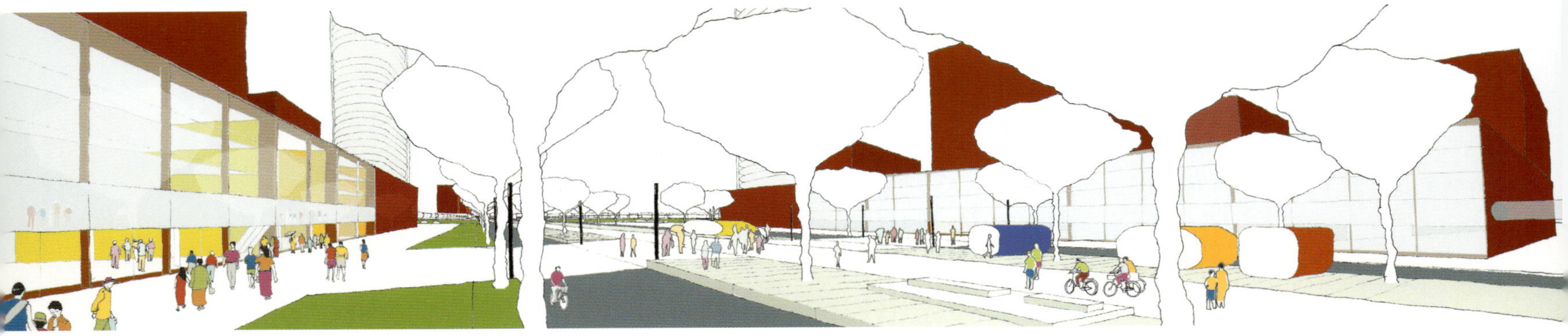

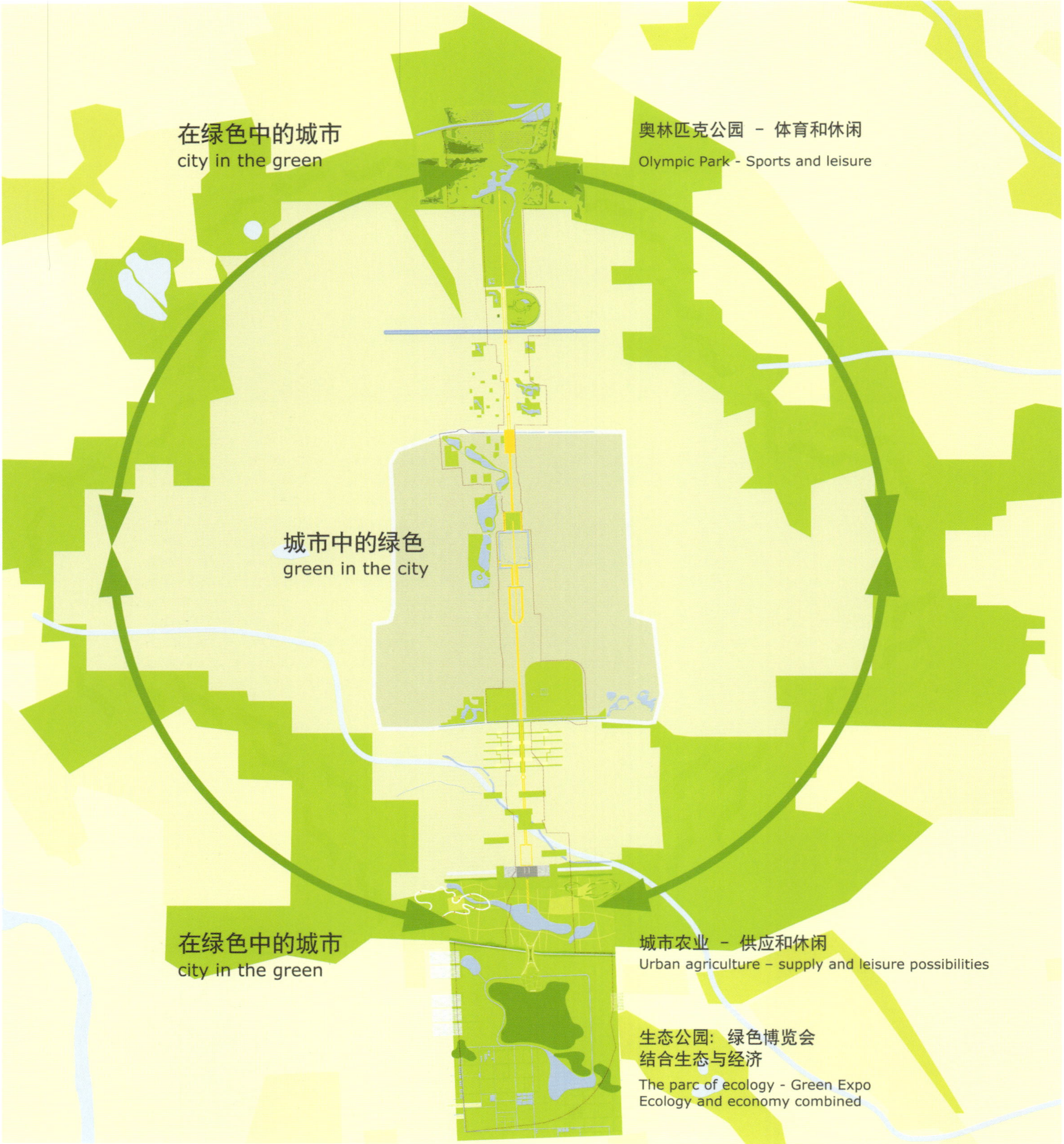
在绿色中的城市
city in the green
奥林匹克公园 – 体育和休闲
Olympic Park - Sports and leisure
城市中的绿色
green in the city
在绿色中的城市
city in the green
城市农业 – 供应和休闲
Urban agriculture – supply and leisure possibilities
生态公园：绿色博览会
结合生态与经济
The parc of ecology - Green Expo
Ecology and economy combined

Das Stadtgebiet wird entlang der Achse durch Frischluftschneisen und innerstädtische Parkanlagen gegliedert, um einen wichtigen Beitrag zur Verbesserung des Mikroklimas zu leisten.

The urban area is subdivided along the 'Axis' by means of air corridors and inner-city parks which will contribute to improving the city's climate.

PROJEKT: Konzept für die Zentrale Achse in Peking
AUFTRAGGEBER: Beijing Municipal Planning Commission
ARCHITEKTEN / PLANER: AS&P – Albert Speer & Partner GmbH, Frankfurt am Main / Shanghai
BERATUNG BEI STADTPLANUNG UND ENTWURF: S8 Architekten, Mainz; Chinese Academy of Sciences, Beijing; Research Center for Eco-Environmental Sciences; Beijing SunZhuo Architectural Consulting Co. Ltd.
LANDSCHAFTSARCHITEKTEN: WGF Werkgemeinschaft Freiraum, Nürnberg
LICHTKONZEPT: Kardorff Ingenieure, Berlin
VISUALISIERUNGEN: Hagen Lorenz, Berlin
PLANUNG: Herbst 2003

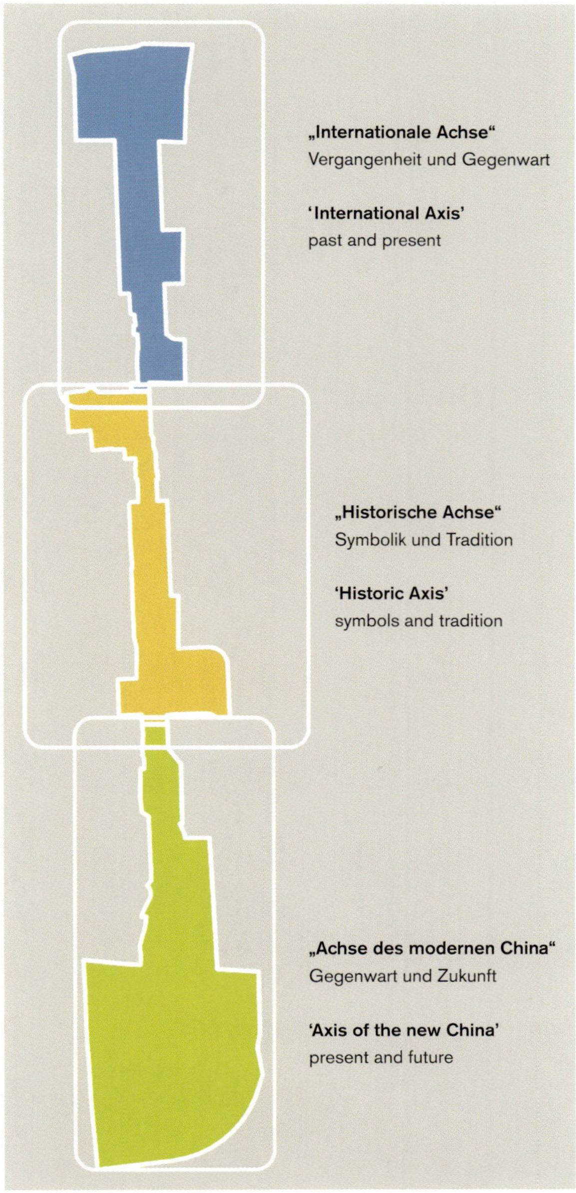

Der zweite wichtige Impuls ist die Vision einer 6 km² großen „ökologischen Stadt der Zukunft". Hier soll Forschung, Ausbildung und Entwicklung für ein harmonisches Leben der Menschen in einer ökologischen Umwelt Experimentierfeld für traditionelle und neue Formen der Landwirtschaft sein. Die intensive Landwirtschaft aus dem „Park der Ökologie" trägt zur Versorgung der Megacity bei. Darüber hinaus könnte die Parkstadt ein wichtiges externes Projekt der Weltausstellung 2010 in Shanghai sein. Auch in den anderen Abschnitten der Zentralen Achse wurden vorhandene Potenziale und natürliche Ressourcen aufgegriffen, um sie mit modernen Hochtechnologien zu kombinieren, Beispiele dafür sind eine Windkraftanlage in einem 3 km² großen Gebiet im Norden der Stadt, die konsequente Nutzung von Solarenergie sowie Konzepte für den sorgsamen Umgang mit Grund- und Regenwasser.

The second important development impulse is the vision of a 6-km² 'ecological city of the future', accommodating educational, research and development institutions active in the field of testing traditional and new forms of agriculture with the aim of securing a peaceful life for the people of the region. The intensive agricultural production of this 'ecological park' will contribute to feeding the millions of the megalopolis. In addition, it could be an important external project of the World Exhibition that is to take place in Shanghai in 2010.

AS&P also identified a number of potentials and resources in the other sections of the Central Axis and suggested combining them with modern technology such as wind power stations in a 3-km² area north of the city, the consistent use of solar energy as well as ground and rain water management systems.

Der neue Entwicklungsschwerpunkt könnte entscheidend dazu beitragen, die historische Altstadt Pekings zu entlasten und zu schützen.

This priority development project could contribute decisively to relieving and preserving Beijing's historic city.

AS&P – ALBERT SPEER & PARTNER, FRANKFURT AM MAIN

GARTENSTADT FOSHAN SANSHUI, GUANGZHOU
FOSHAN SANSHUI GARDEN CITY, GUANGZHOU

Die Region um Kanton gilt als eine der wirtschaftsstärksten in China. Bis vor kurzem wegen der fast ausschließlichen Ausrichtung auf Konsumgüter als „Fabrik der Welt" bezeichnet, findet hier momentan ein Umstrukturierungsprozess von massiven Ausmaßen statt.

Der Preis für diese atemberaubende Entwicklung ist hoch: Umweltverschmutzung unvorstellbaren Ausmaßes, die völlige Zersiedlung fast des gesamten Perlfluss-Deltas mit damit verbundener dauerhafter Zerstörung der naturräumlichen Besonderheiten und eine nach europäischen Maßstäben hochgradig übervölkerte, form- und gesichtslose Hauptstadt.

Rasche Veränderungen haben die Landschaft und ihre Siedlungen ungeplant überformt und einen stark fragmentierten, heterogenen Flickenteppich von unterschiedlichen, teilweise gegensätzlichen Nutzungseinheiten entstehen lassen. Um zukunftsfähige Visionen für das nahe der Provinzhauptstadt Guanghzou liegende Foshan zu entwickeln, wurde 2005 ein internationaler Wettbewerb ausgelobt.

The region of Guangzhou (formerly Canton) is one of the economically strongest in China. Until recently regarded as the 'world factory' – on account of its almost exclusive production of consumer goods –, it is at present undergoing massive restructuring.

A high price is being paid for the region's breathtaking redevelopment: environmental pollution to an unbelievable extent, almost total destruction of the Pearl River's natural delta landscape and topographical identity by new settlements, and a faceless and shapeless capital city that, to European standards, is excessively overpopulated.

Rapid unplanned developments have changed the landscape and the old villages into a fragmented, heterogeneous patchwork of different, in some cases even conflicting, uses. In 2005 an international competition was held to develop viable visions for the future of the region of Foshan near Guangzhou, the capital of Guandong Province.

Sanshui liegt nordwestlich von Hongkong in der Provinz Guandong im Pearl River Delta und kann als einer der bedeutenden „Vororte" der Provinzhauptstadt Guangzhou (Kanton) bezeichnet werden.

Sanshui lies north-west of Hong Kong in Guandong Province in the Pearl River delta region and is one of the major 'suburbs' of Guangzhou (Canton), the capital of Guandong Province.

AUFTRAGGEBER: Sanshui District Construction Bureau, Foshan; Foshan Urban Planning Bureau Sanshui Branch
ARCHITEKTEN / PLANER: AS&P – Albert Speer & Partner GmbH, Frankfurt am Main / Shanghai in Zusammenarbeit mit D. Grösel und D. Chen, Guangzhou (Kanton)
WETTBEWERB: 1. Preis im städtebaulichen Wettbewerb
KONZEPT: M. Stadler, D. Grösel, S. Hornig, B. Mertens (Verkehr)
KOORDINATION: Johannes Dell
AUSARBEITUNG: D. Grösel, D. Chen
PLANGEBIET: 15 km²
PLANUNG: 2004

Hauptziel des Entwurfs war es, Foshan eine neue Identität mit hohem Entwicklungspotenzial zu geben. Dazu wurde eine Struktur mit verbindenden Elementen entwickelt. Die Zuordnung der Nutzungen: Wohnen, Verwaltung, öffentliche Einrichtungen, Dienstleistungen, Sport, Freizeit und Erholung sollte sich an diesem Netzwerk-Gedanken orientieren und aus der vorhandenen Fragmentierung eine vitale Nutzungsmischung machen.

Das Wettbewerbskonzept baut auf den Prinzipien der Nachhaltigkeit auf: Eindämmung weiterer Zersiedlung, Konzentration der städtebaulichen Strukturen auf bereits bestehende Standorte, Verknüpfung der noch vorhandenen Landschaftsräume unter Einbeziehung der erhaltenswerten Dörfer und Siedlungen, Stärkung der Beziehungen zwischen Stadt und Landschaftsraum.

Das verbindende Element des Entwurfes ist ein grünes Band, das sich entlang eines neugestalteten Zuflusses zum Dong Ping River von Süden nach Norden zieht. Dieser Grünzug bildet im Süden einen innerstädtischen Park, an den das neue Stadtzentrum von Sanshui angeschlossen ist. Über „Seitenäste“ werden andere Elemente der Landschaft und der historischen Siedlungen angebunden.

Der Entwurf von AS&P nutzt das symbolträchtige chinesische „Drachen-Motiv“ als assoziatives Element. Das sich schlängelnde grüne Band ist im Plan als „Drachenkörper“, das neue Stadtzentrum als „Drachenkopf“ von Sanshui wahrnehmbar – ein Bild, das bei der Kommunikation des Entwurfes sehr hilfreich ist.

The design primarily aimed to give Foshan a new identity as a place with great development potential by means of a structure with interconnecting elements. The zoning for dwelling, administration, public facilities, services, sports, leisure and recreation was to follow this idea of a network and to change the existing fragmented urban structure into a vital functional urban mix. The competition design builds on sustainability and therefore proposes: restricting further 'urban sprawl'; densifying urban areas already covered by buildings; linking the remaining countryside areas while integrating villages and settlements worthy of preservation; strengthening the relationship between the city and its rural and natural environs.

The integrative design element is a 'green belt' that runs from south to north along the redesigned embankment of a stream which flows into the river Dong Ping. The southern section of this green strip is an inner-city park adjacent to the new city centre of Sanshui. Other sections of landscape and historic settlements are linked to it by 'secondary branches'.

AS&P's design uses the symbolic Chinese dragon motif as an associative element. The green strip undulates like the body of a dragon, with the new city centre as the dragon's head – an image that facilitated the presentation of the design.

Die erste Realisierungsstufe der Automobile City ist die 58 ha große „Core Service, Trade and Exibition Zone", die südlich von Anting auf einer Halbinsel liegt. Sie ist dicht bebaut mit Hochhäusern, die als Wahrzeichen dienen und die Silhouette der SIAC bilden.

The first-phase of the development of the Automobile City is the 58-hectare 'Core Service, Trade and Exhibition Zone' on a peninsula south of Anting. It is densely built up with landmark high-rises which form SIAC's skyline.

AS&P – ALBERT SPEER & PARTNER, FRANKFURT AM MAIN
INTERNATIONALE AUTOMOBILSTADT / ANTING NEW TOWN, SHANGHAI-ANTING
INTERNATIONAL AUTOMOBILE CITY, ANTING NEW TOWN, SHANGHAI-ANTING

Die Shanghai International Automobile City (SIAC) ist Teil einer Strategie der Stadt Shanghai, vier räumlich getrennte Industriestützpunkte im Stadtgebiet zu schaffen: Petrochemie im Süden (Jinshan), Schwerindustrie im Norden (Baoshan), Elektronik / IT im Osten (Pudong) und Automobil im Westen (Anting).

Anting liegt ca. 35 km nordwestlich vom Zentrum Shanghais entfernt. Nach der Öffnung des chinesischen Marktes 1984 hat Volkswagen hier als erstes ausländisches Unternehmen in Joint Venture mit der SAIC (Shanghai Automotive Industry Corporation) ein regionales VW-Fertigungswerk errichtet. Damit gilt Anting als die Wiege der chinesischen Automobilindustrie. Ziel ist es, Anting zum primären Zentrum der zukünftigen chinesischen Automobilindustrie und zum zentralen Geschäftssitz der national und international bekannten Automobilhersteller sowie verwandter Industriezweige auszubauen.

AS&P gewann 2000 den internationalen Wettbewerb für die Shanghai International Automobile City und wurde daraufhin mit dem Masterplan Anting sowie der städtebaulichen Planung für die Autostadt beauftragt. Auf einer Fläche von rund 600 ha entstehen Produktions-, Ausstellungs-, Handels-, Forschungs-, Entwicklungs-, Ausbildungs-, Management- und Unterhaltungsbereiche rund um das Auto. Dazu kommen ergänzende Einrichtungen wie Büros, Hotels, Restaurants, Einkaufsmöglichkeiten, Museen, Unterhaltungs- und Freizeiteinrichtungen. Die Sport- und Erholungseinrichtungen umfassen unter anderem einen Stadionkomplex, einen Golfplatz, eine Formel-1-Rennstrecke und einen Vergnügungspark.

Shanghai International Automobile City (SIAC) is part of the city's strategy to create four separate industrial areas, one to the south (Jinshan) for petrochemical industries; one to the north (Baoshan) for heavy industry; one east (Pudong) for electronics/IT companies, and one west (Anting) for automobile production.

Anting lies about 35 km north-west of downtown Shanghai. Following the opening of the Chinese market in 1984, Volkswagen was the first foreign corporation which built a plant here, as a joint venture with the SAIC (Shanghai Automotive Industry Corporation). This is why Anting is regarded as the cradle of China's automobile industry. Anting is to be developed as the nation's main car-manufacturing centre and seat of Chinese and foreign manufacturers of cars and related products.

In 2000 AS&P won the international competition for SIAC and was subsequently commissioned to design Anting's masterplan and the urban layout of the automobile city. Production, exhibition, trading, research, development, education/training, management and entertainment facilities – all related to the automobile – as well as offices, hotels, restaurants, shopping malls, museums, entertainment venues and leisure amenities will be created on an area of about 600 ha. The sports and recreational structures will include a large stadium, a golf course, a formula-1 racing course and an entertainment park.

Die Architektur reflektiert das Hauptthema des Projektes, Werbung für ein Spitzentechnologieprodukt zum Zwecke der Mobilität des Einzelnen zu machen. Internationale Standards und ein beispielhaftes Energiebewusstsein spiegeln den einzigartigen Zweck und den internationalen Charakter der Automobile City wider.

The architectural design reflects the main theme of the project, i.e. advertising a high-tech product that makes people mobile. International design standards and exemplary energy-efficiency reflect the unique purpose and international character of the Automobile City.

安亭新镇
ANTING
德国建筑艺术与技术的结晶

PROJEKT: Internationale Automobilstadt / Anting New Town
ARCHITEKTEN / PLANER: AS&P – Albert Speer & Partner GmbH, Frankfurt am Main / Shanghai

Mit der „Anting New Town" wird seit 2002 eine komplette Wohnstadt für 50.000 Einwohner realisiert. Aufgrund der Nachbarschaft zum chinesischen VW-Werk wollten die Auftraggeber eine „deutsche Stadt" erbaut sehen – weshalb in der Presse oft fälschlicherweise der Begriff „Klein-Wolfsburg" auftauchte. An die Vorgabe „Deutschland" erinnert der mittelalterlichen Städten entlehnte, eher runde – d.h. im Gegensatz zu traditionellen chinesischen Städten nicht rechteckige, schachbrettartige – Grundriss. Die wichtigsten städtebaulichen Prinzipien und charakteristische Elemente deutscher Bautradition, wie multifunktionale Blockstrukturen, öffentliche Plätze, auf Fußgänger ausgerichtete Straßenräume und die Mischung von Funktionen im Stadtzentrum, sind die Basis für die vitale, nachhaltige und vielfältige Stadtentwicklung.

Glücklicherweise konnte AS&P seine Auftraggeber davon überzeugen, dass man auch bei der Architektur anstatt mit Fachwerk und Butzenscheiben mit qualitativ hochwertiger Gebäudetechnik und Wärmedämmung die Qualitätsmerkmale und den Charakter deutscher Städte transportiert.

So wurden ein Ausstellungszentrum und Modellwohnungen inklusive der Freiräume, Gärten und Parkmöglichkeiten am Rande der New Town geplant und gebaut, die exemplarisch die Entwurfsziele und die architektonischen Standards zeigen.

In dem Ausstellungszentrum werden die städtebaulichen und architektonischen Entwürfe für Anting New Town präsentiert. Dabei werden besondere Aspekte bei der Planung und Entwicklung der New Town gezeigt, einschließlich der Geschichte des deutschen Städtebaus, der Nachhaltigkeit in Bezug auf Infrastruktur und geeignete Baumaterialien, deutscher Entwurfs- und Qualitätsstandards beim Bauen und des Kontextes des Projektes als Teil der Shanghai International Automobile City. Integriert in das Ausstellungszentrum sind außerdem die Hauptgeschäftsstelle des Auftraggebers SIACRE mit etwa 50 Mitarbeitern sowie ein Restaurant mit Terrasse und Dachgarten.

Construction work on Anting New Town – a complete residential town for 50,000 inhabitants – started in 2002. As it is close to the Chinese VW plant, the clients required 'a German town' which is why the press often mistakenly dubbed it 'Little Wolfsburg'. The layout with curving streets is indeed reminiscent of German medieval towns, in contrast to the traditional rectangular, chessboard-type street grids in Chinese towns. The primary urban design principles and characteristic elements of German tradition (multi-functional street blocks, public squares, pedestrian precincts and a mixture of functions in the city centre) form the basis for a vital, sustainable and varied urban development.

Luckily, AS&P were able to convince the clients that the 'German character' of the new development did not have to be expressed in half-timbered houses with crown glass windows, but rather with high-quality installations and heat insulation.

Thus AS&P planned an exhibition centre and model residential units as well as the ambient spaces, gardens and car parks on the edge of the new town which altogether reflect the designers' aims and high architectural standards.

At the time of writing, the urban and architectural designs for Anting New Town were displayed in the exhibition centre, highlighting special planning and development aspects, including a short history of German urban planning; aspects of sustainability in relation to infrastructure and suitable construction materials; German design and construction quality standards, and the project context as part of SIAC. The exhibition centre also includes the headquarters of the client (SIACRE) for about fifty employees, a restaurant with a roof garden and terrace.

PROJEKT: Internationale Automobilstadt / Anting New Town
AUFTRAGGEBER: Shanghai Urban Planning Administration Bureau of the Shanghai Jia Ding District; Shanghai International Autocity Real Estate Development Co. Ltd.
ARCHITEKTEN / PLANER: AS&P – Albert Speer & Partner, Frankfurt am Main / Shanghai in Zusammenarbeit mit ARTFORM Urban Planning & Architecture, Shanghai
LANDSCHAFTSARCHITEKTEN: David Elsworth, Stuttgart (Shanghai International Automobile City); PGW – Wittig – Gast Leyser, Weimar (Anting New Town)
WETTBEWERB: 1. Preis
PLANGEBIET: 600 ha
BGF: 113.000 m^2
PLANUNG: 2000–2005 (Fertigstellung)

Im August 2002 hat die SIACRE fünf renommierte deutsche Architekturbüros eingeladen, Wohnungsbauten und die Gebäude des Stadtkerns von „Anting West" zu entwerfen. Die Büros ABB – Architekten Frankfurt, Auer + Weber + Architekten, Stuttgart, Braun & Schlockermann und Partner, Frankfurt, gmp – von Gerkan, Marg & Partner, Hamburg, AS&P – Albert Speer & Partner, Frankfurt und die Landschaftsplaner PGW – Wittig – Gast Leyser, Weimar, haben in einem Workshop Entwürfe für die verschiedenen Stadtquartieren entwickelt, die inzwischen fast alle realisiert wurden. Der von AS&P geplante und realisierte Anteil umfasst circa 1.000 Wohnungen.

Da bereits jetzt abzusehen ist, dass die Nachfrage nach Grundstücken und Apartments in Anting New Town größer ist als das derzeitige Angebot, ist die Erweiterung „Anting East" bereits in Planung. Auch für „Anting East" erstellt AS&P den Masterplan.

Mit dem Bau von Anting New Town und der Shanghai International Automobile City ist es gelungen, eine beispielhafte Satellitenstadt zu bauen, die deutsche Technologien, Umweltstandards und Qualität einsetzt.

In August 2002, SIACRE invited five well-known German architectural offices to work out proposals for residential buildings and the city centre of 'Anting West'. The following offices participated: ABB Architects, Frankfurt/Main; Auer + Weber + Architekten, Stuttgart; Braun & Schlockermann and Partners, Frankfurt; gmp von Gerkan, Marg & Partners, Hamburg; AS&P Albert Speer & Partners, Frankfurt; and landscape planners PGW Wittig Gast Leyser, Weimer. At a joint workshop, they developed designs for the different urban areas which [by the autumn of 2005] have almost all been built. Roughly 1000 residential units were planned and completed by AS&P.

As it seemed clear by 2005 that the demand for building sites and apartments in Anting New Town would be greater than the supply, the plan was formed to extend the town by 'Anting East' to a masterplan by AS&P.

The new urban developments of Anting New Town and Shanghai International Automobile City now form an exemplary satellite town based on German technologies, environmental and quality standards.

AS&P – ALBERT SPEER & PARTNER, FRANKFURT AM MAIN

VERWALTUNGSGEBÄUDE IM ZHANG JIANG HI-TECH-PARK, SHANGHAI

ADMINISTRATION BUILDING IN 'ZHANG JIANG HI-TECH PARK', SHANGHAI

Nachhaltige Planungen für attraktive Städte und Hi-Tech Architektur

Projects for Sustainable, Attractive Cities and High-tech Architecture

Stadtentwicklung und Modernisierung unter umweltrelevanten Gesichtspunkten wird in China in den nächsten Jahrzehnten eine besondere Relevanz und politische Priorität erhalten. Als Antwort auf die zukünftigen Bedürfnisse hat AS&P gemeinsam mit Fichtner Ingenieuren in den letzten Jahren eine Strategie für ein nachhaltiges, vernetztes Stadtentwicklungs- und Infrastrukturmodell entwickelt – das Konzept für die „Ecological Model Town". Im Zuge von Verhandlungen mit der Betreibergesellschaft des Zhang Jiang Hi-Tech Parks ergab sich die Chance, dieses in seiner Art bisher einzigartige Modell auf ein Projekt im Shanghaier Stadtteil Pudong anzuwenden und dort eine langfristig tragfähige, umweltgerechte Stadtentwicklung einzuleiten. Kernstück ist die Entwicklung eines Masterplans, in dem alle technischen Disziplinen (Wasser, Abwasser, Müll, Energie, Medien) mit Verkehrsinfrastruktur, Stadtplanung und Gebäudetechnologien zu einem Netzwerk zusammengefasst werden. Auf diese Weise werden die Stärken und Vorteile der einzelnen Systeme nachhaltig miteinander verbunden und optimal genutzt. Es entsteht ein für Investoren wie auch Bewohner attraktiver Stadtteil, der gleichzeitig Modellcharakter für die innovative Integration von Umweltschutzaspekten bei der städtebaulichen Planung hat.

In China, in the coming decades, urban development and modernization according to environmental criteria will become a particularly important political priority. In recent years, in response to the country's expected needs, AS&P, partnered by Fichtner Engineers, have devised a strategic proposal for sustainable urban development and infrastructural models and named it 'Ecological Model Town'. Negotiations with the operating company of the 'Zhang Jiang Hi-Tech Park' led to the opportunity of applying this unique model to a project in Shanghai's Pudong district in order to initiate a long-term viable environmental urban development in that area. The most important part of the model was the masterplan which combines and integrates the municipal systems (water, sewerage, waste disposal, energy supplies and communication media) with the traffic infrastructures, urban layout and building services. In this way, the strengths and advantages of the individual systems can be interconnected to provide synergies. The result will be an urban district attractive to both developers and inhabitants and a model of the innovative integration of environmental protection and urban planning.

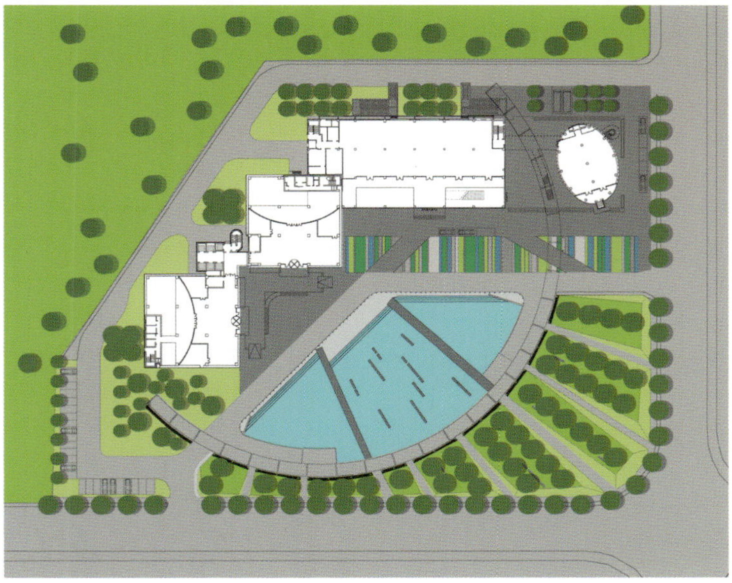

Die Außenanlagen folgen einem streng geometrischen Konzept. Die Gesamtstruktur (Wasser, Beläge, Vegetation) ist auf die Richtung und Koordinaten der Gebäude und des Grundstückes ausgelegt. Das Zentrum der Anlage bildet eine Wasserfläche mit begrünter Pergola und Sitzstufen an der Wasserkante vor dem Gebäude.

The landscaping is strictly geometrical. The overall layout (with water, paved surfaces and greenery) follows the orientation and co-ordinates of both buildings and site. An artificial lake with an arbour overgrown with vines, and steps down to the water forms the centre of the complex.

PROJEKT: Verwaltungsgebäude im Zhang Jiang Hi-Tech Park, Shanghai
AUFTRAGGEBER: Shanghai Zhang Jiang Hi-Tech Park Development Corporation
ARCHITEKTEN / PLANER: AS&P – Albert Speer & Partner GmbH, Frankfurt am Main / Shanghai in Zusammenarbeit mit ECADI, Shanghai und DESHAUS ARCHITECTS, Shanghai
WETTBEWERB: 1. Preis
LEISTUNGSPHASEN: HOAI 1–3, teilw. 5–8
BGF: 35.000 m^2
HÖHE: 18 Geschosse, 95 m
PLANUNG: 2001–2003
FERTIGSTELLUNG: 2004

Der Anspruch des Auftraggebers, sich mit einem zukunftsweisenden Gebäude zu repräsentieren, wird insbesondere an der Fassade sichtbar. Die Doppeltürme sind mit einer zweiten Außenhaut versehen. Bauart und Konstruktion sind nach den aktuellen Erkenntnissen europäischen Fassadendesigns konzipiert und eine Neuheit in Shanghai. Die Vorteile einer von Außenluft durchspülten Doppelfassade sind vielfältig. Es wird nur halb soviel Energie verbraucht wie in einem herkömmlichen chinesischen Bürogebäude mit einfacher Sonnenschutzverglasung. Die Büros sind natürlich zu belüften, da auch in den oberen Geschossen jedes zweite Fenster zu öffnen und dadurch geringere Luftumwälzung von der Klimaanlage zu leisten ist. Im Sommer kommt durch außen liegenden Sonnenschutz weniger Wärme in die Innenräume, wodurch auch weniger Energie zur Kälteerzeugung benötigt wird. Aufgrund des außen liegenden Sonnenschutzes muss kein stark getöntes oder verspiegeltes Sonnenschutzglas verwendet werden, was die Tageslichtausnutzung verbessert.

The clients' wish for self-representation through a seminal building, was fulfilled in particular by the facade design. The twin towers both have a second outer skin. Its texture and type of construction were conceived according to the latest standards of European facade design and are a novelty in Shanghai. A naturally ventilated cavity facade offers many advantages. Buildings fitted with such a facade only use about half the energy of conventional office buildings in China with single anti-sun glazing. The office spaces can be ventilated naturally, as every second window can be opened, even on the upper floors, so that the air-conditioning system uses less energy for mechanical ventilation. In the summer, exterior sunshades help to keep the interiors cooler so that less cooling energy is consumed. As the sunshades are installed in front of the windows, these do not have to be glazed with special anti-sun glass so that they improve the interior natural light conditions.

Die zwei 88 m hohen Türme entfalten ihre städtebauliche Wirkung als Landmarke inmitten einer natürlichen Parklandschaft. Durch die von der Straße zurückgesetzte Lage bietet sich die Möglichkeit der Organisation eines großzügigen Entrees mit repräsentativer Vorfahrt, „Reflecting-Pool" und Landschaftspark.

The 88-metre twin towers act as urban landmarks in a natural parkland. The set-back position of the buildings made it possible to create a spacious driveway, a reflecting pool and a landscape garden.

AS&P – ALBERT SPEER & PARTNER, FRANKFURT AM MAIN

FUDAN UNIVERSITÄT, SHANGHAI

FUDAN UNIVERSITY, SHANGHAI

Die Fudan Universität hat eine lange Tradition als naturwissenschaftlich-technisches Eliteinstitut. 1905 in Shanghai gegründet, besteht die Universität heute aus 17 Fakultäten, in denen insgesamt 36.000 Studenten eingeschrieben sind. Rechtzeitig zum 110-jährigen Gründungsjubiläum im Juni 2005 wurden die neuen Bauten der Fakultät für Informatik und Mikroelektronik in der Wissenschafts- und Ausbildungszone des Zhang Jiang Hi-Tech Park eröffnet.

Der städtebaulich-architektonische Entwurf für die neuen Fakultäten war aus einem internationalen Wettbewerb hervorgegangen, den AS&P in Zusammenarbeit mit den Architekten von ARTFORM, Shanghai 2002 gewonnen hatten. Aufgabe des Wettbewerbs war es, einen neuen Campus zu entwerfen, der in zwei Phasen realisierbar ist. Im ersten Teil wurde bereits die Fakultät für Informatik und Mikroelektronik gebaut, in der zweiten Phase werden das Medizinische Institut und die zugehörige Forschungseinrichtung folgen.

Fudan University in Shanghai has a long tradition as an elite institution teaching natural sciences and technology. Founded in 1905, it now has seventeen faculties and 36,000 matriculated students. 2005 saw the opening of its faculty building for computing science and microelectronics in the science and training zone of the Zhang Jiang Hi-tech Park.

The urban and architectural design of this new faculty building was the result of an international competition for a new university campus to be implemented in two stages, which AS&P won in 2000, together with the architects of ARTFORM, Shanghai. The Medical School and an affiliated research institute will be built in a second phase.

第一教学楼
第二教学楼

PROJEKT: Fudan Universität, Shanghai
AUFTRAGGEBER: Fudan University, Shanghai
ARCHITEKTEN / PLANER: AS&P – Albert Speer & Partner GmbH, Frankfurt am Main / Shanghai in Zusammenarbeit mit ARTFORM Urban Planning & Architecture, Shanghai
BGF: Phase 1: 161.400 m^2, Phase 2: 200.000 m^2
PLANUNG: 2002–2005 (Fertigstellung 1. Bauabschnitt)

Integrative Bestandteile des Campus sind auf unterschiedlichen Höhen gelegene Höfe und ein Landschaftspark, der von Wasserläufen durchzogen wird und damit ein Shanghai-typisches Thema aufgreift.

Die Raumbildung des Campus reflektiert mit geometrisch einfacher, modularer Anordnung der Baukörper und klarer Architektursprache eher die Ästhetik des Bauhauses als die in China weit verbreitete ornamentale Formen- und Farbenvielfalt. Das reduzierte Erscheinungsbild der Gebäude, die Vielgestaltigkeit der landschaftsgärtnerisch gestalteten Freiflächen und die Großzügigkeit der Straßen und Plätze ergänzen sich harmonisch. Dabei werden die Bedürfnisse des Unterrichtens und Lernens genauso berücksichtigt wie die der Freizeit, des Sports und der Entspannung.

Das neue Campusensemble reflektiert den wissenschaftlichen und akademischen Geist der Universität und bildet damit einen würdigen Rahmen für eine selbstbewusste Institution. Die hervorragende Zusammenarbeit zwischen Bauherrn, Behörden und Architekten hat auch in anderer Hinsicht zu einem bemerkenswerten Erfolg geführt: Der erste Bauabschnitt des Campus konnte in etwas mehr als zwei Jahren Planungs- und Bauzeit zu einem auch für chinesische Verhältnisse sehr günstigen Preis fertig gestellt werden.

Courtyards on different levels and a landscape park with water courses running through it form the integrating elements of the campus and a reference to a design theme typical of Shanghai.

The spatial configuration of the campus with its simple geometric and modular arrangement of the buildings and their clear architectural language, reflects the Bauhaus aesthetics rather than the ornamental variety of forms and colours widespread in China. The austere appearance of the buildings, the multiformity of the landscaped ambient areas as well as spacious streets and squares form a harmonious ensemble. The requirements for teaching and studying, as well as for sports and recreation, were treated as equally important.

The new campus breathes the scientific and academic spirit of this self-confident institution of higher learning and forms a worthy frame for it. The excellent teamwork of the clients and public authorities with the architects has produced remarkable results also in another respect: the first stage of the campus was built within little more than two years from planning to completion at very reasonable costs, even according to Chinese standards.

Anlage von Ost.

Overall east view.

AXIS–GROUP.de, BERLIN
FORTUNE PLAZA, CHONGQING
FORTUNE PLAZA, CHONGQING

AUSLOBER: Chongqing HKI Goake Real Development Co.
WETTBEWERB: Entwicklung eines Stadtteilzentrums in der Nordzone von Chongqing: Einkaufs- und Kongresszentrum „Fortune Plaza", Hotels, Boarding-Häuser, Büros, Firmenzentralen, Wohnen, Freizeitzentrum
PLANER / ARCHITEKTEN: Eike Becker_Architekten, Berlin; B. Faskel Architekten, Berlin; Nalbach + Nalbach Architekten, Berlin; R. + R. Rave Architekten, Berlin; M. Stankovic Architekten, Berlin; G. Zamp Kelp, Berlin
ORGANISATION / VERKEHRSKONZEPT: P. Droege, Sydney
KOORDIANTION: G. Blomeyer, Berlin
KONTAKTARCHITEKT: Dr. Y. Rao, Beijing
BAUÖKONOMIE UND BAUTECHNIK: Ingenieursozietät R. Horner + R. Schirmer, Berlin
KLIMA UND LICHT: GLB, Prof. H. Müller, Dortmund; Se'lux, SemperLux AG, Berlin
ÖKOLOGIE: ARUP, Berlin
LANDSCHAFTSARCHITEKTUR: H. Fugmann + M. Janotta

Berliner AXIS-Group.de: 1. Preis für Fortune Plaza in Chongqing, China

Fortune Plaza, Chongqing by AXIS-Group.de Berlin: 1st prize in architectural competition

Chongqing liegt am Jangtze-Fluss oberhalb des fast fertigen, weltgrößten Staudamms. Flächenmäßig ist es die größte Stadt der Welt und sie wächst als neues Zentrum von Westchina sehr schnell. Erste „global players" wie Volkswagen sind schon da. Ziel der Stadt ist es, weitere führende Betriebe aus aller Welt anzusiedeln. Die neue Nordzone ist 20 Quadratkilometer groß. Neben neuen Produktionsstätten für Hightech-Betriebe werden dort auch drei Millionen Quadratmeter Wohnfläche, Parks und Folgeeinrichtungen in den nächsten Jahren entstehen.

The city of Chongqing is situated on the Yangtse, immediately upstream of the huge, almost completed retaining dam, the biggest worldwide. In terms of area, Chongqing is the largest city in the world and is growing at a rapid rate as the new centre of western China. First global players like Volkswagen, for example, have established themselves here. The authorities intend to attract other leading international enterprises to their city. Its new northern district has an area size of 20 km^2. Apart from new high-tech plants, housing estates, parks and related public facilities will be built on 3 million square metres of this quarter in the coming years.

Renhe Tower Fortune Plaza Tower HKI Exhibition Fortune Plaza Hotel Tower Serviced Apartment Tower

Serviced Apartments High rise housing High rise housing and a small office building Dragon's Nest: 2 large and 2 small office buildings Art Office Building Butterfly Office Building

Eines der Zentren der neuen Nordzone ist das Fortune Plaza Projekt. Hier ist eine urbane Mischung vorgesehen: 300.000 m^2 Wohnen, 200.000 m^2 Büros sowie 220.000 m^2 Einkaufen mit einem Ausstellungszentrum und Hotel. Das Herzstück ist ein öffentlicher Platz, der mit einem Park verbunden wird. Der Projektentwickler H.K.I. Development, Hongkong, hat dazu ein internationales Gutachterverfahren durchgeführt.

Den 1. Preis hat AXIS-Group.de aus Berlin gewonnen. Der Entwurf ist eine Kooperation von Eike Becker_Architekten, Faskel Architekten, Architekten Nalbach & Nalbach, Rave Architekten, Stankovic Architekten und Studio Zamp Kelp unter Koordination von Gerald Blomeyer, AXIS-Group.de Berlin, und dem chinesischen Kontaktbüro von Dr. Rao Ying, Beijing.

One of the centres of the new northern district is Fortune Plaza, a mixed-use project with apartments (300,000 m^2), offices (200,000 m^2) and retail areas (220,000 m^2), an exhibition centre and a hotel. The core element is a public square linked to a park.

The Hong Kong project developer, H.K.I. Development, organized a restricted, invited international architectural design competition for the project, and AXIS-Group.de Berlin, submitted the winning design. The design is a co-operative effort by Eike Becker Architects, Faskel Architects, Nalbach & Nalbach, Rave Architects, Stankovic Architects and Studio Zamp Kelp. Gerald Blomeyer of AXIS-Group.de Berlin was responsible for co-ordination with the Beijing partner office of Dr Rao Ying.

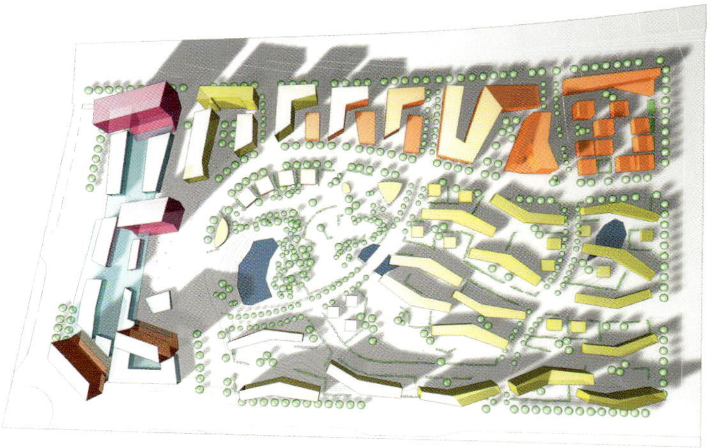

Perspektive Zentrum 1
Centre 1, perspective

Perspektive Zentrum 2
Centre 2, perspective

Bis 2010 wird Shanghai durch dieses große Wohnviertel erweitert. Die Planung eines langen Grüngürtels mit einem See in der Mitte bietet gute Möglichkeiten, das Expo-Thema umzusetzen. Das Stadtentwicklungsgebiet liegt an der äußeren Ringstraße in der Nähe des internationalen Flughafens Hong Qiao und bekommt eine U-Bahn-Station im Bereich des östlichen Geschäftszentrums. Die verschiedenen Abschnitte des neuen Stadtteils werden durch bestehende Straßen, eine innere Ringstraße, einen Grünzug und das begrünte Seeufer miteinander verbunden.

2010 Shanghai has been applied to this large-scale residential area. Planning a long green zone with a large lake in the center of the site is a powerful way of implementing the Expo theme. The site is located on the outer circle city ring. It is close to the Hong Qiao Int. Airport and will have a subway station in the Eastern business node. Besides existing roads and an inner-ring a green belt and the inner green zone along the internal lake connect the different parts of the site.

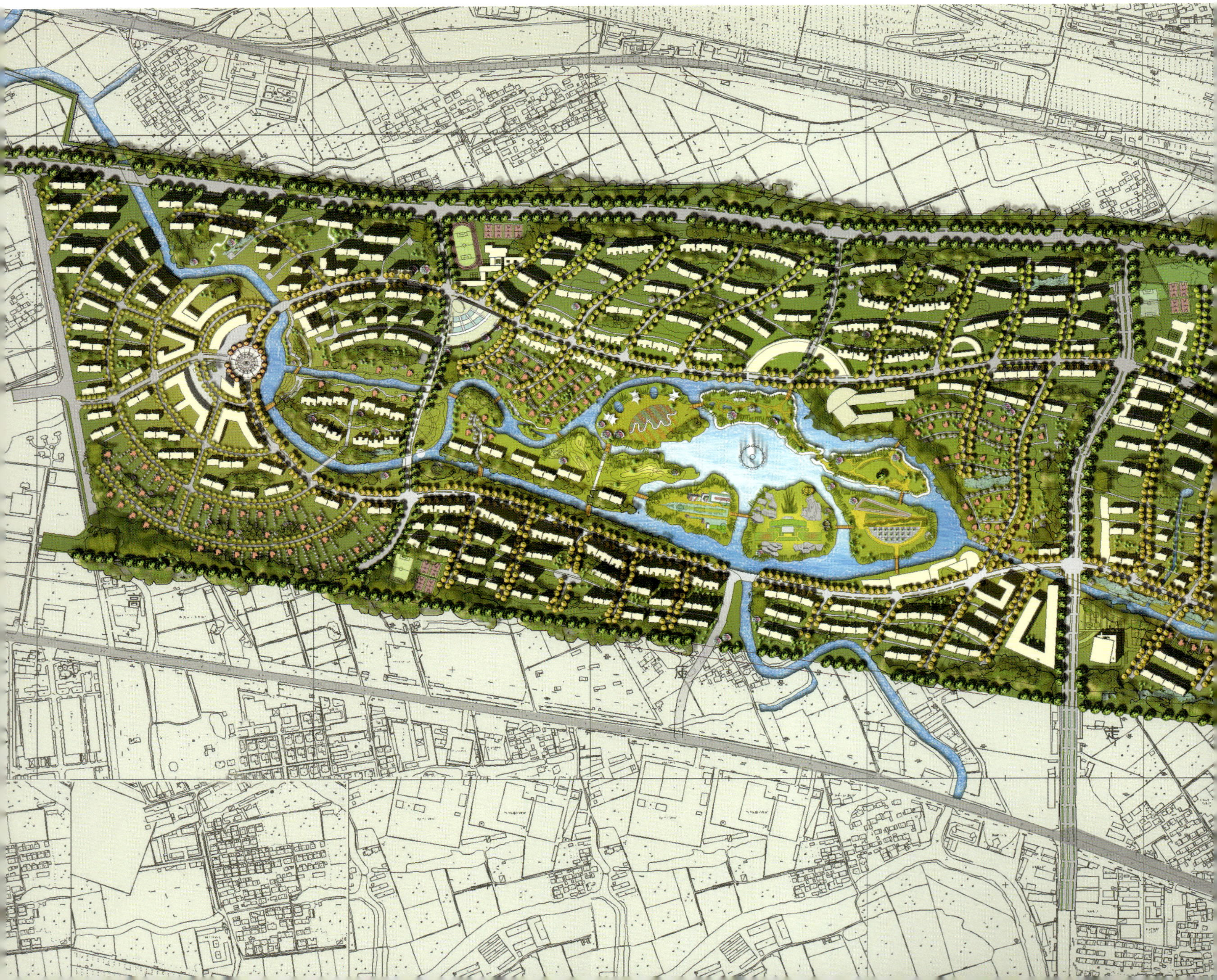

AUSLOBER: Huajiang Construction Development Co., Ltd.
WETTBEWERB: Master Plan for Shanghai Huajiang Residential Estate

BAU.WERK ARCHITEKTEN, MÜNSTER
BRANDENFELS LANDSCAPE + ARCHITECTURE, MÜNSTER

NEUER STADTTEIL HUAJIANG, SHANGHAI
HUAJIANG NEW URBAN DISTRICT, SHANGHAI

Perspektive Themenpark
Theme park, perspective

Das Expo-Thema: Bessere Stadt, Besseres Leben. Das Planungsgebiet wird sozusagen lagenweise bebaut: von Ost nach West mit Bürohochhäusern an beiden Enden und anderen Gebäuden, die zur Mitte hin gestaffelt niedriger werden; von Nord nach Süd mit hohen Mehrfamilienhäusern entlang der Verkehrsarterie, die eine Lärmschutzbarriere darstellen, und schließlich mit einer Villenlandschaft rund um den See.

Das neue Viertel bekommt ein Einkaufszentrum, ein Krankenhaus und ein Clubhaus, die jeweils belebte Zentren im mittleren südlichen Geländeabschnitt bilden.

In den Bürohochhäusern sind auch eine Reihe von Wohnungen vorgesehen, um sicherzustellen, dass dieser Bereich rund um die Uhr belebt ist. Die Grundrisse der Wohneinheiten sind auf den Erhalt des Zusammenwohnens der Generationen angelegt, das für die chinesische Gesellschaft so typisch ist.

The Expo Theme: Better City, Better Life. The development area is layered from east to west – with office towers at both ends and buildings which gradually 'step down' towards the middle – and from north to south with high residential blocks along the arterial road creating an acoustic buffer and with an idyllic high-class residential landscape (free-standing villas) around the lake.

The development includes a shopping centre, a hospital and a club house which form centres of activity in the middle southern section of the area.
The office high-rises also include apartments to ensure that the area remains busy and alive around the clock. The floor plans of the residential units were developed with the aim of sustaining the multi-generational co-habitation typical of Chinese society.

Perspektive Masterplan
Masterplan, perspective

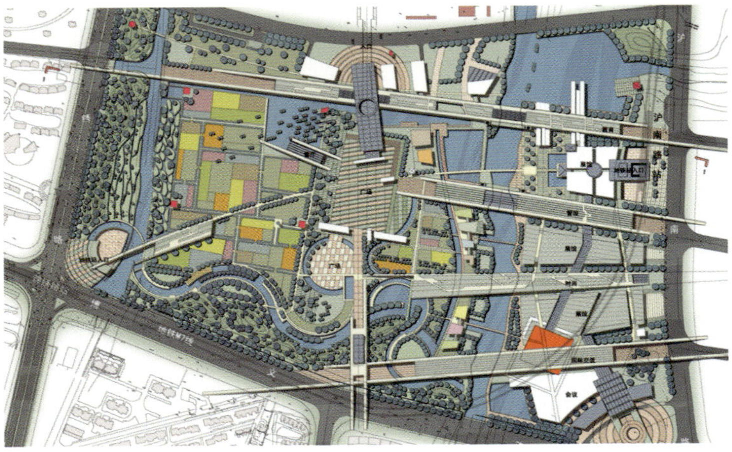

Lageplan
Location plan

Gesamtansicht nachts
Overall night view

In einem Gutachterverfahren wurde die Arbeitsgemeinschaft Peddle Thorp (Melbourne) Architects und brandenfels landscape + architecture aufgefordert, eine Konzeption zu Freizeit, Tourismus, Kunst und Entertainment für die Metropole Shanghai zu erarbeiten. Die 51 ha große Fläche liegt im neuen Stadtteil Pudong und soll als kultureller Trittstein im Stadtgebiet von Shanghai internationale Gäste und Ausstellungen anziehen.

Die Konzeption für das Gelände sieht eine neue Form von Städtebau vor – ein Netz von Ausstellungs-

Following a restricted competition (based on expertises), the project partnership of Peddle Thorp (Melbourne, Australia) and brandenfels landscape + architecture was asked to develop a recreational park with art, leisure and entertainment facilities and other tourist attractions for the metropolis of Shanghai. The 51-hectare project area is situated in the new district of Pudong and was to form a cultural 'stepping stone' attracting international visitors and exhibitions to the city.

AUSLOBER: Shanghai Pudong Development Authority
WETTBEWERB: Shanghai Pudong Cultural Park

PEDDLE THORP MELBOURNE ARCHITECTS, SHANGHAI
BRANDENFELS LANDSCAPE + ARCHITECTURE, MÜNSTER

CULTURE-THEME-PARK, SHANGHAI
CULTURE THEME PARK, SHANGHAI

Vogelperspektive nachts
Bird's-eye view at night

hallen, Künstlerateliers, Hotels und Freizeiteinrichtungen verwoben mit freien Gartenlandschaften, Dachgärten, Promenaden am Wasser, Reminiszenzen an die vorhandene Kulturlandschaft und großzügigen Plätzen.

In dem Gebiet existieren „Creeks", die in ein umfassendes Wassersystem integriert werden: eine Zone zur ökologischen Wasserreinigung wird durchströmt. Dann wird das Wasser durch ein Kanalsystem in einen anderen Bereich geführt und gelangt so zu den Stegen und Inseln, die im westlichen Teil eine Pier-Atmosphäre erzeugen.

The project represents a new type of urban design, i.e. a network of exhibition pavilions, artists' studios, hotels and leisure facilities integrated with landscaped areas, roof gardens, waterside esplanades, reminders of the surrounding cultivated countryside and of spacious open squares.

There are several creeks in the area which have been integrated into a comprehensive hydrological system. The waters of these creeks first flow through a biological water purification bed, are then directed to another area, through a system of channels, and finally reach the piers and islands which create a pleasant seabridge atmosphere in the westen site section.

Zentrum
The centre

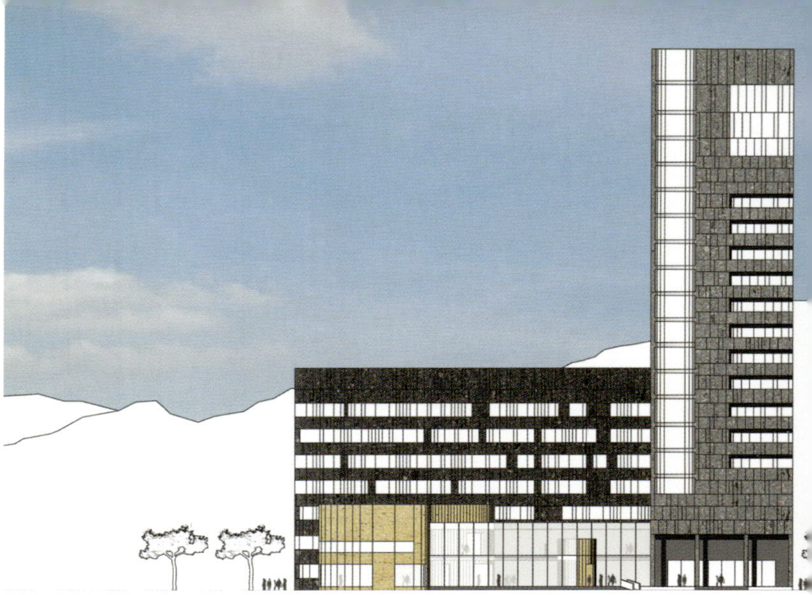

In der nordchinesischen Kleinstadt Liu Lin in der Provinz Shan Xi entsteht derzeit die neue Firmenzentrale eines chinesischen Bergbau-Unternehmens.

Die Konzernzentrale, die ursprünglich von einem chinesischen Planungsbüro entwickelt wurde, besteht aus einem Büro- und Verwaltungsbereich sowie einem zusätzlichen Kongress- und Schulungszentrum. Ergänzt wird das Gebäudeensemble von zwei 21-geschossigen Wohntürmen, die für einen ausgesuchten Teil der über 5.000 Mitarbeiter des Unternehmens vorgesehen sind.

Zusammen mit einer Aufforstungsinitiative und der Anlage eines großen Stausees soll eine flächengreifende Maßnahme zur Rekultivierung der durch den Bergbau stark beeinträchtigten Landschaft beitragen.

Das neue Gebäudeensemble sollte sowohl technisch als auch gestalterisch westlichen Anforderungen entsprechen.

A Chinese mining company is currently building its new corporate headquarters in the northern Chinese town of Liu Lin in the province of Shan Xi.

Originally designed by a Chinese planning firm, the headquarters consist of an office/administration block and a congress and training centre, supplemented by two 21-storey residential towers for a select number of employees of the company with a staff of over 5,000.

In addition, in conjunction with an afforestation project and the creation of a large artificial lake, parts of the landscape damaged by mining were to be restored to its natural state.

In terms of technology and design, the new corporate complex was to correspond to western standards.

BRUNO BRAUN ARCHITEKTEN

BÜROGEBÄUDE, LIU LIN

OFFICE BUILDING, LIU LIN

ORT: Liu Lin, Provinz Shan Xi, VR China
EINWOHNERZAHL: 27.000
GRUNDSTÜCKSFLÄCHE: 42.000 m²
NUTZFLÄCHE GESAMT: 50.100 m²
NUTZFLÄCHE BÜRO / SEMINAR / KONGRESS: 32.600 m²
NUTZFLÄCHE WOHNHÄUSER: 10.500 m²
BAUKOSTEN GESAMT (SCHÄTZUNG): ca. 40,8 Mio. €
BAUKOSTEN UMPLANUNG/AUSBAU: ca. 11 Mio. €

Bruno Braun überarbeiteten gemeinsam mit dem Führungsteam des Unternehmens das Raumprogramm und machten Vorschläge für die Hochhaus-Fassaden. Insbesondere die Organisation der Bürobereiche und der Hotelfunktionen wurde intensiv bearbeitet; Eingangsbereich und Kongressbereich wurden völlig neu entwickelt.

Intensive Beratungsgespräche und gemeinsame Exkursionen zu beispielhaften Projekten in Deutschland waren erforderlich, um die Delegation aus China von einzelnen europäischen Standards und Lösungsvorschlägen zu überzeugen. Während man sich in der Materialwahl schnell darauf einigen konnte, regionale Vorkommen und traditionelle Verwendung zu berücksichtigen, soll nach Wunsch des Bauherren im Innenausbau vorzugsweise europäische Ausstattung zum Einsatz kommen.

Bruno Braun revised the programme in co-operation with the management of the mining company and made design suggestions for the high-rise elevations. The interior organization of the offices and the functional spaces of the congress hotel were revised with particular care. The entrance and congress areas were completely redesigned.

Extensive consultancy and joint excursions to exemplary projects in Germany were necessary to convince the Chinese corporate delegation of certain European standards and solutions. While it was quickly agreed tht the materials should be of local origin and used according to Chinese traditions, the client preferred European design and furbishment for the interiors.

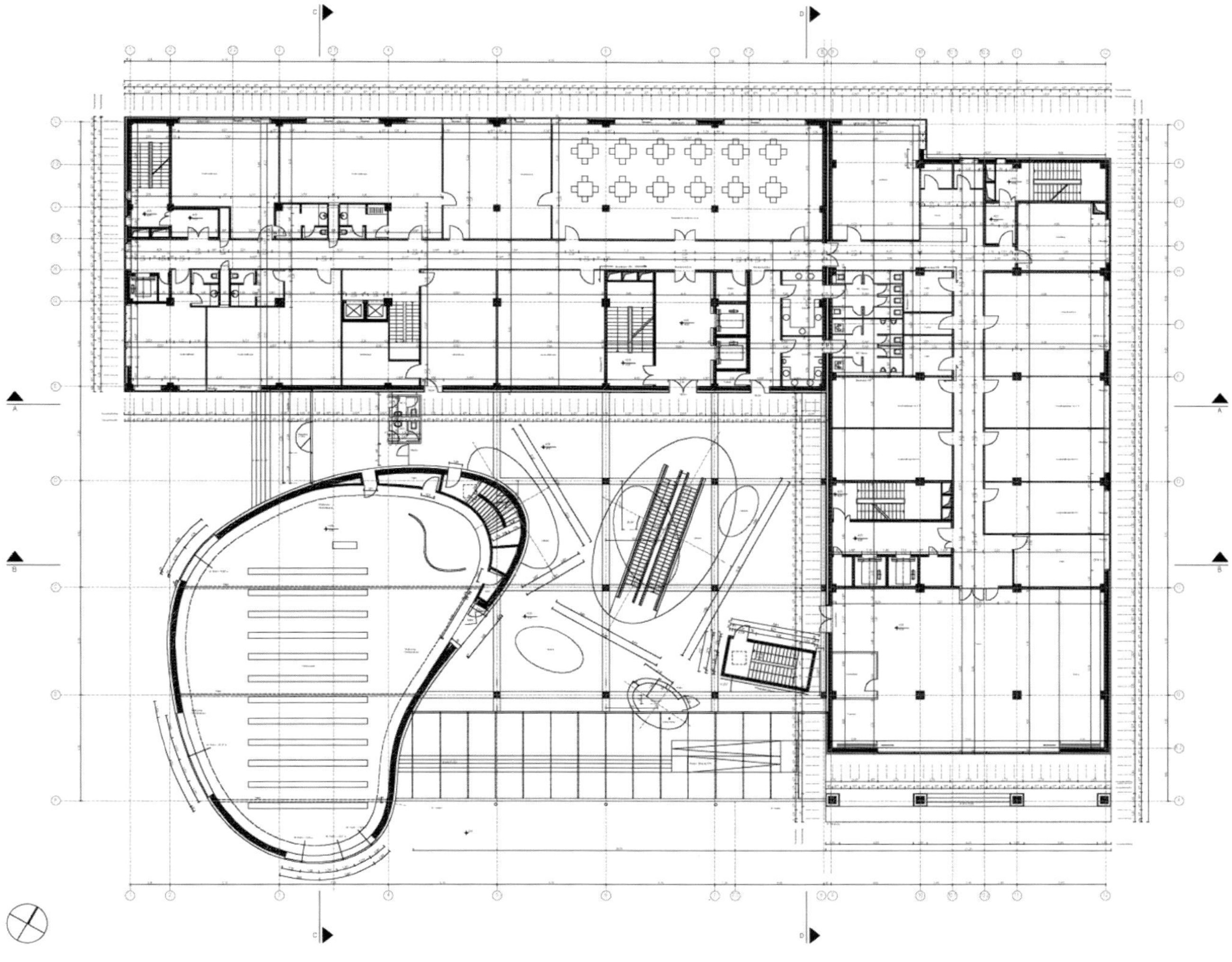

Die Lagune ist ein bedeutender Freiraum an der Gelenkstelle zwischen Meer, Fluss und Stadt. Da der Meeresarm selbst nicht zum Baden geeignet ist, entsteht mit der Lagune durch natürliche Filterung ein sauberer Salzwassersee mit Badestrand und vielfachen Sport- und Erholungsangeboten.

The lagoon is an important open space between the sea, the river and the city. Bathing in the waters of the Qiantang inlet is not advisable, but the lagoon filters and purifies the salty sea water so that it is possible to create a beach for bathing and many forms of sports and leisure activities.

Der Nord-Süd-Grünzug westlich der Feinchemie-Zone wird großflächig mit Waldtypen der subtropischen Küstenregionen entwickelt, eng verwoben mit zahlreichen Wasserflächen. Hier finden bedrohte Tier- und Pflanzenarten Rückzugsräume. Ein Wall im Westen schirmt den Grünzug gegen die Lärmbelastung der Central Road ab.

North-south Green Belt. This green belt west of the fine-chemical zone is generously planted with native trees of this sub-tropical coastal region, and interspersed with numerous bodies of water. Here, endangered animal and plant species will find new places of refuge. An embankment on its western side protects this wooded area from the noise of the Central Road.

Baumgruppen und Waldpflanzungen im Estuary Park im Nordwesten der neuen Stadt bilden eine tiefe Kulisse zum Fluss hin, Schneisen ermöglichen Durchblicke auf die Wiesen am Ufer. Die intensiv genutzten Bereiche mit Spiel- und Sportflächen sowie Schmuck- und Picknickplätzen liegen an der Stadtkante oder eingebettet zwischen sanften Hügeln im Inneren des Parks.

The groves and woods of the Estuary Park in the north-western development area separate the latter from the river, but paths through the forest afford views of the riverside meadows. The intensively utilized areas with playgrounds and sports fields as well as decorative gardens and picnic areas either line the city's edge or are embedded in between the rolling hills in the middle of the park.

Aufgabe der Freiraumplanung ist es, die grundlegenden ökologischen Funktionen wie ausreichende Durchlüftung, Bereitstellung von Retentionsflächen, Erhalt wertvoller Wattgebiete, Entwicklung von Waldflächen etc. sicherzustellen und ein übergeordnetes Freiraumsystem zu entwickeln.

The landscape design was geared to safeguard the basic ecological functions of and requirements for the area – green lungs for the city, rainwater retention areas, conservation of precious tidelands, planting of forests, etc. – and to develop an overriding landscape design.

IRENE BURKHARDT LANDSCHAFTSARCHITEKTEN, MÜNCHEN

FREIFLÄCHEN-KONZEPT UND WASSER-MANAGEMENT SYNIA

LANDSCAPING DESIGN AND WATER MANAGEMENT CONCEPT, SYNIA

Freiflächen-Konzept

Landscaping Design

Am Golf von Hangzhou, etwa 250 km südlich von Shanghai, entsteht eines der größten Industriegebiete Chinas. Hier sollen in den nächsten zwei Jahrzehnten 250 km^2 Polderland zu einer hoch produktiven Stadt- und Industrielandschaft mit unterschiedlichen Branchen wie z.B. Feinchemie, Hightech, Textil- und Leichtindustrie entwickelt werden.

Einzigartig an dem Konzept ist die Neugründung einer Stadt mit ca. 700.000 Einwohnern parallel zur Entwicklung der Industriegebiete. Breite Grünzüge stellen das Rückgrat für eine nachhaltige Entwicklung dar. Ziel ist, eine vielseitige Industrielandschaft mit urbanem Flair und der Möglichkeit zur Naherholung bis hin zu touristischen Attraktionen zu entwickeln.

Die an das Gebiet grenzenden Siedlungsbereiche wurden mit in die Planung einbezogen, sodass insgesamt eine Fläche von 400 km^2 bearbeitet wurde.

One of the largest industrial centres of China is being developed on the Bay of Hangzhou (Hangchow), roughly 250 km south of Shanghai. Over the coming two decades, 250 km^2 of polder land are to be transformed into a highly productive urban and industrial landscape with different larger and smaller plants producing, among others, fine chemicals, high-tech and textiles.

This is a unique urban project for a new city of approximately 700,000 inhabitants parallel to developing industrial estates. Wide green belts represent the 'spines' of a sustainable urban development. The project aims to create a multi-faceted industrial agglomerate with urban flair, near-by recreational areas/facilities and even tourist attractions.

The adjacent settlement areas were included in the project which enlarged the overall planning area to a total of 400 km^2.

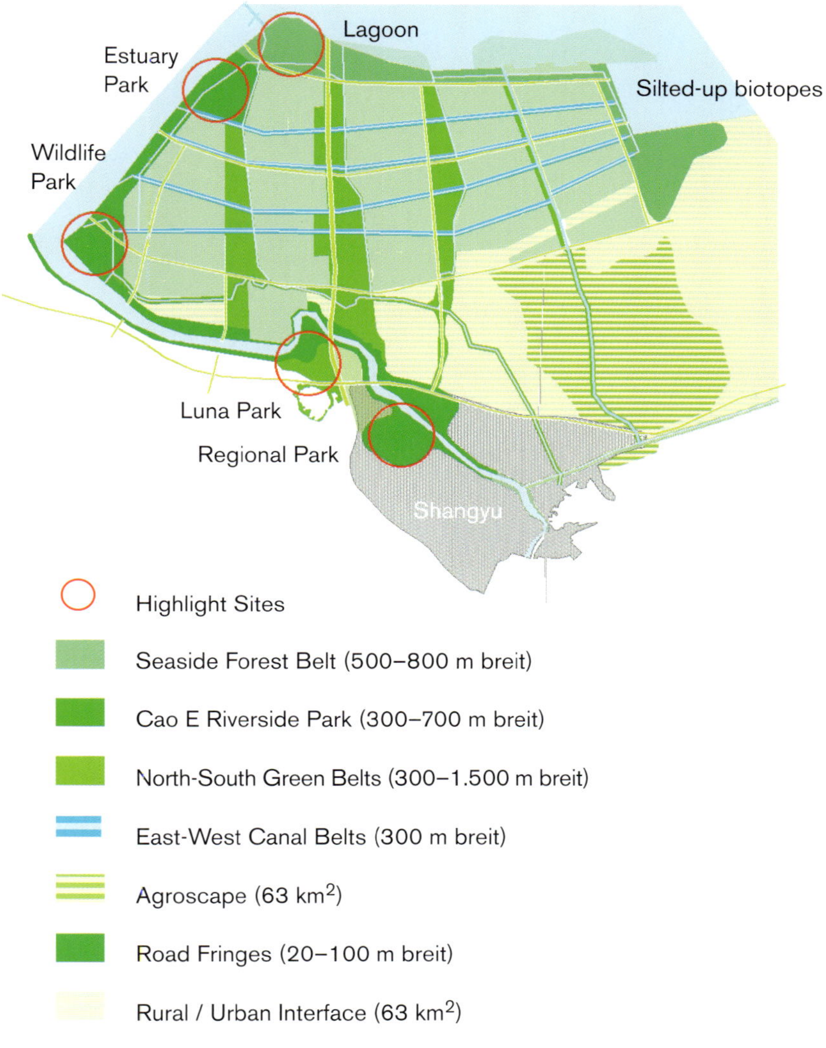

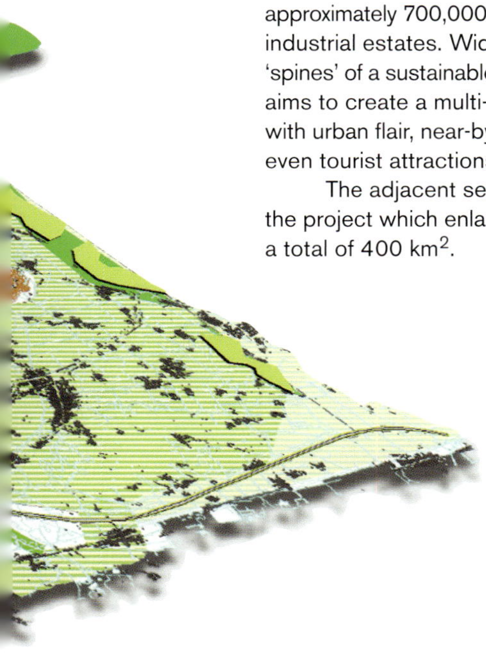

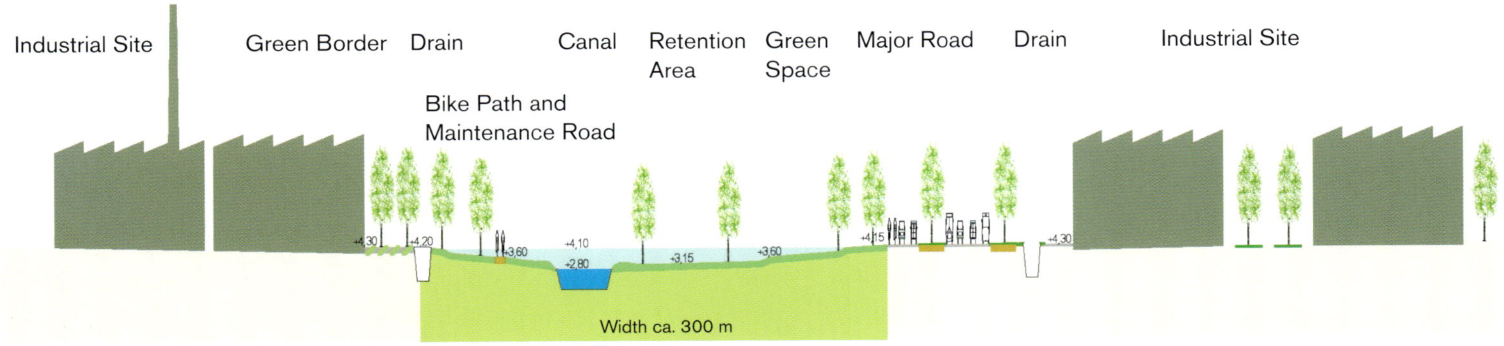

Freiraum am Entwässerungskanal innerhalb eines Industriequartiers (5 x überhöht).

Canal Green Space in Industrial Quarter (Height 5 x multiplied).

Entlang des zentral gelegenen schiffbaren Hauptkanals befinden sich zwei Brauchwasserentnahmestellen mit je einer Aufbereitungsanlage. In den Grünzügen wird das Wasser durch Schilfgürtel, Teiche und Feuchtgebiete biologisch gereinigt. Als Nebeneffekt entstehen hochwertige Lebens- und Erholungsräume. Das Gesamtgebiet wird bei Ebbe durch Sieltore entwässert.

Along the central navigable canal, there are two process water draw-off points, each equipped with a water treatment/recycling plant. Waste water is biologically purified in reed belts, ponds and marshes. As a side effect, this creates high-quality habitats and recreational zones. Under outgoing tides, the entire area is drained via tide gates.

GESAMTGEBIET: 400 km^2
NEUPLANUNG: 250 km^2
PARTNER: Fink + Jocher Architekten, München; TRANSVER Transport System Planners, München; taraske consult Infrastructure Planners, Frankfurt + Leipzig

Wasser-Management

Water Management

Das Wassermanagement ist die zentrale Aufgabenstellung für die sichere Entwicklung des Gebiets. Einerseits müssen für die Industriegebiete enorme Mengen an Brauchwasser aus dem Kanalsystem entnommen werden, andererseits gehen bei starken Monsunregen bis zu 20 Mio. m^3 Regen in 24 Stunden auf das Gebiet nieder, sodass ausreichend große Retentionsflächen erforderlich sind.

Das Gebiet liegt ca. vier Meter über dem Meeresspiegel, bei Flut und Sturmfluten jedoch bis zu vier Metern darunter. Es ist daher durch Deiche zu sichern. Die planerische Herausforderung bestand in der engen Verknüpfung von Brauchwasserentnahme, Abführung von Tagwasser und Retention, wobei die naturnah gestalteten Retentionsflächen zugleich der Naherholung dienen und das Landschaftsbild prägen.

Water management was a central task to be accomplished for the safe urban development of this area. On the one hand, the industries established here need enormous amounts of process water from the urban sewers and canal system, on the other, strong monsoon downpours produce up to 20 million cubic metres of rainwater per 24 hours so that sufficient retention areas are indispensable.

The ground here is about 4 m above sea level, but in times of high and storm tides submerge 4 m under water. This is why it must be secured by dikes. The challenge to planners consisted in the need to combine the systems for process water supplies, stormwater drainage and retention while landscaping the retention areas naturally so as to turn them into recreational spaces for the local population.

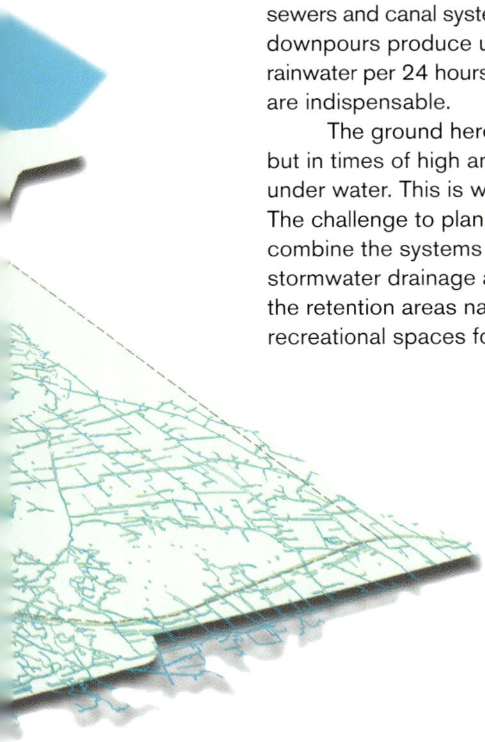

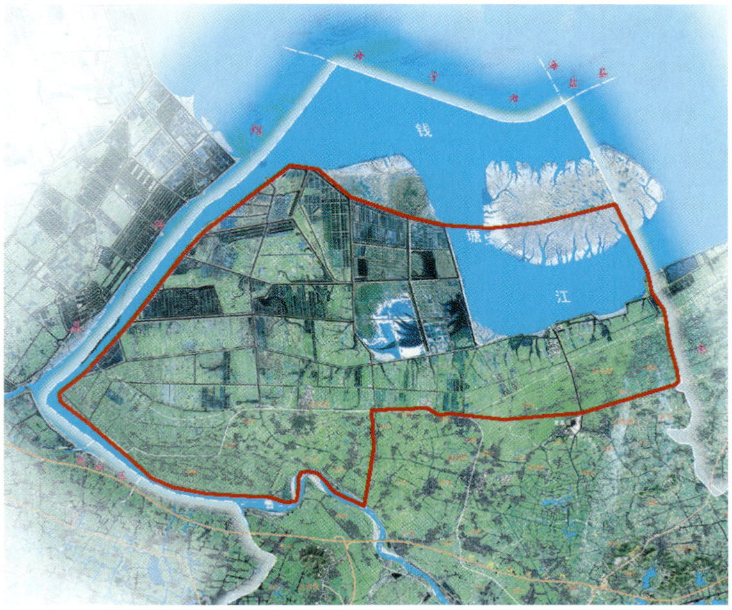

Die Sedimentfracht des Flusses CaoE wird durch einen Sandfang und nachgeschaltete Absetzteiche spürbar gesenkt. Anfallendes Tagwasser kann in kurzer Zeit von den Vorflutern aufgenommen und gegebenenfalls in die Retentionsflächen abgeleitet werden. Diese sind so dimensioniert, dass selbst bei Sturmflut und gleichzeitigem Monsunregen die Aufnahmekapazität mindestens drei Tage ausreicht.

The sediment load carried along by the river Cao'e is substantially reduced by a sand catcher, followed by sediment tanks. Storm water is quickly absorbed by draining ditches and if need be, fed into the retention areas. These have been designed with a capacity large enough to retain, for at least three days, not only stormtide waters, but also monsoon rain falling at the same time.

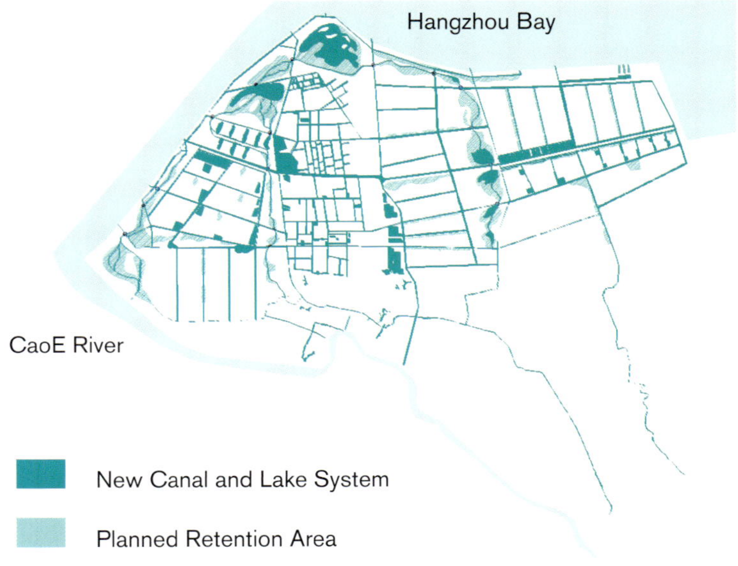

Fassade des Wettbewerbsentwurfs an der West Chang an Avenue, östlich der „Großen Halle des Volkes“ und südlich der „Verbotenen Stadt“. Additiv nebeneinander Eingangsfassade der Konzerthalle, des Schauspielhauses und der großen Oper.

Façade of the competition project towards West Chang-an Avenue, east of the Great Hall of the People and south of the Forbidden City; in linear sequence: the entrance façades of the concert hall, the theatre and the opera house.

Blick in das Foyer des Opernhauses mit den offenen Vertikalerschließungen der drei Ränge. Daneben in der Übereck-Ansicht (Ost-Süd) der kleine Veranstaltungssaal (Auditorium 4) und die Bühnenbetriebsbereiche der verschiedenen „Häuser“.

Interior view of the main opera foyer with the open vertical access to the three upper circles. Left: Corner (southeast) view of the small hall (auditorium 4) and the backstage sections of the different ‘houses’.

PROF. HARALD DEILMANN

WETTBEWERB „NATIONAL GRAND THEATRE, BEIJING 1998“

COMPETITION OF THE NATIONAL GRAND THEATRE, BEIJING 1998

Gesamtansicht des Baukomplexes mit den Foyers der Auditorien, die nach den unterschiedlichen Zweckbestimmungen gegliedert sind, charakterisiert durch den traditionellen Sandstein und rot gestrichenes Holzwerk. Die betont plastische Gliederung soll das große Gebäudevolumen maßstäblich in Erscheinung treten lassen. Sie entspricht den für erforderlich gehaltenen Erschließungsstraßen.

General view of the building complex with the foyer of the auditoria; organized according to their different purposes; characterized by the traditional sandstone and woodwork painted red. The markedly sculptural organization is to give prominence to the scale and dimensions of the large building mass and corresponds to the required access roads.

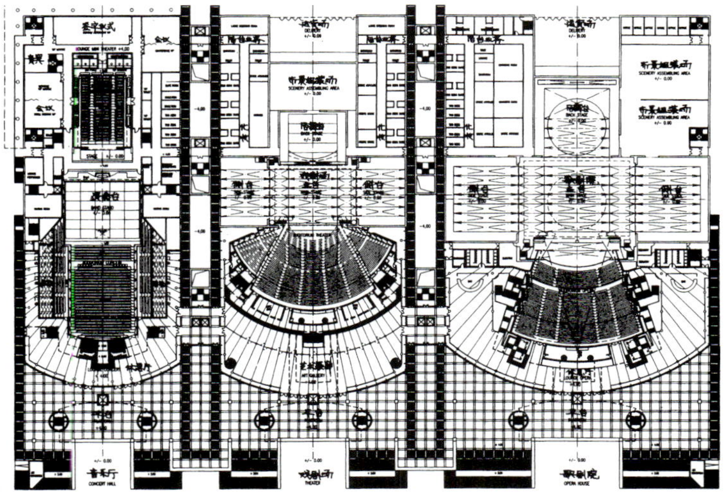

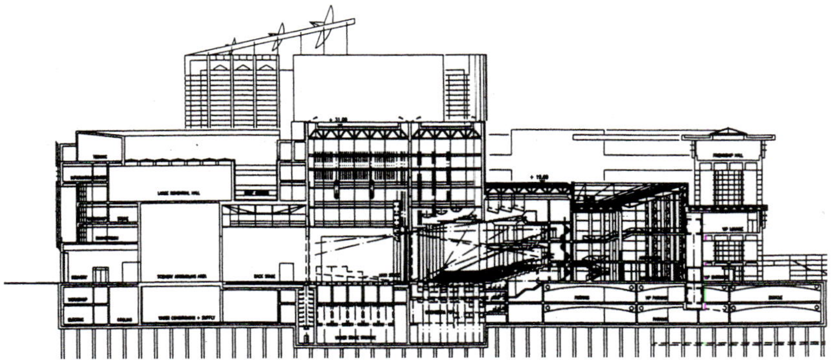

Längsschnitt durch das Opernhaus mit Foyer, dem Auditorium, Vorbühne, Hauptbühne, Hinterbühne, Bühnenbetriebsräumen und Bühnenturm.

Longitudinal section of opera house (with foyer, auditorium, proscenium, main stage, backstage, stage-technical controls rooms and stage house.

Wettbewerb „National Grand Theatre Beijing, 1998“ überarbeitete Fassung – zweiter Entwurf

National Grand Theatre, Beijing Competition design, revised version

Blick aus dem Foyer des Opernhauses in das – im Bild nur angedeutete – Zentralfoyer. Dieses befindet sich im ersten Obergeschoss des Gebäudes mit großzügiger Oberlichtbeleuchtung.

View from the opera foyer into the central foyer (only sketched in this illustration) located on the generously top-lit first upper level of the building.

Der Gebäudekomplex in der Abendbeleuchtung von der West Chang an Avenue aus. Die rechts liegende Außenfassade enthält die elektronisch gesteuerte Programmanzeige.

The illuminated complex at night, seen from West Chang-an Avenue with an electronically controlled programme billboard on the facade (right).

AUFTRAGGEBER: Proprietor Committee of the National Grand Theater, Beijing
WETTBEWERB: Internationaler Wettbewerb 1998
AUFTRAGNEHMER: Obermeyer Planen + Beraten, München
ENTWURF: Prof. Dipl.-Ing. Harald Deilmann

In einer zweiten Überarbeitungsstufe wurde für die Gestaltung eine Bezugnahme auf die „Große Halle des Volkes“ verlangt und in der inneren Gliederung eine zentrale Erschließung der Publikumsbereiche. Die damit verbundene Aufgabe der einander zugeordneten Hinterbühnenbereiche hat im Inneren eine vorteilhafte Kommunikationsmöglichkeit der Publikumsbereiche ergeben.

For a second, revision, stage of the competition, the client insisted that the theatre should relate to the Great Hall of the People and include an interior central access to the public spaces. This made it possible to rearrange and improve the interconnections between the back-stage areas which, in turn, improved the communication between the different public areas.

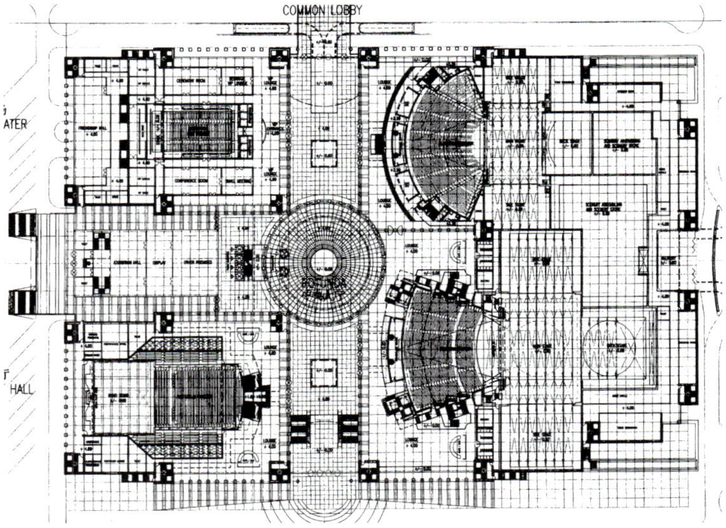

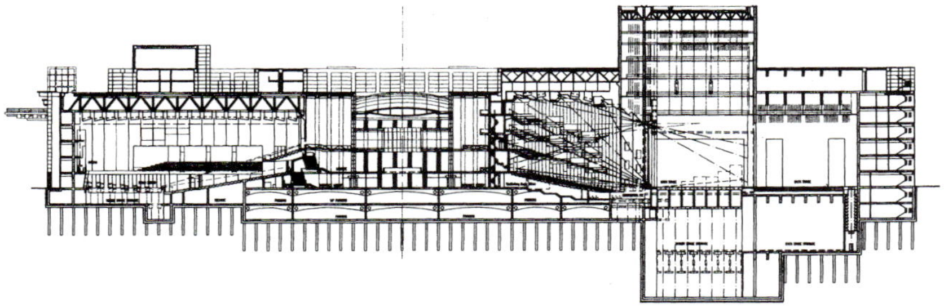

Schnittzeichnung durch – von links – das Konzerthaus, das zentrale Foyer und das dreirangige Opernhaus. Die Auditorien entsprechen dem ersten Wettbewerbsentwurf.

Sectional drawing of (from left to right): concert hall, central foyer and three-circle opera house (with auditoria corresponding to the first competition design).

Golfspiel am Rande eines Bambuswaldes – der Landschaft gewordene Traum des Verfassers

Playing golf next to a bamboo forest – the designer's dream turned landscape

Das Wettbewerbsgebiet ist Teil einer 11 km² großen National Holiday Area, die eine halbe Fahrstunde von Shanghai entfernt liegt.

In der ansonsten flachen Umgebung von Shanghai sind die Erhöhungen des Hügellandes von Sheshan von prägnanter und dominanter Bedeutung.

Diese Besonderheit erhält im Wettbewerbsgebiet eine Antwort durch eine Hügellandschaft, die gleichermaßen für das Golfspiel und den Schwerpunkt der Siedlung, das Clubhaus, einen überhöhten Rahmen bildet und so zum gestalterischen Highlight der Anlage wird.

The competition site is part of an 11 km² 'national holiday area' half an hour's drive from Shanghai. The hills of Sheshan are the literally outstanding features that dominate the otherwise flat countryside around Shanghai.

The competition design responds to them with an equally hilly topography which forms a raised frame for the golf course and the club house and thus becomes the highlight of the design.

Das Clubhaus in seinem markanten Stil ist mit Bezug zum Wasser so platziert worden, dass es als Markenzeichen weithin sichtbar und von prägnanter Bedeutung ist.

The club house with its distinctive architectural style was placed in relation to the lake in such a way as to make it a significant landmark, visible from afar.

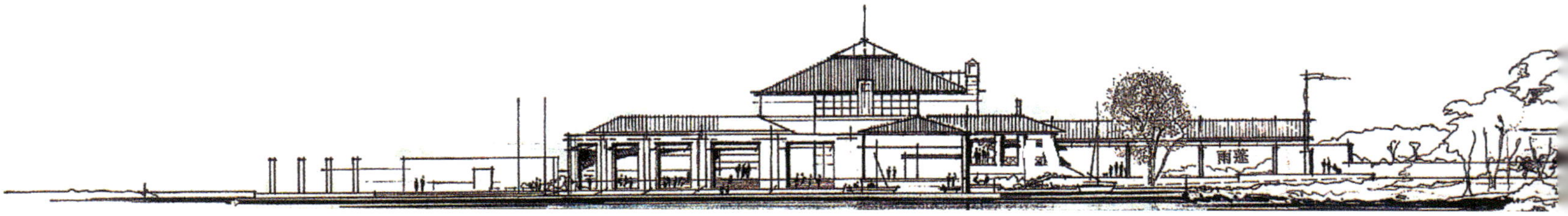

DEUTSCHE GOLF CONSULT

IN ZUSAMMENARBEIT MIT V & B ARCHITEKTENGEMEINSCHAFT, DÜSSELDORF

INT. WETTBEWERB SHANGHAI SHESHAN GOLF PARK

SHESHAN GOLF PARK, SHANGHAI, INTERNATIONAL COMPETITION

Durch die Schaffung weiterer Anhöhungen wird der Reiz für das Auge und das Golfspiel gesteigert und eine dreidimensionale Kulisse gezaubert.

Im Zusammenspiel von bewegter Landschaft, Wasser im Überfluss, blühenden Gehölzen und Stauden und zusätzlichen Golfelementen wie Bunker und nicht zuletzt dem Steinbruch bieten die drei Halbrunden ein unvergessliches Golferlebnis.

Further artificial hills enhance the visual attraction and scenic beauty of the golf course and form a three-dimensional stage set for the players to act on. The interplay of undulating landscape, an abundance of water, flowering shrubs and perennials, additional small golfing elements like bunkers and, last but not least, the existing quarry and the three hemicycles of the design offer an unforgettable golfing experience.

Der Masterplan zeigt die gelungene Symbiose einer Wohnlandschaft in einer Golfanlage mit reizvollen Bezügen zum Wasser.

The masterplan shows the successful merger of a residential estate and a golf course in an attractive lacustrine neighbourhood.

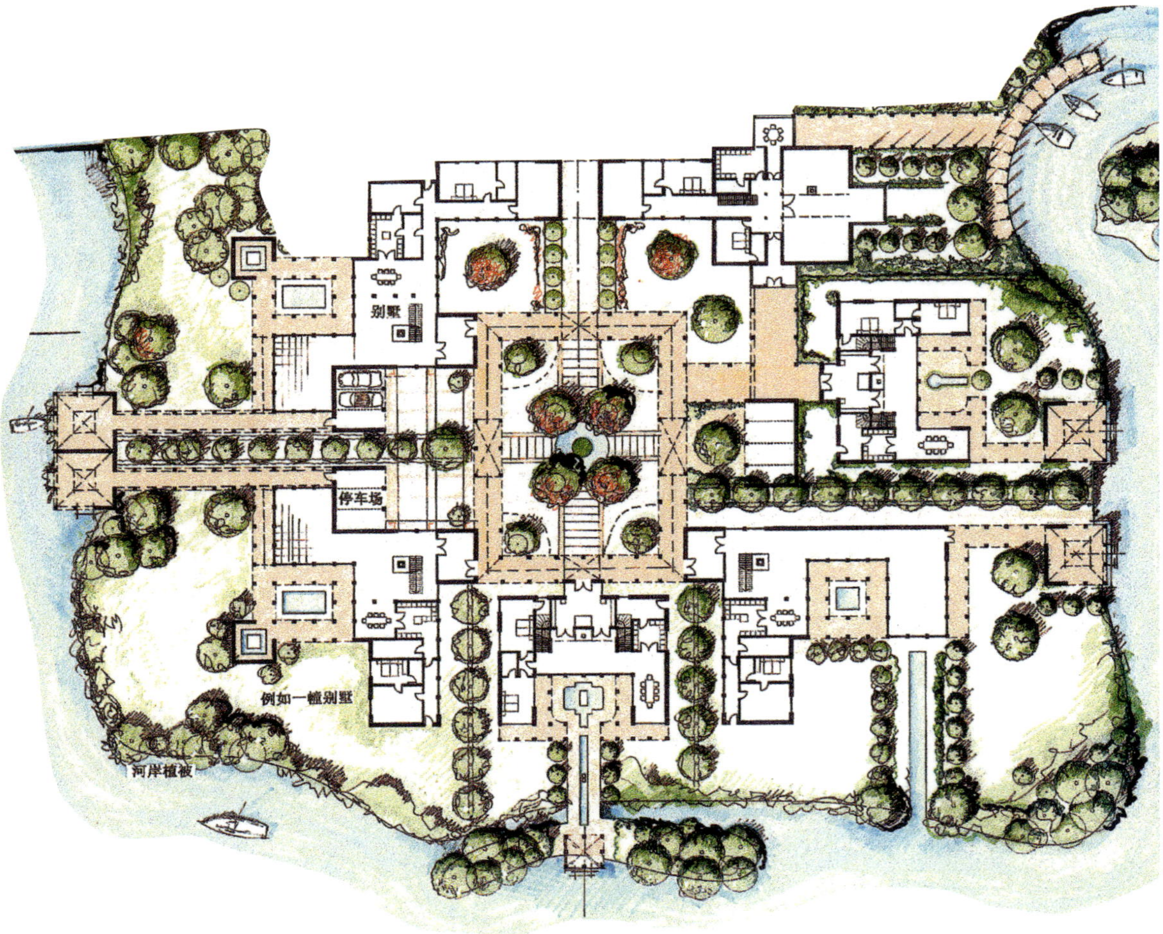

Prof. Volkamer hat es meisterhaft verstanden, den Wohngruppen, die dem traditionellen Wohnen im alten China sehr nahe kommen, eine individuelle elegante Handschrift mitzugeben.

In masterly fashion, Professor Volkamer put an elegant signature style stamp on the residential clusters which emulate the traditional Chinese form of living.

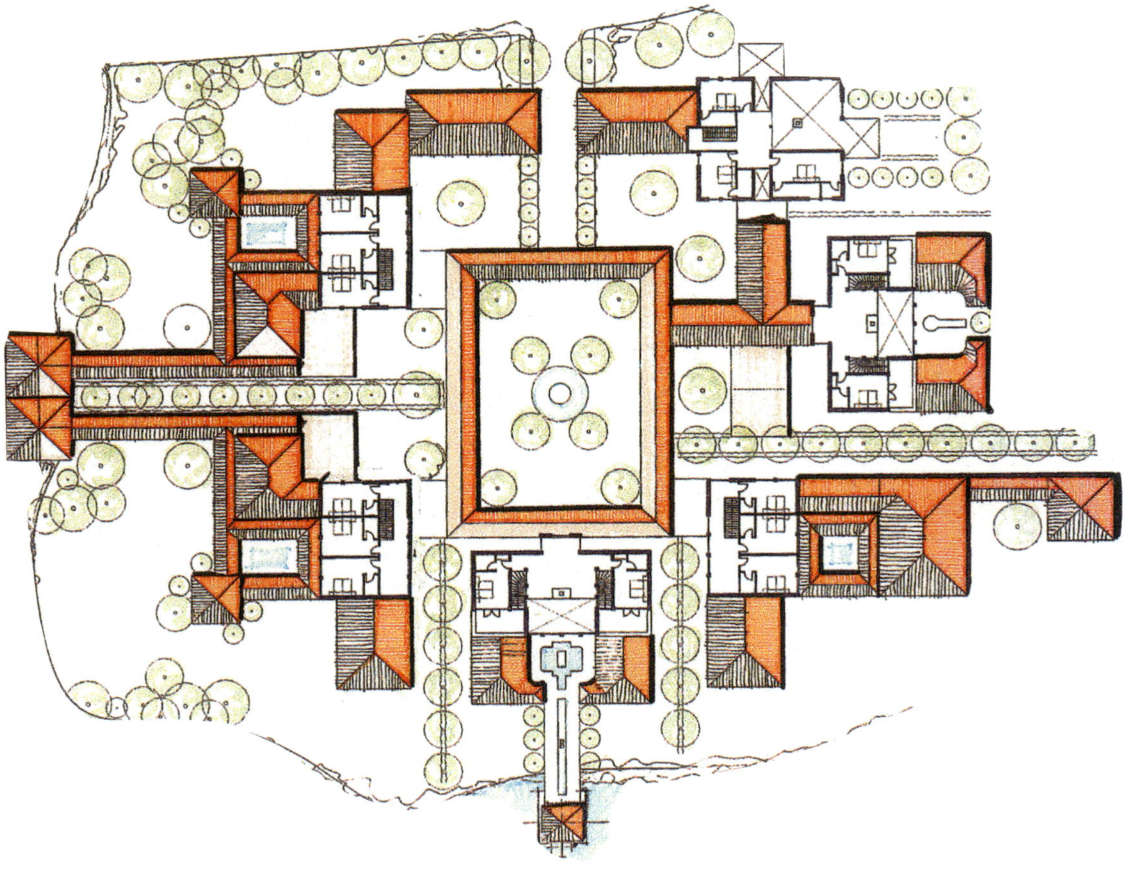

Die Wohngruppen am Wasser und das Clubhaus sind die Markenzeichen der Anlage

The lakeside residential clusters and the club house form the landmarks of the golf course

Die Villenanlage und das Clubhaus entsprechen – wie die Qualität der Golflandschaft – höchstem europäischem Niveau.

Das Clubhaus liegt am Ende der Zufahrt und steht erhöht und eindrucksvoll über dem Gelände, so dass man einen weiten Blick über große Teile der Landschaft und der Villenanlage genießt.

Die Villen sind so angeordnet, dass der größte Teil der Grundstücke Kontakt zum Wasser hat und über das Wasser einen ebenso herrlichen Blick über den Golfplatz.

So ist nicht nur golf- und wasserzugewandtes Wohnen möglich, sondern durch eine häufige Südwestorientierung der Grundstücke auch ein Genuss der Nachmittags- und Abendsonne gesichert.

Die Erschließung des Golf-Parks mitsamt seiner Wohnbebauung von Süden von einer Zufahrt mit Torhaus aus unterstreicht dabei den individuellen und intimen Charakter der Anlage.

The lakeside clusters of houses and the club house as well as the golf course landscape represent the highest European quality standards.

The club house is located at the end of the drive and raised above the site so that it affords a panoramic view of the countryside and the residential neighbourhood.

The houses are placed in such a way that they overlook the lake and the golf course beyond. Most of them are oriented southwest so that they benefit from the afternoon and evening sun.

Both the golf park and the residential area are accessed from the south via a gatehouse and drive. This type of access underlines the individuality and intimate character of the development.

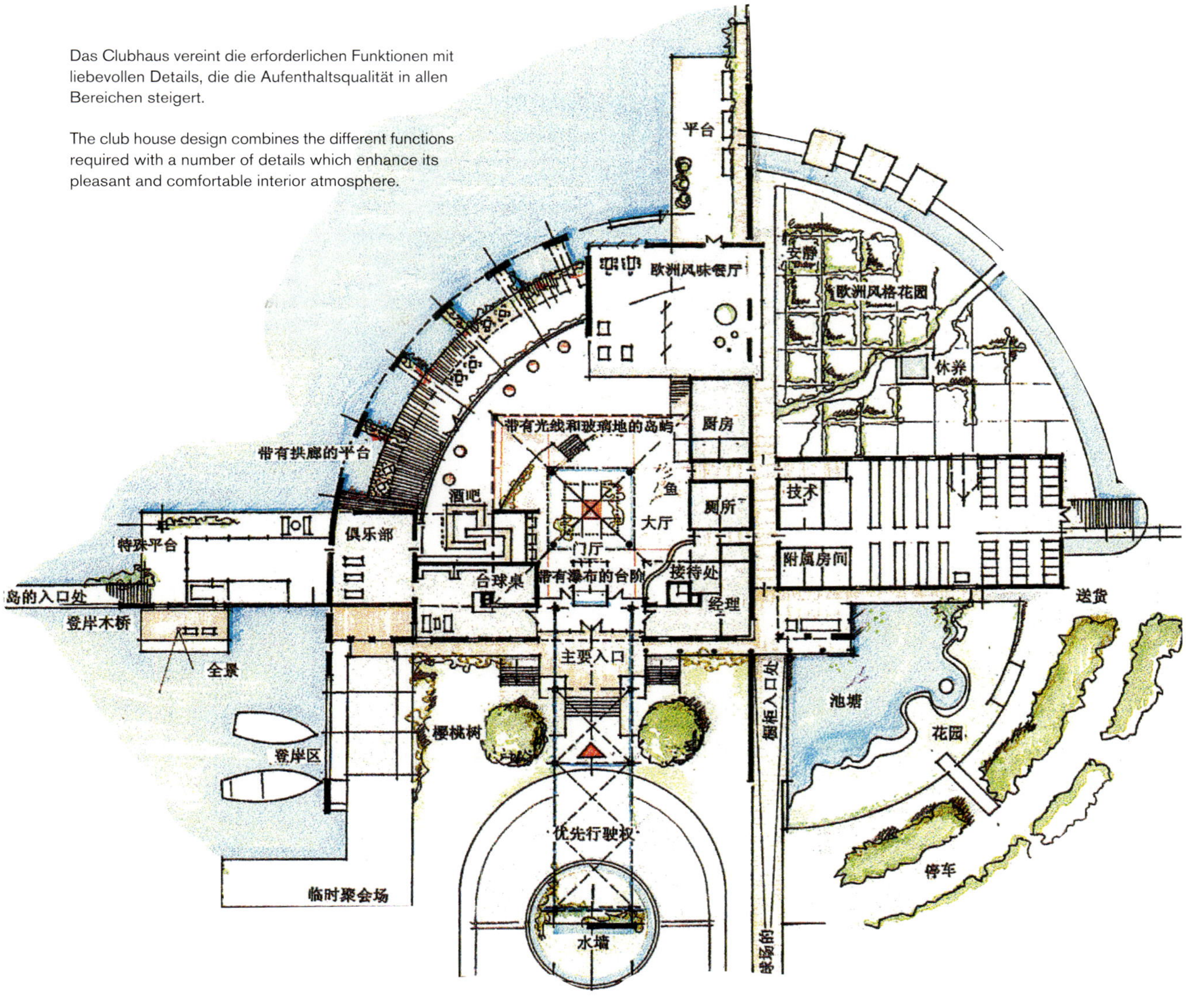

Das Clubhaus vereint die erforderlichen Funktionen mit liebevollen Details, die die Aufenthaltsqualität in allen Bereichen steigert.

The club house design combines the different functions required with a number of details which enhance its pleasant and comfortable interior atmosphere.

Die Hengdian Group Holding Co Ltd. entwickelt ein Wohn- und Freizeitresort für ihre leitenden Angestellten

The Hengdian Group Holding Co. Ltd. is building a residential and leisure resort for its managerial staff

Als markante Erhebung ragt der Vulkankegel aus der Ebene am Rande von Hengdian.

Die Hengdian Group Holding will zur Attraktivitätssteigerung der Movie and TV Tourism City eine Wohnerlebnislandschaft der besonderen Art entwickeln. Die Besiedlung der Hänge eines schlafenden Vulkans ist in dieser Form sicherlich einmalig und lädt zum experimentellen Bau von Häusern in Steilhanglage ein. Die Kombination mit zwei 18-Loch-Golfanlagen verspricht zusätzliche Reize, die sich aus der teilweise klüftigen und rauen Landschaft entwickeln lassen – ein absolutes Unikat.

A cone-shaped volcano rises out of the flat countryside near Hengdian. The Hengdian Group Holding wishes to increase the attraction of its Movie and TV Tourism City by means of an unusual type of inspiring and exciting residential landscape. Building on a sleeping volcano is certainly unique und challenged designers to experiment with building houses stepping down a steep hillside. Combining this terraced residential development with two 18-hole golf courses on levelled site areas promises additional attractions partly derived from the rugged mountain landscape. Altogether an absolute unicum.

Die Landschaft um den schlafenden Vulkan erhält eine gestaffelte Hangbebauung und zwei 18-Loch-Golfplätze in den verebneten Bereichen.

The hilly site at the foot of the inactive volcano was built up with houses stepping down the hillside, and an 18-hole golf course was laid out on the level sections of ground.

DEUTSCHE GOLF CONSULT

INT. GOLF AND LEISURE RESORT HENGDIAN MOVIE AND TV TOURISM CITY

INT. GOLF AND LEISURE RESORT HENGDIAN MOVIE AND TV TOURISM CITY

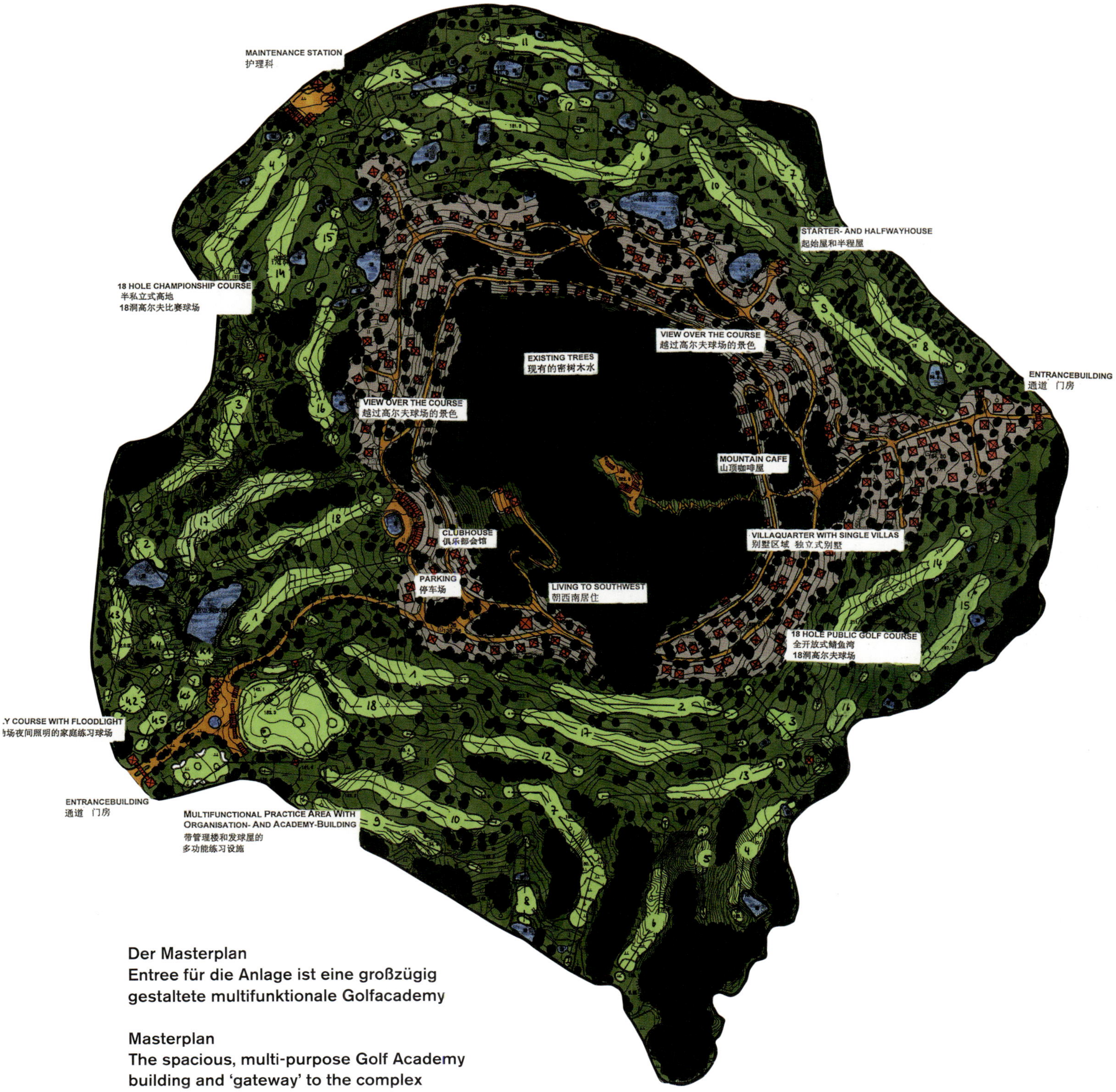

Der Masterplan
Entree für die Anlage ist eine großzügig gestaltete multifunktionale Golfacademy

Masterplan
The spacious, multi-purpose Golf Academy building and 'gateway' to the complex

GRUNDSTÜCKSFLÄCHE: 120.000 m²
WETTBEWERB: 2004, 1. Preisgruppe

JO. FRANZKE ARCHITEKTEN, FRANKFURT AM MAIN

JINMEN TOWER UND KONZERTHAUS, TIANJIN
JINMEN TOWER AND CONCERT HALL, TIANJIN

Auf der Grundlage der Ergebnisse eines städtebaulichen Wettbewerbs waren ein Torhaus, eine kreisförmige Fußgängerbrücke sowie ein Konzerthaus im Stadtzentrum von Tianjin zu entwickeln. Das 254 m hohe Torhaus für Hotel- und Konferenznutzung sowie die dreigeschossigen Sockelgebäude markieren den Abschluss einer 100 m breiten Grün- und Verkehrsachse am Schnittpunkt der Hauptgeschäftszonen. Die als Pylon ausgebildeten Zwillingstürme tragen die hängende Brücke, die beide Ufer des Hai-River verbindet – ein Brückenschlag zum gläsernen Konzerthaus im Zentrum des „Wasserplatzes" mit uferbegleitenden öffentlichen Zonen, Plätzen und Parks. Die um 15° geneigte Hochhaus-Spitze ist das Ergebnis eines optimierten Tragwerkskonzeptes im Dialog zwischen dem Torhaus und der Brücke.

The urban design competition was for a gate house, a circular pedestrian bridge and a concert hall in the city centre of Tianjin. The 254-metre gate house, used as a hotel and conference centre, marks the end of a green,100 m wide, and traffic axis which runs between two main business and shopping areas. The circular bridge across the River Hai is suspended from pylon-type twin towers and leads to the glass concert hall in the middle of the 'water square' and the adjoining public squares and parks along the embankment. The twin-tower top is inclined by 15 degrees and is the result of an optimized structural design in dialogue with the gate house and the bridge.

EVOLUTION
HISTORY

CINEMA

GRUNDSTÜCKSFLÄCHE: 55.000 m^2
WETTBEWERB: 2004, 2. Preis

JO. FRANZKE ARCHITEKTEN, FRANKFURT AM MAIN

HOHHOT – STÄDTEBAULICHE ÜBERLEGUNGEN
URBAN DESIGN IDEAS FOR HOHHOT

In der Nähe des Regierungsviertels plant die Stadt Hohhot ein Opernhaus mit zwei großen Kinos und einem 50.000 m^2 großen Museum.

Im Westen grenzt das Areal an ein Wohngebiet, im Norden schließen sich 5-geschossige Zeilenbauten an. Selbst bei einer großzügig bemessenen, niedrigen Bauweise besetzen die Gebäude der Oper und des Museums nur einen geringen Teil des Planungsfeldes. Sieht man sie jedoch als Beginn eines so genannten „Kulturforums", dem weitere Bauten für die Öffentlichkeit, wie z.B. ein Konzertsaal oder ein Kongresszentrum, folgen könnten, so bilden sie den Nukleus einer neuen Stadtentwicklung.

Die Platzgestaltung entspricht den städtebaulichen Fluchtlinien der Gebäude. So wird die Rahmung durch die Platzkanten im Fußbodenbelag aufgenommen und durch unterschiedliche Beläge unterstrichen. Durch Grünstreifen erfolgt eine Längsorientierung zur Platzmitte.

Alle Gebäude werden zentral vom Platz aus erschlossen. Sie sind sowohl Solitärgebäude als auch Teil einer städtebaulichen Einheit. Lebhaft und extrovertiert von Inhalt und äußerer Gestalt her bilden Oper und Kinocenter den Ausgleich zum eher introvertierten Museum. Aus diesem Kontrastprogramm bezieht der Platz seine Spannung.

Der Grundriss des Museums ist geprägt durch die zentral liegende Rotunde, um die über drei Geschosse die Ausstellungshallen und weitere Nutzungen angeordnet sind. Wesentliches Gestaltungsmerkmal ist die Konstruktion der Rotunde in Form und Material einer Jurte als kultureller Bestandteil des Lebens in der Region. Um die Rotunde laufen spiralförmig die Rampen, von denen man in die Ausstellungshallen gelangt.

The city of Hohhot plans to build an opera house, which also contains two large cinemas, and a museum with 50,000 m^2 of floor space close to the government district.

To the west, the area borders on a residential neighbourhood and to the north on an area with five-storey ribbon blocks. Even though they are generously dimensioned and low, the opera and museum buildings cover only a small section of the entire building site. Seen as the beginning of the so-called 'cultural forum' which could be built up with additional public buildings, such as a concert hall or congress centre, they form the nucleus of a new urban development.

The design of the square retraces and extends the building lines of the urban environment and marks them with lines and areas of different paving materials. Strips of greenery run lengthwise to the centre of the plaza.

All the buildings – both free-standing and attached – are accessible from this public space. The opera and cinema complex appears lively and extrovert, both in terms of shape and content, and thus forms a contrast to the rather introvert museum. The plaza draws its appeal from this striking contrast.

A three-storey central rotunda, surrounded by the exhibition galleries and other spaces, dominates the plan of the museum. In shape and materials, the rotunda was modelled on the yurta, the essential part of the culture and life of this region. It is surrounded by the helical ramp which gives access to the exhibition galleries.

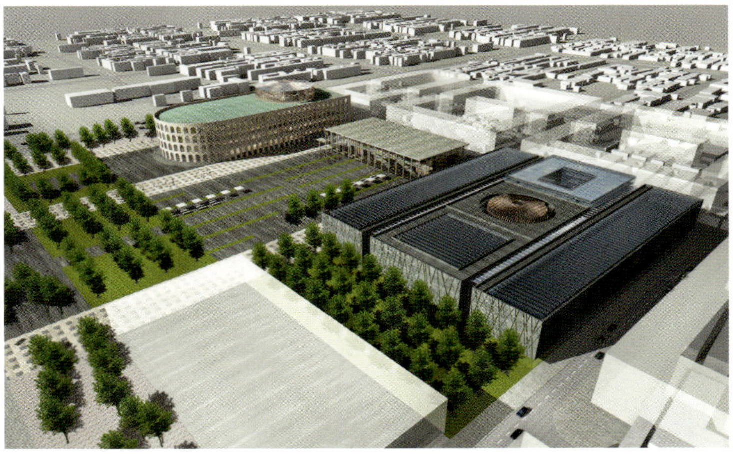

Aus der Korrespondenz der beiden für das kulturelle und städtische Leben Hohhots wesentlichen Bauten, Oper und Museum, ergibt sich ihre innere und äußere Ordnung. Die Oper rahmt den Platz im Süden, das Museum bildet den Abschluss im Norden, und die Kinos stellen das Bindeglied zwischen beiden her.

The correspondence between the two buildings essential to the cultural and urban life of Hohhot – i.e. the opera house and the museum – generates both their interior organization and façade structure. To the south, the square is closed off by the opera house, to the north by the museum; the cinemas form the link between both.

Flowers
Gifts
Travel
Food
Modern living
StyleShop
Shoes
Books

GRUNDSTÜCKSFLÄCHE: 81.500 m²
GUTACHTEN: 2004

JO. FRANZKE ARCHITEKTEN, FRANKFURT AM MAIN

ZHAO LIN HOTEL & BÜROGEBÄUDE (PROJEKT), PEKING

ZHAO LIN HOTEL & OFFICE BUILDING (PROJECT), BEIJING

Das Planungsgebiet weist eine dünne Bebauung aus Wohn- und Büroquartieren auf. Die städtebaulichen Überlegungen legen ein strenges Raster aus Straßen und Quartieren für Wohnen, Büro und Freizeit. Da die Vorgaben für die beiden Hochhäuser den östlichen Teil des Grundstücks vorgaben, erstreckt sich die Bebauung in einer Breite von 90 m und einer Länge von 190 m entlang der inneren Erschließungsstraße.

Die Erschließung für das Hotel, das Bürogebäude und die Mall wurde nach Osten gelegt, da so auf dem westlichen Grundstücksteil Platz für einen Park geschaffen werden konnte, der die Fortsetzung des Hotelgartens darstellt. Die Erschließung im Osten bietet Zufahrten zur Tiefgarage und eine Umfahrung des Grundstücks mit der Anlieferung im Norden.

Über einer 2-geschossigen Tiefgarage erhebt sich ein 4-geschossiger Sockelbau, der zwei 25-geschossige Hochhäuser und den innen liegenden Garten rahmt. Das Erdgeschoss öffnet sich zum Park und zu den umliegenden Straßen und bietet überdachte Zugänge zum Konferenzbereich im Bürohochhaus, zum Hotel und den Passagen der Mall als horizontale Erweiterung der beiden Hochhäuser.

Die beiden Hochhäuser haben kleeblattförmige Grundrisse. Beide Türme verfügen über Empfangshallen und innen liegende Foyers. Während das Konferenzzentrum den Sockel des Bürohochhauses beherrscht, sind es im Hotel Restaurants, Bars und der Ballsaal. Umgeben sind sie von Läden. Im 4. Obergeschoss liegt der Wellnessbereich des Hotels. Im Bereich der Einschnürungen beider Türme springen die Fassaden nach außen, sodass sich rings um das vertikale Foyer drei Lufträume ergeben.

Die Farbigkeit der Fassaden wird durch den innen liegenden Sonnenschutz unterstützt: Während beim Büroturm kühle Blautöne gewählt wurden, sind es beim Hotelturm warme Rottöne. Der Kontrast zwischen dem Sockelgebäude und den filigranen und lebhaften Türmen bildete einen wesentlichen Entwurfsparameter.

The development area is sparsely dotted with residential and office clusters. The urban design envisages a rigid grid of streets as well as residential, business and leisure zones. The client required the two high-rises to be placed on the eastern site section; for this reason, the overall complex extends over 90 m (width) and 190 m along the inner access road.

The access drive to the hotel, the office building and the mall was aligned on the eastern side so that the western section could be designed as a park, as extension of the hotel gardens. A site road leads to the entrance of the underground garage from the west, and continues around the site to the delivery yard on the north side of the complex.

A four-storey base structure, which frames two twenty-five-storey high-rises and an inner garden patio, rises above the two-level underground car park. The ground-floor spaces open to the park and the surrounding streets and have canopied entrances to the conference centre in the office tower, to the hotel and the shopping mall.

The two towers on clover-leaf footprint plans each have a reception hall with a foyer behind it. While the conference centre occupies most of the base structure of the office tower, the hotel section also contains restaurants, bars and a ballroom. Both are surrounded by shops. The hotel's spa facilities are on the 4th floor. Where the towers are 'constricted', the façades project outward to create three air spaces above the vertical foyer.

The colours of the façade are enhanced from inside by the interior colour scheme. Cool shades of blue were chosen for the office tower, and warm red hues for the hotel. The contrast between the solid base structure and the filigree vibrancy of the towers was a determining design factor.

Während das Sockelgebäude eine Fassade aus einem dunklen, farbkräftigen Naturstein erhält, haben die Türme transparente Glasfassaden, die in ihrer Doppelschaligkeit klimatischen Ansprüchen Rechnung tragen.

The base was clad with a dark-coloured stone; the towers have double façades of transparent glass which help to create the required pleasant interior climates.

Der strenge Masterplan für das Ningbo Eastern New City Center prägt den Entwurf für das Technologiemuseum.

Dreiseitig von geradlinigen Kanälen gerahmt und im Süden über die Ost-Zhongshan-Straße erschlossen, fügt es sich als scharf konturierter Bau dem Grundstück ein. Alle Stellplätze sowie die Einfahrt zur Tiefgarage wurden entlang der Straße angeordnet, sodass mit Ausnahme notwendiger Transporte von Ausstellungsgütern kein Verkehr die Landschaftsgestaltung beeinträchtigt.

Ebenso wie das Gebäude reagiert auch die Modellierung des Landschaftsgartens um das Museum auf den Masterplan. Es ist ein Versuch, das Pittoreske einer Landschaftlichkeit mit dem strengen Raster des Planes und mit der Strenge des Gebäudes zu verbinden.

Der äußere Aufbau des Gebäudekubus folgt der Gliederung des Programms. Auf einem 2-geschossigen Sockel lagern die beiden Hauptausstellungsgeschosse,

The reduced rigid masterplan of Ningbo's Eastern New City Centre served as a model for the design of the city's museum of technology. Framed on three sides by straight canals and accesses from East Zhongshan Road to the south, it is a sharp-edged volume. The parking lots and the entrance to the underground garage were placed along the street so that, except for delivery vans, cars do not spoil the view of the landscaped grounds.

Apart from the building design, the modelling of the landscape gardens also responds to the masterplan. It is an attempt to combine picturesque parkland qualities with the strict orthogonality of the urban map and the austerity of the building.

The façade structure of the museum cube follows the interior organization. The two main exhibition floors (which include the cinemas) rest on a two-storey 'plinth'. The third, attic, level contains administration offices and lecture halls, which enclose a roof terrace.

GRUNDSTÜCKSFLÄCHE: 35.000 m²
WETTBEWERB: 2004/2005, 1. Preisgruppe

JO. FRANZKE ARCHITEKTEN, FRANKFURT AM MAIN

NINGBO TECHNOLOGIEMUSEUM
NINGBO TECHNOLOGICAL MUSEUM

die auch die Kinos beinhalten. Überkrönt werden sie von einem Dachgeschoss mit Verwaltung und Vortragssälen, die eine weitere Terrassenfläche umschließen.

Alle Hallen, Labore, Büros, Kinos und Versammlungsräume umschließen in ihrer Mitte die kreisförmige Eingangshalle, die magistralenartig Norden und Süden, Osten und Westen über die Hauptverkehrsachsen verbindet. In beide Richtungen durchschneiden sie 3-geschosshoch das Gebäude. In den Lufträumen kreuzen sich Rampen und Wege, die die Hallen miteinander verbinden.

Im Inneren der Halle schwebt als Zitat von Boullées Kenotaph für Newton eine 42 Meter hohe Kugel, die wie ein Nukleus in die Gesamtanlage eingebettet ist. Ihre Fernwirkung entfaltet sie besonders nachts durch ihre obere Hälfte, die die Eingangshalle als Kuppel überwölbt. Treppen, Rampen und Fahrtreppen verbinden die Eingangshalle mit der Kugel und den übrigen Ausstellungsebenen.

All the halls, laboratories, offices, cinemas and other auditoria are grouped around the central circular entrance hall which serves as the hub of the 'main interior thoroughfares' to the north and south, east and west entrances/exits. These corridors are three storeys high and criss-crossed at different levels by ramps and bridges. ((Rest ô, da überflüssig und unklar, welche Hallen gemeint sind))

A spherical gallery with a diameter of 42 m is suspended in the entrance hall. It is a 'quote' from Boullée's cenotaph for Isaac Newton, embedded in the complex as if it were its nucleus. The upper half of the sphere, which is also the domed roof of the entrance hall, unfolds its long-distance effect especially at night. Flights of stairs, ramps and escalators link the entrance hall with the spherical space and the exhibition levels.

Auf die Oberfläche der Kugel werden die Exponate des Museums projiziert, während der Innenraum Platz für übergroße Exponate bietet. Auf der inneren Kugelfläche kann mittels LCD-Technik der neueste Stand aller technischen Entwicklungen weltweit aufgezeigt werden.

Images of the museum's exhibits are projected onto the sphere's surface while its interior offers space for oversized exhibits. The walls of the spherical gallery include LCD stations with which visitors may call up information on the state of international technological developments.

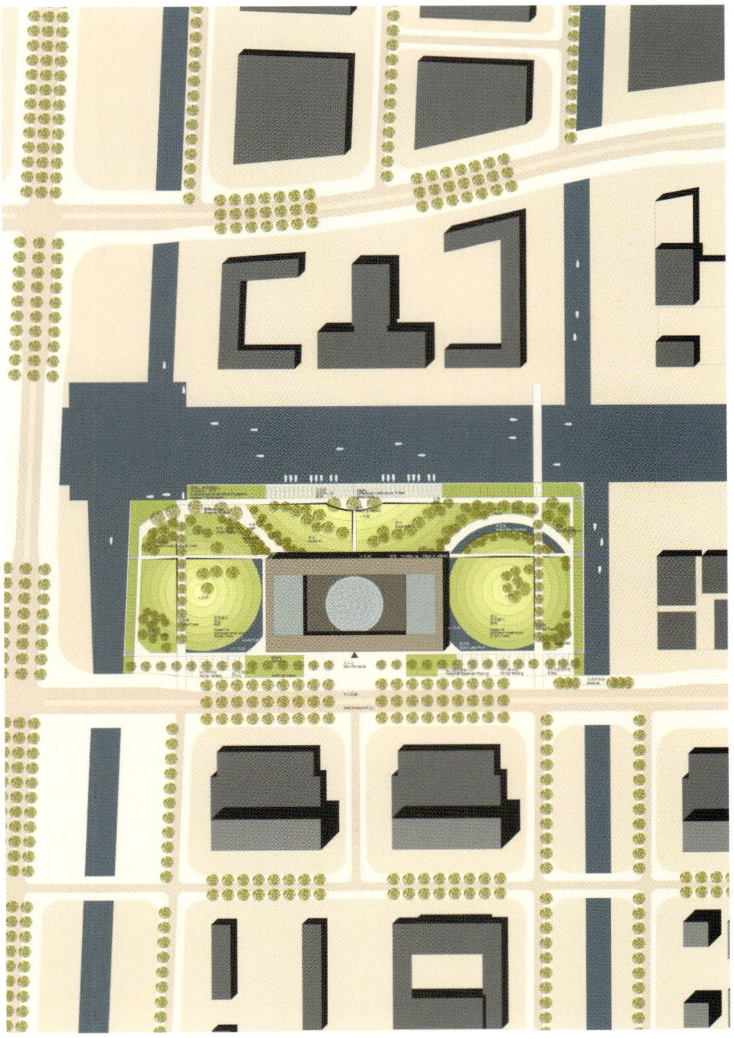

Die Achse des Haupteingangs führt über den zentralen Mittelpunkt des Campusareals. Vis-a-vis entlang der He-Jian-Lu befinden sich das allgemeine Lehrgebäude und das Technologiegebäude, die beide auch über den weiträumigen Campusplatz erschlossen werden.

The axis from the main entrance runs across the centre of the campus. At its opposite end, on He-Jian-Lu Road, are the general lecture hall and the technology institute, both of them also accessed via the spacious central campus area.

GRUNDSTÜCKSFLÄCHE: 76.000 m²
WETTBEWERB: 2005, 3. Preis

JO. FRANZKE ARCHITEKTEN, FRANKFURT AM MAIN

SHANGHAI UNIVERSITY OF ELECTRONIC POWER

SHANGHAI UNIVERSITY OF ELECTRONIC POWER

Das zwischen He-Jian-Lu und Chang-Yang-Lu gelegene neue Areal der Shanghai University of Electronic Power soll in zwei Bauabschnitten mit sechs Gebäuden realisiert werden.

Alle Gebäude orientieren sich zur begrünten Platzmitte. An seiner Schmalseite am Übergang zum gegenwärtigen Universitätscampus entsteht das Mediengebäude, verbunden mit einem seitlichen Stadtplatz und dem Fußgängerübergang zum südlichen Campus. Das Mediengebäude wird gesäumt von zwei Stadtloggien als Teehaus / Bistro oder Orangerie. Sie schließen das Areal zu seiner heterogenen Nachbarschaft im Südwesten ab und trennen den Versorgungsverkehr vom zentralen Campus.

Zwei Türme bilden mit einem gläsernen Querriegel ein kompaktes Wohngebäudeensemble. Das Medienzentrum für Bild und Text besteht aus zwei 6-geschossigen Baukörpern, in deren Mitte sich der zentrale Lesesaal befindet. Das markante Gebäude bildet Kopf und Gelenk zwischen beiden Campusflächen.

The new campus of Shanghai University of Electronic Power is situated between He-Jian-Lu and Chang-Cang-Lu roads and consists of six buildings constructed in two stages. All six buildings face the green centre of the campus. The media institute with an urban square to one side and a pedestrian precinct to the other marks the point of transition to the old campus south of the new site. It is flanked by two 'urban loggias': a tea house and perhaps a snackbar or an orangery. These 'loggias' close the campus off from the heterogeneous neighbourhood southwest of it and separate the delivery traffic from the central campus area.

Two towers waith a glazed connecting structure form a compact residential ensemble. The media centre for text and image consists of two six-storey volumes and a reading room in between. This striking building forms the head and joint between the two campuses.

Auf dem Areal des Musikkonservatoriums in Shanghai soll ein Ensemble aus Bestandsgebäuden und neuen Einrichtungen entstehen. Durch die neue Achsstruktur, die Alt und Neu verbindet und eine übergeordnete Ordnung schafft, wird ein urbanes Campusgelände gestaltet, das modernen Anforderungen gerecht wird.

Die Ordnungsstruktur ist Ausgangspunkt für die Anordnung der Gebäude (Theater, Lehrgebäude, Mensa, Sporthalle und Studentenzentrum sowie das unterirdische Museum für orientalische Musikinstrumente). Entlang der Ost-West-Achsen entstehen unterschiedliche Plätze. So ist der südlichen Achse ein Park zugedacht, während der nördlichen Achse ein städtischer Platz entspringt. Wie in der Musiktheorie verkörpert das Sinnbild „Thema und Variation“ den Entwurfsgedanken.

The site of the Conservatory in Shanghai is to be redeveloped by refurbishing the existing old buildings and supplementing them with new ones. A new circulation axis connects the old and the new structures and unifies them in an urbane campus that meets modern requirements.

This organizational element was the start for placing the buildings (theatre, the conservatory proper, canteen, sports hall, student centre and underground museum of oriental instruments). A number of different public areas line the east-west circulation axes, the southern-most axis is accompanied by a garden; an urban square extends from the northern-most axis. By analogy with musical theory, the basic design idea was 'theme and variations'. Thus, the buildings with their

GRUNDSTÜCKSFLÄCHE: 50.000 m²
WETTBEWERB: 2004, 2. Phase, 1. Preis

JO. FRANZKE ARCHITEKTEN, FRANKFURT AM MAIN

MUSIKKONSERVATORIUM SHANGHAI
SHANGHAI CONSERVATORY

So beziehen sich die Gebäude in ihren Steinfassaden aufeinander, ohne Monotonie zu erzeugen.

Das Theatergebäude an der Wei-Hei-Lu bildet die nördliche Begrenzung des Campus. Eine transparente Hülle umschließt die Körper für Theatersaal, Bühne und Entree des Musikinstrumenten-Museums.

Der unterirdische Bau des Museums für orientalische Musikinstrumente wird durch das Foyer im Theatergebäude erschlossen.

Im Süden des Areals entstehen die Sporthalle und das Studentenzentrum. Während die Sporthalle von einem flachen steinernen Kubus umschlossen wird, ragt das Studentenzentrum als Pendant zur angrenzenden Hochhausarchitektur mit einem 7-geschossigen Turm in die Höhe.

Das Bibliotheks- und Mediengebäude erhält eine Fassadengliederung, die mit einfachen Mitteln entsteht. Das 2-geschossige Sockelgebäude bindet das Bestandsgebäude in das Ensemble ein.

stone façades refer to each other, without becoming monotonous.

The theatre building on Wei-Hei-Lu Road forms the northern border of the campus. It has a transparent skin and houses not only the theatre and stage, but also the museum of oriental musical instruments in the basement which is accessed via the theatre foyer.

The sports hall and student centre are sited on the southern campus section. While the sports hall is enclosed by a flat stone cube, the student building has seven storeys and forms a counterpart of the neighbouring high-rise architecture.

The library and media building has a façade that has been structured by simple means, and the two-storey 'plinth' integrates the existing building into the new ensemble.

Das Lehrgebäude an der Ostseite des Campusgeländes markiert mit dem Theatergebäude die Nord-Süd-Achse, die in ihrem Schnittpunkt mit der Fen-Yang-Lu den Haupteingang der Universität bildet.

The teaching building on the east side of the campus and the theatre accentuate the north-south axis. Its point of intersection with Fen-Yang-Lu Road marks the main entrance to the university.

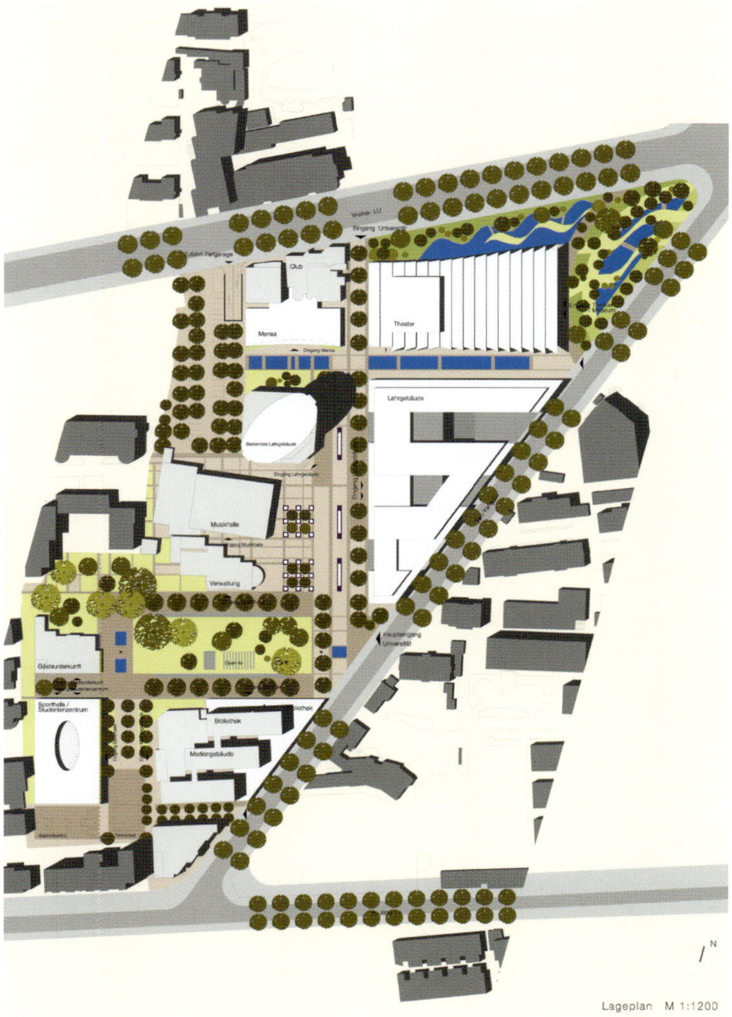

Lageplan M 1:1200

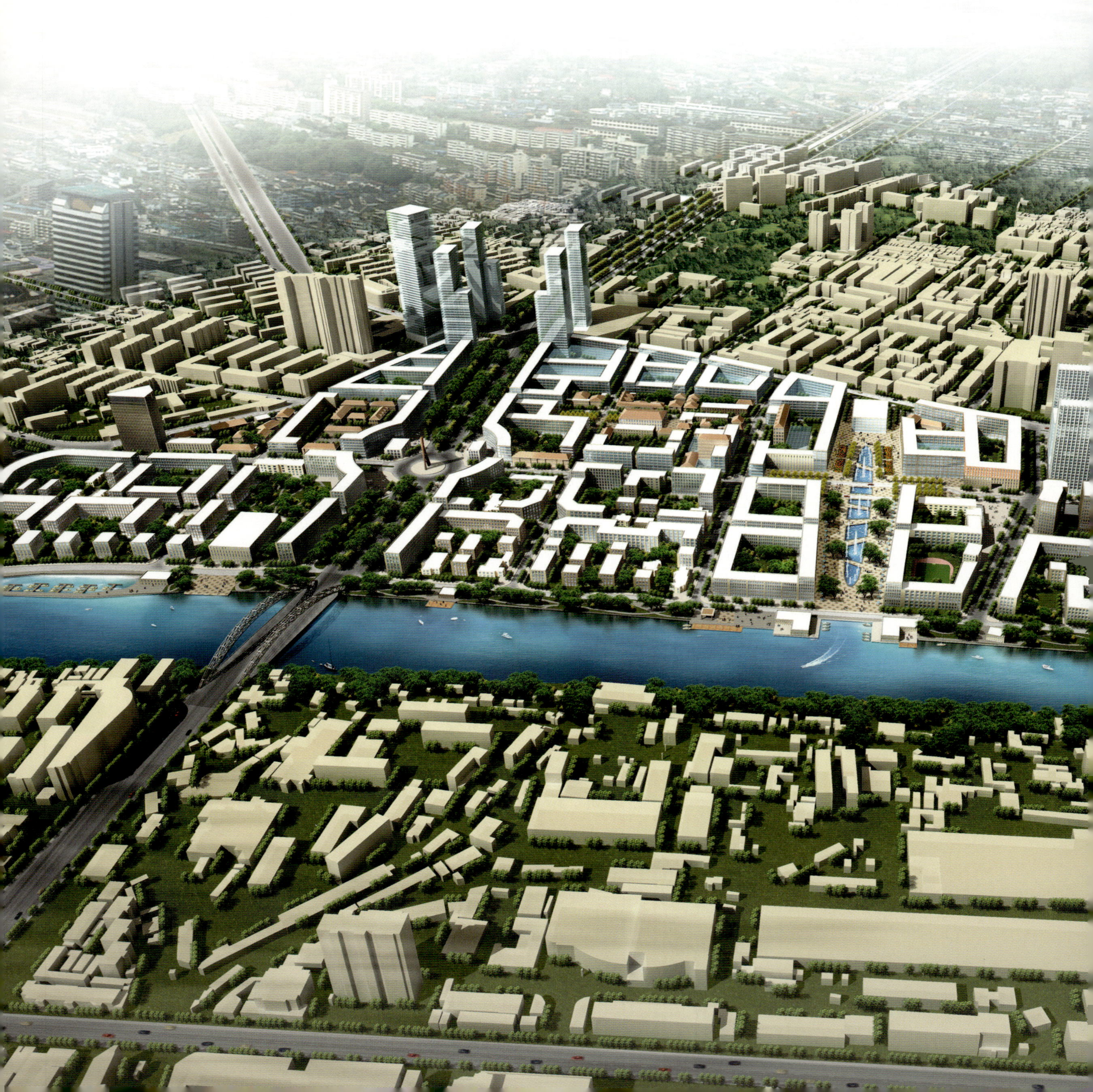

GRUNDSTÜCKSFLÄCHE: 1,4 Mio. m^2
WETTBEWERB: 2004/2005, 1. Preisgruppe

JO. FRANZKE ARCHITEKTEN, FRANKFURT AM MAIN

DEUTSCHES VIERTEL TIANJIN
GERMAN DISTRICT OF TIANJIN

Die Idee ist, ein Viertel in der Stadt Tianjin gemessen an seinem historischen Kontext als „Deutsches Viertel" weiterzuentwickeln und ihm eine eigene Identität zu geben, die zugleich die Geschichte der Stadt und des Viertels reflektiert.

Die Nutzungen der einzelnen Quartiere des Viertels sind Mischnutzungen, die ein pulsierendes und belebtes Viertel ermöglichen. Besonderheiten bilden vor allem die Randbereiche. Ist die Randbebauung entlang der parkähnlichen Uferzone dem Wohnen vorbehalten, so finden sich entlang der westlichen Quartierskante Büronutzungen und Flächen für Handel sowie Sondernutzungen.

Leitmotiv ist die zentrale Kulturachse, die in den Erdgeschossbereichen Flächen für Handel und Gastronomie vorsieht. Wie an einer Perlenschnur reihen sich ergänzend dazu Gebäude und Plätze für kulturelle Einrichtungen auf. Die in Ost-West-Richtung verlaufenden Querachsen verknüpfen die Uferzone und die Randbezirke mit dem „Deutschen Viertel".

The project started from the idea to redevelop one area of Tianjin as the 'German District', following on from the history of the city – to give it a new identity which at the same time reflects the history of both the city and this particular neighbourhood.

There are different areas of mixed uses in this district so that it is always full of life and variety. Its edge areas are places apart, with residential buildings along the green embankment of the river Pei-ho and offices as well as trade facilities and special functional buildings along the western edge of the district.

The guiding design element is the central 'cultural axis' with ground-floor spaces for retail and catering outlets, supplemented like a string of pearls by buildings and open areas designed for cultural purposes. The east-west transverse axes connect the riverside and the outer edge zones with the centre of the 'German District'.

Die historischen Bauten bleiben geschützt und sind Ausgangspunkt für eine nachhaltige städtebauliche Sanierung. Neubauten werden in das Gefüge eingepasst. Erhaltenswerte Gebäude können räumlich versetzt werden – es entstehen intakte Quartiere von hohem städtebaulichen Wert.

The historic buildings have been preserved and form the basis of the sustainable urban redevelopment, with new structures being integrated with the old ones. Buildings worthy of preservation can be moved to other sites. The result of all these measures is an urban area of high design quality.

gmp – VON GERKAN, MARG UND PARTNER, HAMBURG

INTERNATIONALES MESSE- UND KONGRESSZENTRUM, NANNING
NANNING INTERNATIONAL CONVENTION & EXHIBITION CENTRE

Das am Hang gelegene Grundstück mit einer Höhendifferenz von 45 m befindet sich am Rand von Nanning inmitten eines die Stadt umgebenden Grüngürtels.

Eine multifunktionale Halle bildet mit ihrem gefalteten Kuppeltragwerk mit einer Gesamthöhe von 70 m und einem Durchmesser von 48 m den Kopf der Messeanlage und ragt als Landmarke über die Silhouette der Stadt hinaus. Ihre Dachkonstruktion besteht aus einem filigranen Stahltragwerk, das beidseitig mit einer transluzenten Membran bespannt ist. Die kreisrunde Halle kann aufgrund ihrer zentralen Lage auch getrennt vom Ausstellungs- und Konferenzbetrieb genutzt werden. Als Rotunde bietet sie in idealer Weise Platz für Ausstellungen, große Konferenzen, Theateraufführungen, Konzerte und Eröffnungszeremonien.

The site on a slope with a height difference of 45 m is located on the outskirts of Nanning within the green belt surrounding the city.

A multi-functional hall with a folded domical roof, 70 m high and 48 m in diameter, forms the head of the exhibition complex and rises above the city silhouette as a landmark. The roof is conceived as a filigree load-bearing steel structure, which is on both sides covered with a translucent membrane. Due to its central location the circular hall can be used separately from the exhibition and conference operations. As a rotunda it provides an ideal space for exhibitions, large conventions, theatre plays, concerts, and opening ceremonies.

INTERNATIONALER WETTBEWERB: 1999 – 1. Preis
ENTWURF: Meinhard von Gerkan und Nikolaus Goetze
PROJEKTLEITUNG: Dirk Heller, Karen Schroeder
CHINESISCHES PARTNERBÜRO: Guangxi Architectural Comprehensive Design & Research Institute, Nanning
STATIK: Schlaich Bergermann und Partner
HAUSTECHNIK: HL-Technik
LANDSCHAFTSPLANUNG: Breimann + Bruun
BAUHERR: Nanning International Convention & Exhibition Co., Ltd.
BGF: ca. 90.000 m^2 (Erweiterung bis 2005 auf 130.000m^2)
BRI: ca. 1.200.000 m^3
BAUZEIT: 1999–2003

Unterhalb der Halle befindet sich das ebenfalls separat nutzbare Kongresszentrum mit fünf Sälen und einem angrenzenden Restaurant.

Die Ausstellungshallen schließen an die Rotunde an und werden zu beiden Seiten eines zweigeschossigen Foyers erschlossen. Die neun Hallen des ersten Bauabschnitts, die jeweils über zwei Ausstellungsebenen verfügen, können auf beiden Ebenen zu Gruppen zusammengeschlossen werden, sodass Veranstaltungen unterschiedlichster Größe möglich sind. Die Größe der Hallen variiert zwischen 2.100 und 3.200 m^2, ergänzt um eine Halle mit einer Fläche von 5.000 m^2. Alle Hallen werden über zwei Seiten mit Tageslicht versorgt und können bei Bedarf verdunkelt werden.

Ein Natursteinsockel bildet das optische Fundament; während der Veranstaltungen kann er als Freiterrasse und Ausstellungsfläche genutzt werden. Stahlbetonstützen, die vor den aufsteigenden Natursteinsockeln stehen, erstrecken sich über die volle Höhe der beiden Hallenebenen und tragen das signifikante Dach, das durch die Einschnitte der Kerne, in denen sich die haustechnischen Anlagen befinden, rhythmisch gegliedert wird.

Natürliche Materialien und Oberflächen mit den ihnen eigenen haptischen und ästhetischen Qualitäten bestimmen die Erscheinung des Messe- und Kongresszentrums. Außen wie auch im Innenraum überwiegen Naturstein, Glas und Beton, Farben wurden nur sparsam und zur Akzentuierung besonderer Funktionen eingesetzt.

Im Jahr 2005 wurde die zweite Bauphase mit weiteren sechs Hallen in südlicher Richtung und einem Verwaltungsgebäude abgeschlossen.

Im Flusstal am Fuße der Messe wurde der Bau durch ein Open-Air-Theater arrondiert. Das ovale Theater mit ca. 35.000 Plätzen ist in einen Hang eingebettet und öffnet sich in Richtung Messe. Diese bildet den Hintergrund für das jährlich stattfindende Nanning Folksong-Festival.

The convention centre comprising of five halls and an adjoining restaurant is located underneath the hall und can be used separately.

The exhibition halls adjoining the rotunda are accessible from both sides of a two-storeyed foyer. The nine halls realized during the first construction phase, all of them designed with two exhibition levels, can be interlinked on both levels as groups, providing for a variety of events. The dimension of the halls varies between 2,100 m^2 and 3,200 m^2, complemented by one hall with a floor area of 5,000 m^2. The halls are naturally lit on two sides and can be blacked out when required.

A stone plinth forms the visual foundation; during events it can be used as an open-air terrace and exhibition area. Reinforced concrete columns, positioned in front of the ascending stone socle, stretch across the complete height of both hall levels and support the distinct roof, which is rhythmically structured by the recesses of the cores accommodating the technical plant and services.

Natural materials and surfaces with their inherent haptic and aesthetic qualities characterize the appearance of the exhibition and convention centre. Externally and internally stone, glass and concrete are the predominately used materials; colours were scarcely used and only applied for the accentuation of special functions.

In 2005, the second construction phase comprising of another six halls located to the south and an administration building was completed.

In the river valley at the foot of the exhibition centre the building was realigned with an open-air theatre. The oval theatre with approximately 35,000 seats is embedded into a slope and opens up towards the exhibition centre, which forms the backdrop for the annual Nanning Folksong Festival.

构建文明
和谐新浦东
努力争创
全国文明城区

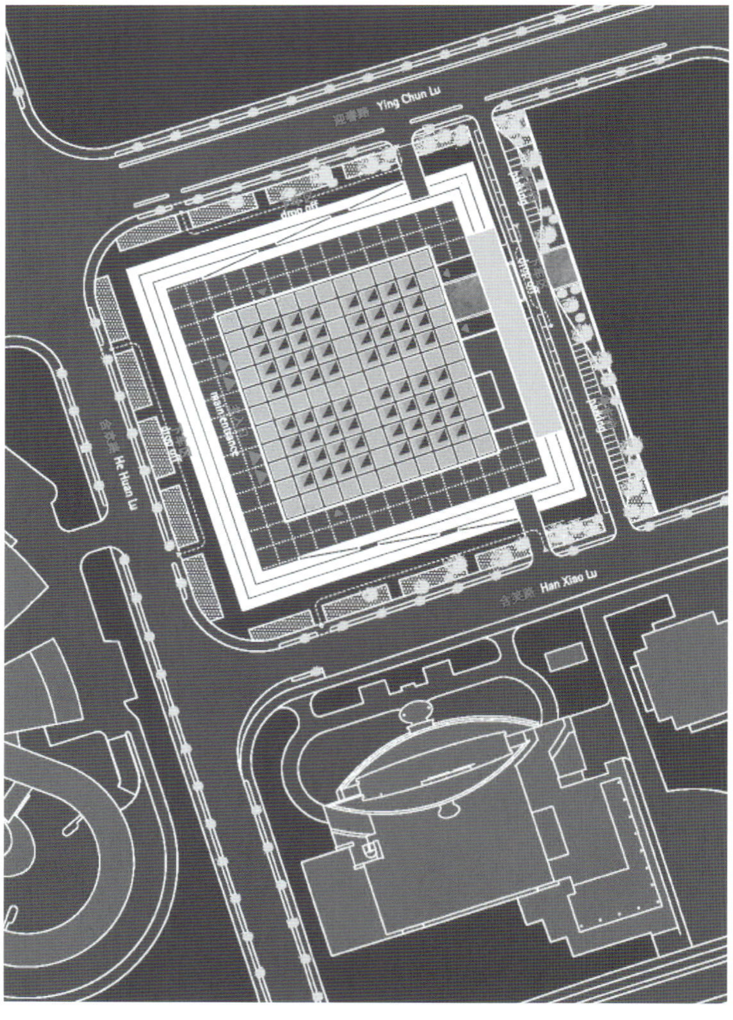
Ying Chun Lu
drop off
main entrance
drop off
He Huan Lu
Han Xiao Lu

WETTBEWERB: 2002 – 1. Preis
ENTWURF: Meinhard von Gerkan
BAUHERR: City of Shanghai, New District Pudong
BGF: 41.000 m²
BAUZEIT: 2003–2005

gmp – VON GERKAN, MARG UND PARTNER, HAMBURG

MUSEUM SHANGHAI-PUDONG

MUSEUM, SHANGHAI-PUDONG

Das Museum Shanghai-Pudong zählt zu den wichtigsten städtischen Projekten des neuen Distrikts. Gegenüber der historisch gewachsenen Kernstadt von Shanghai entsteht derzeit auf der anderen Flussseite ein neues „Manhattan": der Stadtteil Shanghai-Pudong mit dem zur Zeit höchsten Büro- und Hotelgebäude Chinas.

Das Museum soll die Geschichte des Stadtbezirks und seine Entwicklung umfassend dokumentieren und archivieren. Gleichzeitig sollen moderne, multifunktionale und offene Ausstellungsflächen entstehen, die die Öffentlichkeit mit einer ständigen Ausstellung und mit Sonderausstellungen zu ausgewählten Themen über die Stadtgeschichte und Stadtentwicklung informieren.

Der Sockel hebt das Hauptgebäude mit den Ausstellungshallen vom Niveau der umgebenden Straßen ab und unterstreicht die zentrale Bedeutung des Komplexes. Einfachheit und Reduktion der Materialien bestimmen den Kubus. Die Gebäudekomposition setzt sich aus drei Elementen zusammen: dem quadratischen Hauptgebäude mit zentralen Funktionen, einem deutlich breiteren, 4 m hohen Sockel mit umlaufenden Treppen, der die Archive beherbergt, und einem Gebäuderiegel an der östlichen Seite mit Räumen für die Verwaltung.

Die Fassade des oberen, geschlossenen Teils des Hauptgebäudes dient nicht nur als Wetterschutz, sondern auch als Kommunikationsfläche. Sie setzt sich aus zwei parallelen Fassadenebenen zusammen, wobei die äußere aus Glas besteht und die innere Fassade aus raumhohen, geschlossenen Wandpaneelen. Diese Elemente sind entlang ihrer Längsachse drehbar und können – entsprechend dem jeweiligen Ausstellungskonzept – geschlossen oder geöffnet werden, sodass Sichtbeziehungen von innen nach außen entstehen.

Die äußere Fassade fungiert als Medium zwischen Museum und Öffentlichkeit: Die transparente Glashaut wird mit aufgerasterten Bildern aus dem Bestand des Archivs bedruckt, die aus der Entfernung gesehen wiederum ein Großbild ergeben. An exponierten Stellen sollen auf semi-transparentem Glas mittels im Fassadenzwischenraum angeordneter Projektoren Bilder, Filme oder Texte projiziert werden.

The Museum in Shanghai-Pudong is one of the most important urban projects in this new district. Opposite the historically grown city centre of Shanghai a new 'Manhattan' comes into being on the other side of the river: The district Shanghai-Pudong with the highest office and hotel building at present in China.

The new Museum in Shanghai-Pudong is supposed to document and archive the district's history and development comprehensively. At the same time modern, multifunctional and open exhibition spaces are developed to inform the public with a permanent exhibition and special exhibitions about the city's history and development.

The base as one of the main architectural features of the museum lifts the main building with the exhibition halls above the level of the surrounding streets and emphasizes the central importance of the complex. Simplicity and reduction of the materials dominate the clear cube that is based on a square floor layout. Three elements form the building complex: the square-shaped main building with central functions, a much broader, 4 metres high base with surrounding stairs, which accommodates the archives and a bar-shaped building on the eastern side for the administration.

The façade of the upper, closed part of the main building not only serves as weather protection but also as a communication surface. It is made of two parallel façade-layers. The outer layer consists of glass and the inner one of room-high closed wall panels.

These elements can be rotated along their longitudinal axis and can be opened or closed, according to the particular requirements of the exhibition concept, so that views from the inside to the outside and vice versa are generated.

The outer façade serves as a medium between museum and public: the transparent glass skin displays the content of the archive in small patterned pictures, which form a big picture when seen from a distance. In some exposed spaces pictures, movies or texts will be projected onto semi-transparent glass by video projectors mounted in wall recesses.

gmp – VON GERKAN, MARG UND PARTNER, HAMBURG

CHINESISCHES NATIONALMUSEUM, PEKING
NATIONAL MUSEUM OF CHINA, BEIJING

Das Chinesische Nationalmuseum ist die Vereinigung des vormaligen „Chinese History Museum" und des „Chinese Revolutionary Museum" und somit Schaufenster der Geschichte und Kunst einer der ältesten Kulturen der Menschheit.

Der Neubau des Museums liegt an der kulturellen und politischen Mitte Chinas, dem „Platz des Himmlischen Friedens" vis-a-vis der „Verbotenen Stadt" und der „Großen Halle des Volkes".

Schwerpunkt der Entwurfsaufgabe ist die sensible Integration eines 170.000 m^2 großen Neubaus in das weltbekannte Platzensemble unter Mitnutzung einiger Teile des bestehenden Museums.

Der bestehende Bau zeigt Großzügigkeit und Würde durch seine gebäudehohen Kolonnaden, gleichzeitig fehlt es ihm jedoch an Offenheit und Transparenz im Inneren, da es durch das zentrale Eingangsgebäude blockiert ist.

Der Entwurf sieht vor, die vereinigten Museumsbauten durch ein Dach zu symbolisierten, das den öffentlichen Raum bedeckt und damit Wetterschutz für die Menschen bietet, die auf dem Vorplatz stehen.

The Chinese National Museum of China is the union of the former 'Chinese History Museum' and the 'Chinese Revolutionary Museum', and thus the showcase of the history and culture of one of the eldest cultures of mankind.

The new building is sited at the cultural and political centre of china, the 'Square of Heavenly Peace', opposite the 'Forbidden Town' and the 'Great Hall of the People'.

Focal point of the design is the sensitive integration of the 170,000 m^2 large new building in this world famous square ensemble using several parts of the existing museum.

The current building offers generosity and dignity by the building high colonnades but at the same time it lacks openness and transparency inside because it is blocked by the central entrance building.

The comprehensive museum is symbolized by a roof volume which covers the public space and provides weather protection for the people staying in that space.

WETTBEWERB: 2004 – 1. Preis
ENTWURF: Meinhard von Gerkan mit Stephan Schütz
MITARBEITER: Stephan Rewolle, Doris Schäffler, Gregor Hoheisel, Katrin Kanus, Ralf Sieber, Du Peng, Chunsong Dong
BAUHERR: The National Museum of China
BGF: 170.000 m^2
BAUZEIT: 2005–2007

Die Dachtraufe liegt in einer Höhe von 34,50 m, sodass die „Große Halle des Volkes" und das Chinesische Nationalmuseum in Höhe und Proportion ausbalanciert sind. Die geradlinige Silhouette des Daches versucht nicht, der Gebäudeerscheinung eine expressive oder sensationelle Geste hinzuzufügen. Es soll sich der Proportion des Platzes anpassen und sich auf die dialogische Beziehung zur „Großen Halle des Volkes" fokussieren. Somit wird die räumliche Qualität des Tiananmen-Platzes eindeutig verbessert.

The eave of the roof is located on a height of 34.50 m so that the Great Hall of the People and the National Museum of China are balanced in height and proportion. The straight silhouette of the roofing does not pretend to add an expressive and sensational architectural gesture to the appearance of the building. It intends to adjust the proportion of the square as well as to focus on the dialogue relationship to the Great Hall of the People.

Majestätisch und erhaben liegt das „Grand Theatre“ auf einer Landzunge oberhalb des Yangtse, vis-a-vis des business districts der Metropole Chongqing. Durch diese Einzigartigkeit des Ortes, des Panoramablickes auf die imposante Skyline der Stadt in Verbindung mit der skulpturalen Architektur wird dieses Theater zu einem internationalen Wahrzeichen, zu einem Ort weltweiter kultureller Begegnung.

Eine steinerne Sockelplattform bildet die Basis für die gläserne Skulptur, Grund- und Aufriss folgen trotz scheinbar willkürlicher Expressivität und maritimen Analogien streng den funktionalen Anforderungen.

Das Grand Theatre ist kein Gebäude mit üblicher Fassade aus Wand- und Fensterflächen. Das von innen nach außen dringende Licht, die Reflexion von Sonne, Wolken und Wasser auf den vielschichtig geneigten und gebrochenen Glasflächen lassen den Baukörper in immer wieder neuen, geheimnisvoll mystischen Lichtstimmungen erscheinen und erstrahlen.

The ‘Grand Theater’ is situated on a headland, majestic and lofty above the Yangtse, directly opposite the business district of the Chongqing metropolis. The uniqueness of the location and the panoramic view of the imposing cityscape, together with the building’s sculptural architecture, will make the theater an international landmark, a place for cultural encounters from around the world.

A stone platform base supports the glass sculpture; the ground plan and elevation are subject to strict functional requirements despite their seemingly arbitrary expressiveness and maritime analogy.

The ‘Grand Theatre’ does not have the typical façades made up of wall and window surfaces. Due to the light that urges its way out from the inside, and the reflection of the sun, clouds and water on the complex-angled and broken glass surfaces, the building appears to glow in new moods created by the light.

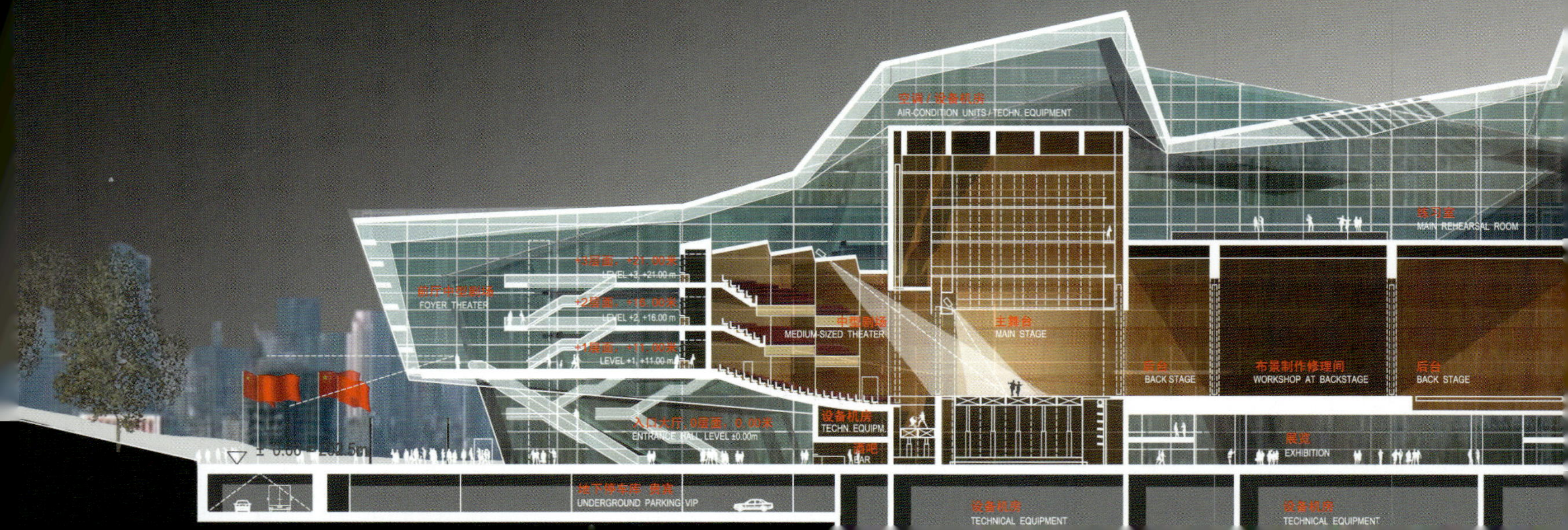

gmp – VON GERKAN, MARG UND PARTNER, HAMBURG

GRAND THEATER CHONGQING

GRAND THEATRE, CHONGQING

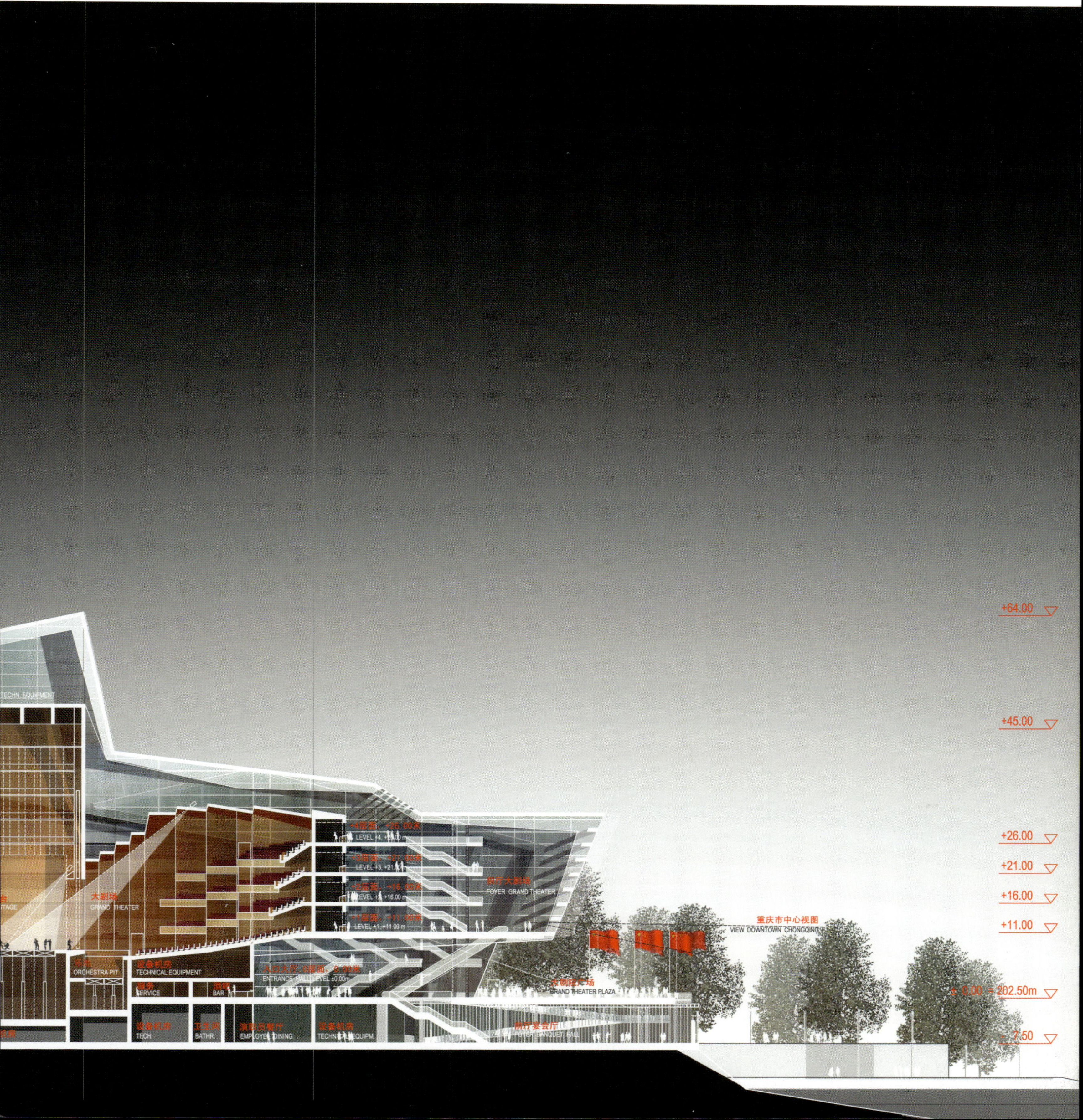

WETTBEWERB: 2004 – 1. Preis
ENTWURF: Meinhard von Gerkan mit Klaus Lenz
PARTNER: Nikolaus Goetze
PROJEKTLEITUNG: Volkmar Sievers
MITARBEITER ENTWURF: Heiko Thiess, Monika van Vught, Robert Friedrichs, Matthias Ismael, Tobias Jortzick, Dominik Reh, Christian Dahle, Julia Gronbach
MITARBEITER AUSFÜHRUNG: Knut Maass, Kerstin Steinfatt, Jan Stolte, Nils Dethlefs
BAUHERR: Chongqing Urban Construction Investment
BGF: 70.000 m^2
BAUZEIT: 2005–2007

Wo immer Tageslicht und Sonne in das Innere des Gebäudes dringt, ist die gläserne Hülle die Klimahaut, gewährt Einblick und Ausblick, verbindet das Innen mit dem Außen. Dort wo das Innere verborgen bleiben soll, z.B. im Bereich der hohen Bühnentürme, bildet eine zweite massive Hülle den nötigen Schutz. Beide Konzertsäle mit ihren zugeordneten Foyers liegen auf der Längsachse, gleichsam auf der ‚Kiellinie' eines Schiffes, und bilden so am Bug und Heck die Eingangsbereiche aus. Mittig zu diesen beiden Eingangsbereichen liegt die Exhibition Hall, die somit alle Foyerflächen des Theaters miteinander verbindet. Es können nun unabhängig alle denkbaren Aufführungen und Veranstaltungen parallel zeitgleich durchgeführt werden.

Die Konzertsaalgeometrie folgt der traditionellen Hufeisenform, mit zwei bzw. drei Rängen. Die Saalproportionen im Hinblick auf Akustik und Sichtachsen lassen unterschiedlichste Musik- und Sprachveranstaltungen zu. Hiermit sind Sing- und Tanzveranstaltungen, Sprechtheater, Orchester- und Kammermusik, aber auch internationale Operninszenierungen durchführbar.

Der zentrale Block von Haupt-, Neben-, Seiten- und Unterbühnen bildet die Schnittstelle zwischen dem Publikumsbereich und der internen Arbeits- und Künstlerwelt des Grand Theatre. Oberhalb der Seiten- und Hinterbühnen sind alle Rehearsal und Probebühneneinrichtungen vorgesehen. Diese Räumlichkeiten sind für halböffentliche Veranstaltungen mit Eingangsfoyer über eine Aufzugs- und Treppenanlage angebunden.

Wherever daylight and sunshine make its way into the building's interior, the glass shell becomes a climatic skin allowing for views in and out of the building, connecting the interior and the exterior.
In the areas were the interior should remain hidden, e.g. in the tall stage towers, a second, massive shell provides the necessary protection. Both concert halls with their respective foyers are situated in the longitudinal axis, similar to the 'keel line' of a ship, thus forming entrance areas at the bow and the stern.

In the centre of these entrance areas, is the exhibition hall, which joins all the theatre foyers together. All kinds of performances and events can take place simultaneously, independent of one another.

The concert halls, with their two-to-three-tiered seatings, are in the traditional shape of a horseshoe. With regard to acoustics and angles of visibility, the hall-proportions can facilitate different kinds of musical and non-musical events. This includes song and dance events, spoken theater, orchestra and chamber music and international opera performances. The central block, made up of the main-, auxiliary-, side-, and substages forms the interface between the audience and the internal working world and artist's world at the 'Grand Theater'.

Beyond the side and backstage areas, there is an area intended for all rehearsal and practice stage facilities. These areas are connected to the entrance hall via elevators and stairways for semi-public events.

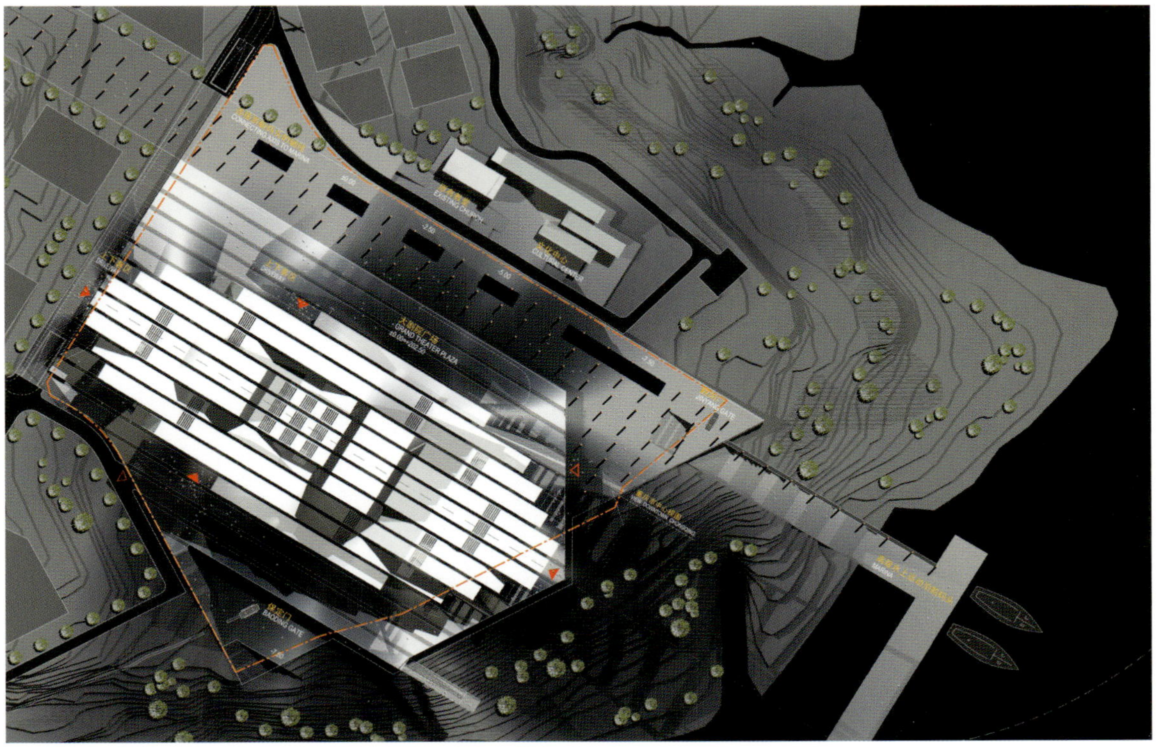

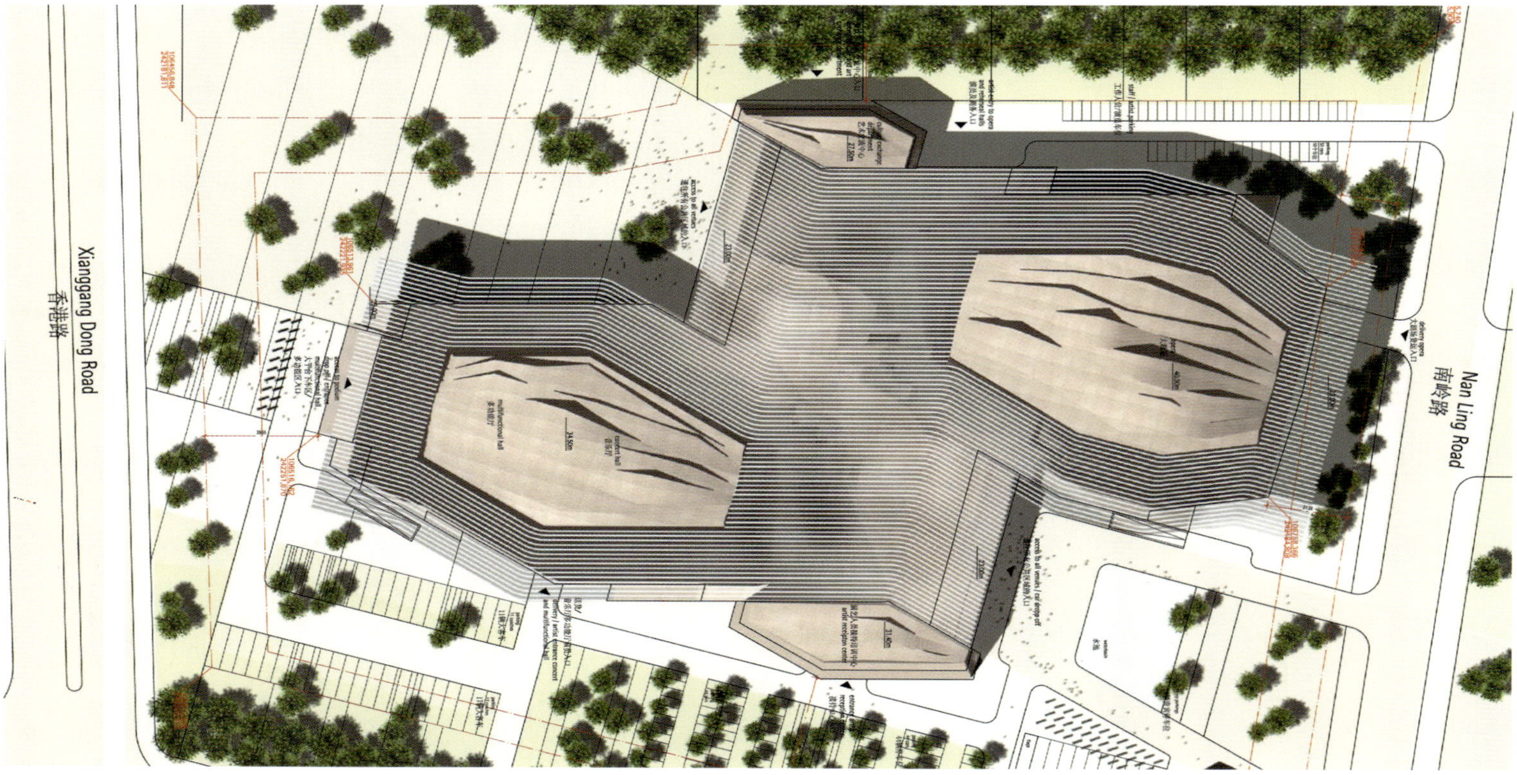
Xianggang Dong Road
香港东路
Nan Ling Road
南岭路

WETTBEWERB: 2004 – 1. Preis
ENTWURF: Meinhard von Gerkan und Stephan Schütz
BAUHERR: Qingdao Conson Industrial Corporation
BGF: 60.000 m^2
BAUZEIT: 2005–2007

gmp – VON GERKAN, MARG UND PARTNER, HAMBURG

GRAND THEATER, QINGDAO

GRAND THEATRE, QINGDAO

Mit seiner höchsten Erhebung von 1.134 m über dem Meeresspiegel ist das Laoshan-Gebirge das landschaftlich reizvollste und aus diesem Grund das bekannteste Gebirgsmassiv entlang der chinesischen Ostküste. Aufgrund der einzigartigen Lage des Massivs direkt am Meer sind die Berge des Laoshan oftmals in Wolken gehüllt, die der Landschaft eine mystische Atmosphäre verleihen.

Berge und Wolken: Es ist das Ziel des Entwurfes, Landschaft und Naturgewalten in die Sprache der Architektur zu übertragen. Wie ein Gebirgsmassiv erhebt sich das Gebäude aus der Landschaft, während ein schwebendes, wolkengleiches Dach die Baukörper umgibt. Auf diese Weise entsteht ein einzigartiges Ensemble aus dem Bezug zum Genius Loci. Wie ein Gebirgsplateau erhebt sich eine öffentliche Terrasse aus dem umgebenden Park und lässt eine großzügige Platzfläche entstehen, die sich gleichermaßen zum Meer im Südwesten und zu den Bergen im Nordosten orientiert. Durch die Anhebung der Terrasse auf +4,50 m und durch eine leichte Verdrehung zur zentralen Parkachse entstehen attraktive Blickbeziehungen in die umgebende Landschaft. Die bergartigen Baukörper beinhalten die hauptsächlichen Funktionsbereiche des Theaters:

1. das Opernhaus
2. die Konzert- und Multifunktionshalle
3. das Medienzentrum
4. das Hotel

Das Wolkendach setzt dieses Naturschauspiel der wolkendurchzogenen Berggipfel in ein einzigartiges Architekturbild um, welches dem Entwurf Wiedererkennbarkeit und Identität verleiht: Schwere und Massivität der „Berge" auf der einen Seite, Leichtigkeit und Eleganz der „Wolke" auf der anderen Seite treten in einen spannenden Dialog.

With its highest peak rising 1134 meters above the sea level the mount Laoshan and the surrounding peaks are situated in the southeastern Shandong peninsula. Due to the unique climatic situation the Laoshan mountains are very often wrapped in clouds, which lend a particularly mystic atmosphere to the scenery.

Mountains and clouds: Aim of the design is to transform landscape and the power of nature into architectural language. Like a mountain plateau an open terrace raises up from the park and forms a generous public square, which is orientated to the sea in the southwest and to the mountains in the northeast. The terrace forms an open space of underneath the floating cloud like roof. By raising the plateau by 4.5 m and turning it slightly to the sea and to the Laoshan Mountains a clear visual relation to the most scenic spots of Laoshan is produced. From the platform the major functions of the Grand Theatre up grow like granite rocks, which is the local stone:

1. the opera house in the north,
2. the concert and multifunctional hall in the south,
3. the media centre in the west ,
4. the Artist Reception and Training Centre in the east.

Analogue to the predominant weather situation in the Laoshan Mountains the roof of the Grand Theatre appears like a cloud drifting along the mountain like volumes of singular buildings. That way a most poetic architectural image is created which makes the buildings recognizable all over the world. The expressive and massive rocks of the architectural landscape and the light and elegant cloud like roof form an exciting architectural dialogue.

WETTBEWERB: 2003 – 1. Preis
ENTWURF: Meinhard von Gerkan
BAUHERR: Dalian Commodity Exchange
BGF: 353.000 m^2
BAUZEIT: 2004–2007

gmp – VON GERKAN, MARG UND PARTNER, HAMBURG

TWIN TOWERS, DALIAN

TWIN TOWERS, DALIAN

Die Twin Towers erreichen mit 62 oberirdischen Geschossen eine Höhe von über 280 Metern. Beide Türme, deren mittige Rücksprünge durch große Verglasungen zu Wintergärten werden, basieren auf rechteckigen Grundrissen. Die „Skylobbies" fassen jeweils acht Geschosse zusammen und erlauben auch in den oberen Geschossen großzügige Hallen und Foyers, sodass Besucher angemessen empfangen werden können.

Die Gestaltung der Fassade ist aus der statischen Struktur des Gebäudes abgeleitet: einem tragenden Stahlbetonkern in der Mitte des Gebäudes mit einer als „Gitterhülle" vorgestellten Außenhaut.

Die Twin-Towers bilden zusammen mit ihren Sockelbauten einen rechteckigen Platz, der die nach Norden geöffnete Form des angrenzenden Messegebäudes abschließt. Der Vorplatz bildet das Entree zu den Hochhäusern. Die öffentliche Platzfläche wird mit organisch geformten Wasserbecken und Grünflächen gestaltet, die zwischen den Türmen hindurch nach Norden bis in die Fußgängerzone geführt werden.

With 62 floors above ground the Twin Towers reach an overall height of 280 m. Both Towers are based on a rectangular floor plans, with full height conservatories recessed into the centre of each. Within the conservatories sky lobbies span the height of eight floors each, allowing for spacious lobby and entrance situations to suitably welcome visitors to all floors.

The design of the façade is based on the structural composition of the building: The concrete core within and the grid like shell outside are load bearing.

The Twin Towers with their base buildings open up a rectangular public square complementing the trade fair building next door. The piazza forms the entrance to the towers. The public areas are landscaped by free form water surfaces and areas of green reaching through between the towers into the pedestrian zone in the North.

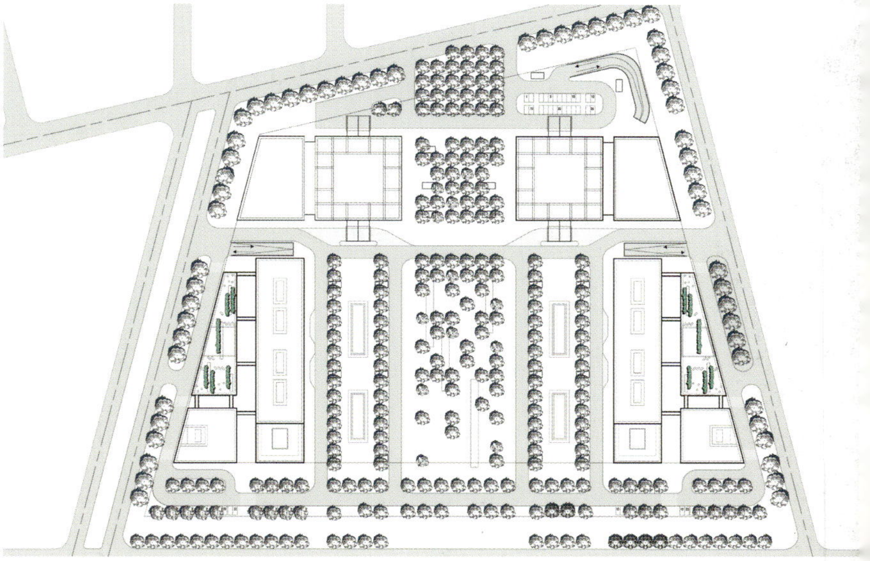

中国建築

ENTWURF: Meinhard von Gerkan mit Doris Schäffler und Stephan Schütz
BAUHERR: China CYTS Tours Holding Co., Ltd.
BGF: 65.000 m²
BAUZEIT: 2004–2005

gmp – VON GERKAN, MARG UND PARTNER, HAMBURG

CYTS TOWER, PEKING

CYTS TOWER, BEIJING

Office building of a tourist company

Bürohochhaus eines Tourismusunternehmens

Die 2. Ring Road markiert den Übergang von der Pekinger Altstadt zu den moderneren Stadtvierteln. Vor allem an ihrem östlichen Abschnitt erfährt die 2. Ring Road derzeit (2005) tiefgreifende Veränderungen, da das Gebiet als zentrales Geschäftsviertel für chinesische und ausländische Firmen neu bebaut wird. Der Dongcheng District in erstklassiger Stadtlage umfasst moderne Gebäudekomplexe entlang der 2. Ring Road, aber auch historische Baudenkmäler wie den Lama-Tempel.

Hauptelement des Entwurfs ist das gebäudehohe Atrium, das den Ost- und den Westflügel des Hochhauses miteinander verbindet und als Durchgangsbereich von einem zum anderen dient. Dieser eindrucksvolle Raum besteht eigentlich aus zwei viergeschossigen Glashallen, die in ein rechteckiges Volumen eingestellt sind. Aufgrund ihrer Ausrichtung und Platzierung bestimmen diese Hallen den L-förmigen Grundriss der beiden Seitenflügel, die das gesamte Raumprogramm enthalten. Die klare konstruktive Ordnung des Projekts ist das direkte Ergebnis der „CYTS-Philosophie“: klar und transparent, innovativ und effizient. Brücken und Panoramaaufzüge sind in die zwei Hallen eingebaut, sodass sie Besuchern und Beschäftigten nicht nur den Blick über diese Räume, sondern zugleich auch über die Stadt bieten.

Die viergeschossigen Glashallen dienen als Kommunikationsräume für alle, die im CYTS arbeiten, und bürgen mit üppiger Bepflanzung für angenehme Aufenthaltsqualität. Die Außenfassaden des Hochhauses sind vertikal betont gegliedert; die konstruktiven Teile bestehen aus dunklem Aluminium. Die horizontalen Balken der Atriumfassaden sind in die Gesamtgestaltung eingebunden und sorgen für ein ausgewogenes ästhetisches Erscheinungsbild. Die „Ausfachungen“ bestehen überwiegend aus Glas.

The 2nd Ring Road marks the transition between Beijing's historic city centre and its modern extensions. Especially the eastern section of the 2nd Ring Road area is currently undergoing a radical change as it is being redeveloped as a modern business district with headquarters of national and international companies. Dong-cheng District is in a prime urban location and comprises modern complexes on 2nd Ring Road, but also historic architectural monuments like the Lama Temple.

The main element of the project is an atrium (as tall as the building) which forms a link and passageway betweeen the building's eastern and western sections. This exciting architectural space actually consists of two four-storey glass halls inscribed in a rectangular volume. The orientation and location of these volumes determined the layout of the two l-shaped wings, which contain the entire functional programme.

The clear structural order of this scheme is the direct result of the 'CYTS philosophy': clear and transparent, innovative and efficient. Bridges and panorama lifts are placed inside the two halls so that the space and the view over the city can be experiences by both employees and visitors.

The central four-storey glass halls serve as communication zones for all the people working in the CYTS building. With lush green plantings, these zones provide a pleasant atmosphere. The building's façades consist of strongly vertically structured modules of dark aluminium. At the same time, the horizontal structural members of the atrium façades are integrated into the overall order of the building and give it a well-balanced appearance. The structural modules are filled in with panels, most of them of glass.

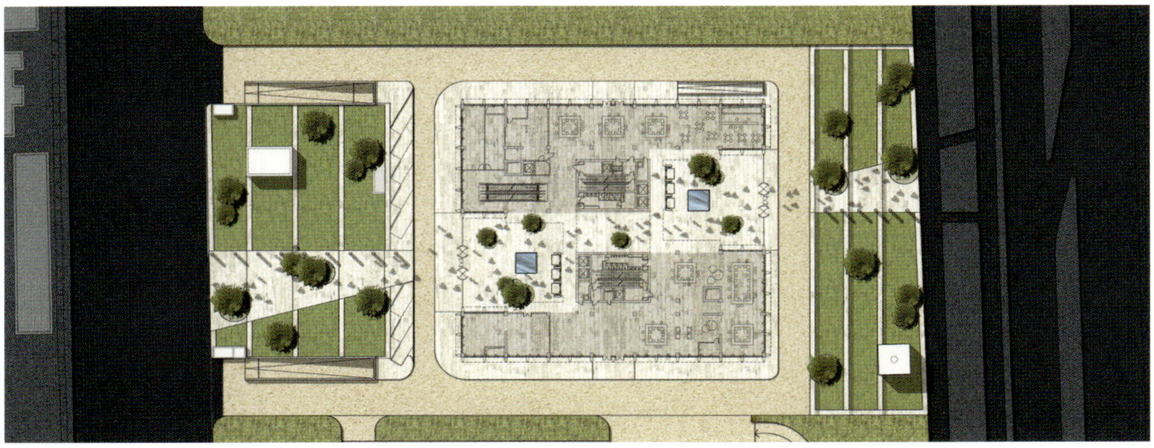

WETTBEWERB: 2001 – 1. Preis
ENTWURF: Meinhard von Gerkan
BAUHERR: Guangzhou Developing New City Investment Co., Ltd.
BGF: 78.600 m²
BAUZEIT: 2002–2005

gmp – VON GERKAN, MARG UND PARTNER, HAMBURG

GUANGZHOU DEVELOPMENT CENTRAL BUILDING

GUANGZHOU DEVELOPMENT CENTRAL BUILDING

Das Guangzhou Development Central Building befindet sich an einer besonderen Stelle innerhalb der Zhu Jiang New City von Guangzhou: Als „Eckpfeiler" bildet das Hochhaus die südwestliche Spitze des neuen Stadtteils in unmittelbarer Nähe zum Pearl River.

Das Gebäude ist in drei vertikale Scheiben unterteilt. Im Kontrast zu dem gläsernen Mittelteil sind die flankierenden Seitenflügel von einer Rasterstruktur geprägt. Jeweils zwei Geschosse werden in großen Fensteröffnungen zusammengefasst. Senkrechte, drehbar gelagerte Verschatter können entsprechend den Licht- und Schattenverhältnissen gesteuert werden. Das Gebäude steht auf einem sechsgeschossigen Sockel und ist an der höchsten Stelle, dem Hubschrauberlandeplatz auf dem Mittelteil, 127 m hoch. Die beiden Seitenteile haben eine Höhe von 111 m.

Mit der Reduzierung des Versorgungskernes auf das Innere des Mittelschiffes bieten die seitlichen Flügel eine freie Aufteilung in Großraum-, Kombi- oder Einzelbüros, die flexibel miteinander kombinierbar sind. Die meisten Büros befinden sich direkt an der Fassade, so dass die Arbeitsplätze natürlich belichtet sind.

Das gewählte Materialkonzept basiert auf der Idee, im und am Gebäude wenige, aber hochwertige Materialien einzusetzen: Sowohl die Fassaden als auch die Fußböden der Sockelgeschosse sind in hellgrauem Naturstein ausgeführt. Hierzu werden im Inneren kontrastierend Wandflächen aus warmem Edelholz gesetzt. Dieses Holz findet sich in den Türen und Möbeln der Verkehrsbereiche wieder.

Die Außenanlagen sind im Norden einheitlich mit Laubbäumen bepflanzt, im Osten befindet sich ein öffentlicher Boulevard. Große Wasserflächen mit Wasserspielen und Fontänen werden seitlich von Baumreihen begrenzt.

The Guangzhou Development Central Building occupies a special place in Guangzhou's Zhu-jiang New City. It is a high-rise which forms the south-western 'corner stone' of the new urban district in the immediate proximity of the Pearl River.

The building consists of three vertical 'slabs': a fully glazed one in the middle, flanked by two slabs the façades of which have a grid structure. Two storeys together share large double-height windows. Vertical revolvable shading slats can be controlled to adapt to prevailing light conditions. The tower rises from a six-storey base; the middle section is 127 m high and supports a heliport, the two side sections are both 111 m high.

By concentrating vertical circulation and media ducts in the middle of the central section, it was possible to sub-divide the interiors into open-plan, combination or cellular offices that can be freely combined. Most office spaces are arranged behind / along the façades so that work stations receive natural light.

The materials chosen were deliberately reduced to just a few high-quality ones: light grey stone for the façades and the floors of the base levels, contrasted by wall claddings of one kind of luxury wood for the doors and furniture in the concourse areas.

The exterior areas to the north are planted with deciduous trees; to the east there is a public boulevard. Large reflecting pools with waterworks and individual fountains are flanked by rows of trees.

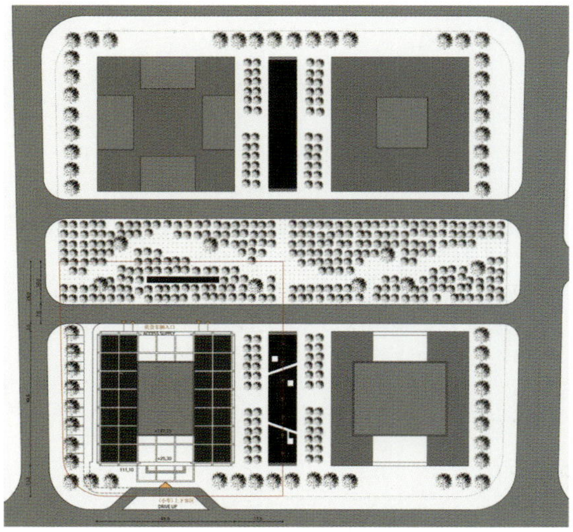

鑫兆佳园 23

ENTWURF: Meinhard von Gerkan und Nikolaus Goetze
BAUHERR: Beijing Xinzhao Real Development Co.; Beijing Town-Country Houses Construction Development Co.
BGF: 235.000 m^2 – 2.163 Wohnungen
BAUZEIT: 2001–2004

gmp – VON GERKAN, MARG UND PARTNER, HAMBURG

WOHNUNGSBAU XINZHAO, PEKING
XINZHAO RESIDENTIAL AREA, BEIJING

Ein Achsenkreuz unterteilt das nahezu quadratische Gebiet in vier große Quartiere. Von Norden nach Süden erstreckt sich mittig eine Aktions- und Erlebnisachse mit einer durch Baumreihen gesäumten Platzabfolge, die mit dem Schulgelände im Süden ihren Abschluss findet. Eine landschaftlich geprägte Parkanlage, in der sich freie Baumgruppen mit kleinen Lichtungen abwechseln, durchzieht das Gelände von West nach Ost und bildet eine grüne Achse im Zentrum des Wohngebietes.

Die Wohnquartiere sind linear strukturiert mit parallel gestaffelten, zeilenartigen Gebäuden, die von West nach Ost verlaufen und eine maximale Anzahl Nord-Süd-orientierter Wohnungen ermöglichen. Teile der Gebäudezeilen sind gegeneinander versetzt, sodass die Freiräume dazwischen in ihrer Breite variieren und eine Vielzahl von Hofräumen unterschiedlicher Größe bilden. Die grüne Hauptachse und die kleineren Innenhöfe bieten Freiräume und gliedern den Stadtraum sukzessive vom Großen ins Kleine.

Turmartige Wohnhochhäuser, die sich aus unterschiedlich hohen, gegeneinander versetzten Gebäudescheiben zusammensetzen, betonen die geschwungene südliche Kante der Parklandschaft und bilden einen Kontrast zu den rechtwinkligen Strukturen der Quartiersblöcke, die an den Rändern zu allen Seiten geschlossen sind. Über den Boulevard in der Mitte und den südlich der Hochhäuser verlaufenden „Parkdrive" werden alle Quartiere miteinander vernetzt und von dort aus schleifenförmig erschlossen. Für Fußgänger ist ein durchgehendes Wegenetz geplant, das die grünen Höfe in nord-südlicher Richtung durchzieht und sie über Durchgänge miteinander verzahnt.

Ein Einkaufszentrum im Südosten sowie die gewerbliche Nutzung in den Erdgeschossen entlang der Straßen bieten eine optimale Versorgung der Bewohner mit den Gütern des täglichen Bedarfs.

A coordinate axis divides the almost square area in four large districts. A centrally positioned activity axis with a tree-lined sequence of squares stretches from north to south, which terminates with the school premises in the south. A landscape park, in which freely positioned groups of trees alternate with small clearings, runs through the grounds from west to east and forms a green strip in the centre of the residential area.

The residential districts are structured in a linear fashion with a parallel staggered ribbon development, which runs from west to east and consequently allows for a maximum of north-south orientated apartments. The linear structure is alternated in some areas, thus varying the width of the open spaces between the building rows and forming a large number of courtyards of various scale. The main green axis and the smaller courtyards provide open spaces in immediate proximity to the apartments and successively divide the urban space to a reduced dimension.

Tower-like residential blocks, which are composed from building slabs of various height and alternated positioning, emphasize the curved southern edge of the park landscape and form a contrast to the rectangular structures of the district blocks with massive edges on all sides. All districts are interlinked via the central boulevard and 'park drive' running south of the tower blocks and are accessible from these roads in a loop-shaped circulation. A continuous network of footpaths is planned for pedestrians, which runs through the green courtyards in a north-south direction and is interlinked with passages in the rows of buildings.

A shopping centre in the south-east as well as the commercial use on the ground floors along the roads provide an ideal supply of the residents with everyday facilities and services.

ORIENT

ENTWURF: Meinhard von Gerkan mit Magdalene Weiß
BAUHERR: Beijing Shoulu-Huayuan Property Co., Ltd.
BGF: 69.000 m^2
BAUZEIT: 2003–2005

gmp – VON GERKAN, MARG UND PARTNER, HAMBURG

BEIJING CHÂTEAU, PEKING
BEIJING CHÂTEAU

Als selbstbewusstes und dominantes Gebäude wird das Beijing Château einen besonderen Ort und eine eigene Identität im Stadtbild definieren. Hier entstehen Wohnungen bis zu einer Größe von 1.000 m^2 für eine neue Generation von Bewohnern der aufstrebenden Weltstadt, die einen urbanen und großzügig-luxuriösen Lebensstil pflegen. Es wird eine Symbiose aus der chinesischen Lebensart und westlichem Standard entstehen. In diesem Sinne verbinden sich in dem Gebäude horizontal geschwungene Grundrissformen mit vertikalen Schichtungen und Einschnürungen, die dem Gebäude Maßstab und Dimension im Stadtbild geben. Die weich fließende Außenkontur des Baukörpers spiegelt die Idee wider, die Bewegung des Wassers im nahen Fluss und die das Grundstück geschäftig umspülenden Verkehrsadern in die Architektursprache des Gebäudes zu übersetzen.

Das Beijing Château, im Herzen des Verwaltungs- und Botschaftsviertels gelegen, erscheint mit den glänzenden, gerundeten Doppelfassaden als signifikante Baukörperskulptur. Das gläsern und metallisch glänzende, luxuriös wirkende äußere Erscheinungsbild setzt sich im Inneren fort mit eleganten zweigeschossigen Apartements, die ein Maximum an Qualität und Lebensstil bieten. Die Hightech-Fassade bietet Panoramaaussicht für jedes Apartement in alle Richtungen, während gleichzeitig durch den integrierten hölzernen Sonnenschutz individuell gesteuert Schließungen und Raumabschlüsse möglich sind. Jedes Apartment hat Zugang zu einem Terrassendeck. Die Serviceeinrichtungen des Wellnessbereichs und des Schwimmbades sowie die exklusiven Clubräume und das Restaurant im Erdgeschoss werden ausschließlich von den Bewohnern genutzt.

Die Idee des Projektes ist es, ein einmaliges und einprägsames Wohngebäude in einer pulsierenden modernen Großstadt zu schaffen, in der sich Vergangenheit und Zukunft verbinden. Es entsteht ein High-end-Luxusapartmenthaus, das den Bewohnern Behaglichkeit und Wohnkomfort bietet und dabei modernste Technik mit höchstem Lebensstandard verbindet.

As a self-confident and remarkable building for extraordinary requirements, Beijing Château defines a special place and a strong own identity within the townscape. Beijing Château offers luxury apartments of up to 1,000 m^2 for a new generation of inhabitants in this rising metropolitan city. It is due to create a symbiosis of Asiatic harmony with western standard of living. In this sense flowing sketch forms connect themselves with layerings and constrictions, which give the building scale and dimension in the townscape.

The design is influenced by the idea to transform the flow of the nearby river and the busy surrounding roads into architecture.

The Beijing Château building is a unique curved glazing sculpture excellently located in the heart of the largest administrative area of Beijing. The luxury appearance of the outside continues inside where elegant duplex apartments with high standard facilities offer maximum quality and lifestyle. The high-tech façade enables a panorama view from each apartment into all directions whereas integrated wooden shading elements are available to please sunprotective needs. Each of the apartments has access to a balcony following the idea of a luxury yacht deck.

The idea behind the project is to create a powerful and remarkable landmark building within a lively and modern metropolitan city where history and future form a unit. It is a residential building with high-end luxury apartments in order to combine state of the art domestic engineering with highest quality and standards for living.

gmp – VON GERKAN, MARG UND PARTNER, HAMBURG

CENTURY LOTUS SPORTS CENTER, FOSHAN

CENTURY LOTUS SPORTS CENTRE, FOSHAN

Im Rahmen der 12. Guangdong Provinzfestspiele 2006 wird sich Foshan mit einem neuen Sportpark einer breiten Öffentlichkeit als moderne und aufstrebende Stadt präsentieren. Ein Multifunktionsstadion und eine Schwimmhalle bieten internationalen Wettkampfstandard, während weitere Trainings- und Freizeitsportanlagen auch den Besuchern zur Verfügung stehen.

Das kreisrunde Stadion überragt mit seinem riesigen, weißen Membrandach den Sportpark und gleicht – gelegen auf einem begrünten Hügel und umgeben von einem ringförmigen Wasserbecken – einer Lotusblüte im See.

Die Speichenradkonstruktion des Stadiondaches mit der gefalteten Membrandeckung misst 350 m im Durchmesser und überdeckt sowohl die Tribünen als auch die äußeren Umgänge. Über dem Spielfeld kann das Dach je nach Bedarf geöffnet oder geschlossen werden. Mit einer großen Geste verbindet es die Stadionschüssel mit dem umgebenden Park und wird mit seiner Unverwechselbarkeit zum Symbol der Spiele 2006 werden.

On the occasion of the 12th Guangdong Province Sports Meeting 2006 Foshan will present itself to the public as a modern and growing city. A multipurpose stadium and a swimming hall will serve all demands of international sports competitions, while training and leisure sports facilities offer a large variety of activities to the visitors.

The circular stadium dominates the silhouette of the sports park with its huge, white membrane roof. Being situated on a green hill and surrounded by a circular ring of water it looks like a lotus blossom in a lake. The stadium's spokes-wheel roof construction with the folded membrane covering measures 350 m in diameter and covers not just the stands but the outer concourses as well.

Above the field the roof can be opened and closed according to demand. With a grand and generous gesture it links the stadium bowl to the surrounding park and will turn into a symbol for the games of 2006.

Das Dach der Schwimmhalle ist ebenfalls mit einer leichten, transluzenten Membran gedeckt. Die Halle selbst ist in das Gelände eingegraben und stellt die städtebauliche Dominanz des Stadions nicht infrage; das Dach nimmt jedoch die grundlegende Entwurfsidee auf und lässt beide Gebäude als architektonisches Ensemble erscheinen.

The roof of the swimming hall is as well covered by a lightweight and translucent membrane roof. Embedded in the landscape it does not question the urban domination of the stadium, but its roof structure takes up the very architectural design idea creating the strong and lasting impression of the two buildings as an architectural ensemble.

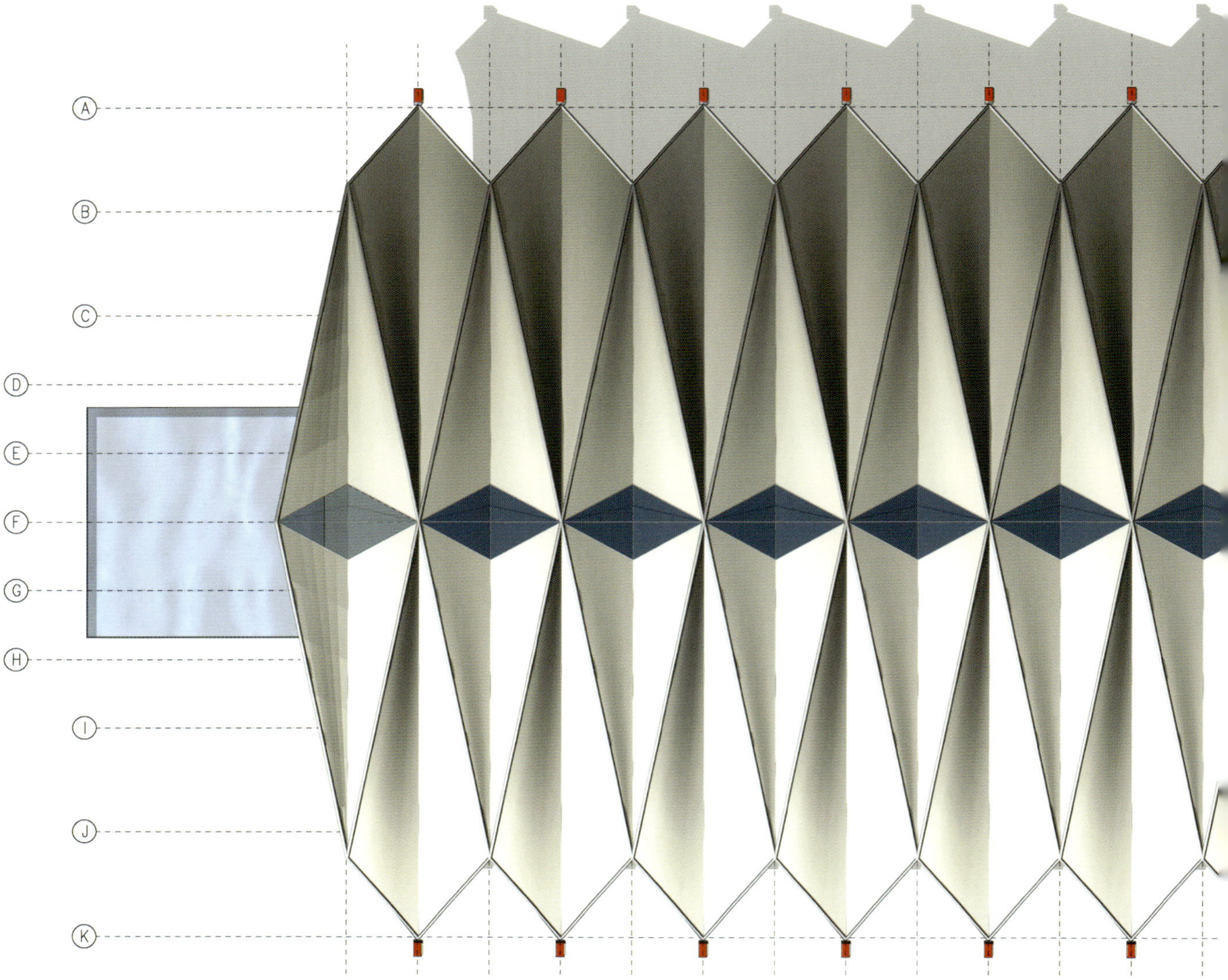

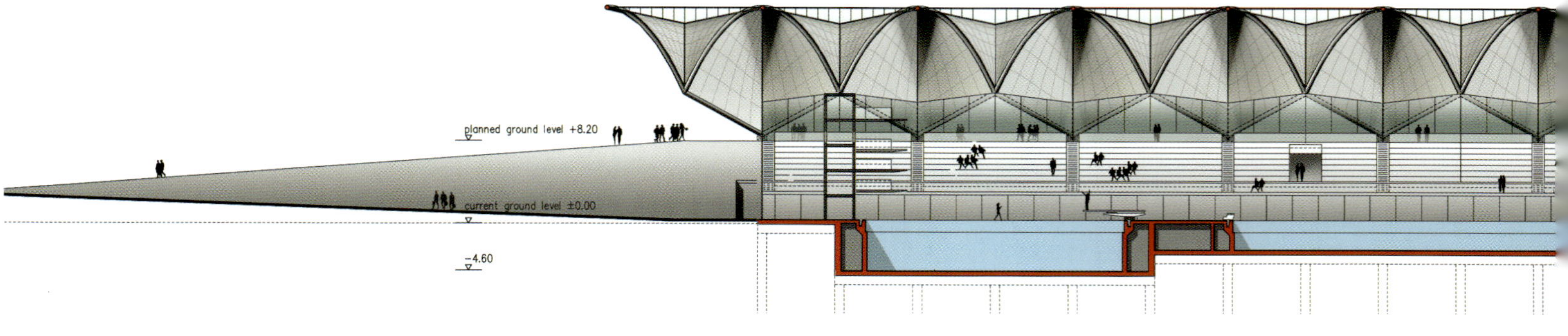

WETTBEWERB: 2003 – 2. Preis und Beauftragung
ENTWURF: Volkwin Marg mit Marek Nowak
PARTNER: Nikolaus Goetze
STATIK: Schlaich Bergermann und Partner
BAUHERR: Foshan Construction Bureau/Foshan Sports Bureau
SITZPLÄTZE STADION: 36.000
SITZPLÄTZE SCHWIMMHALLE: 2.800
BAUZEIT: 2004–2006

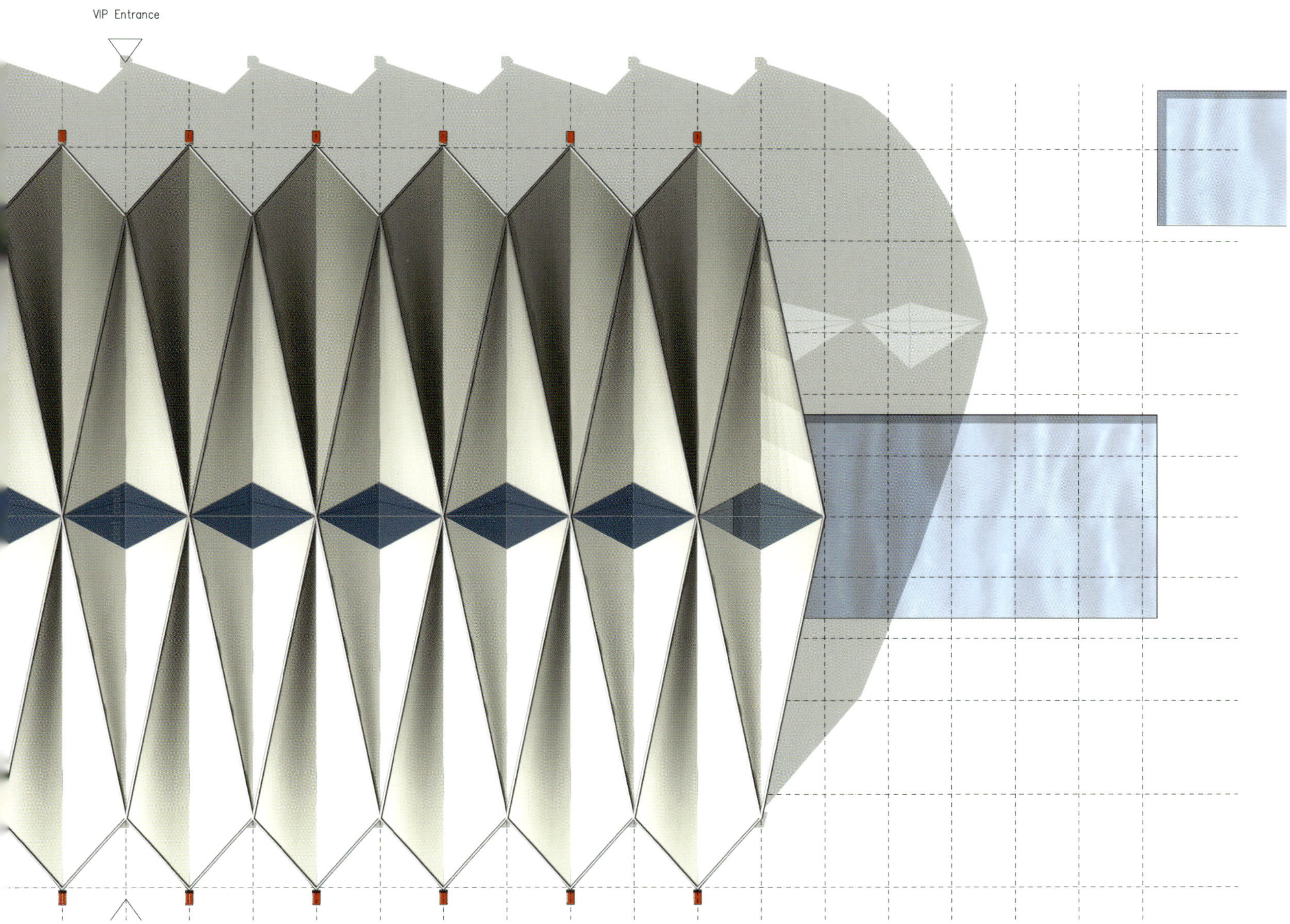

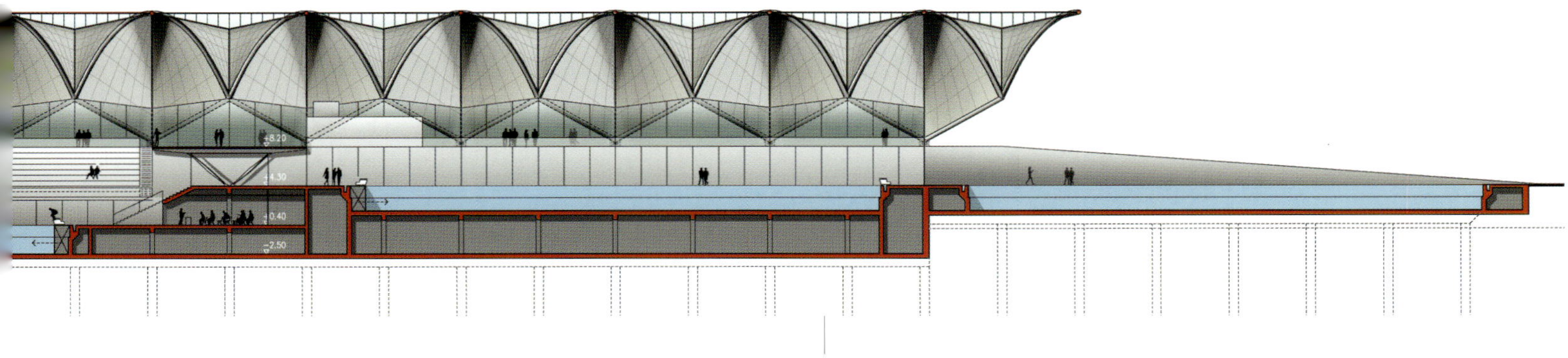

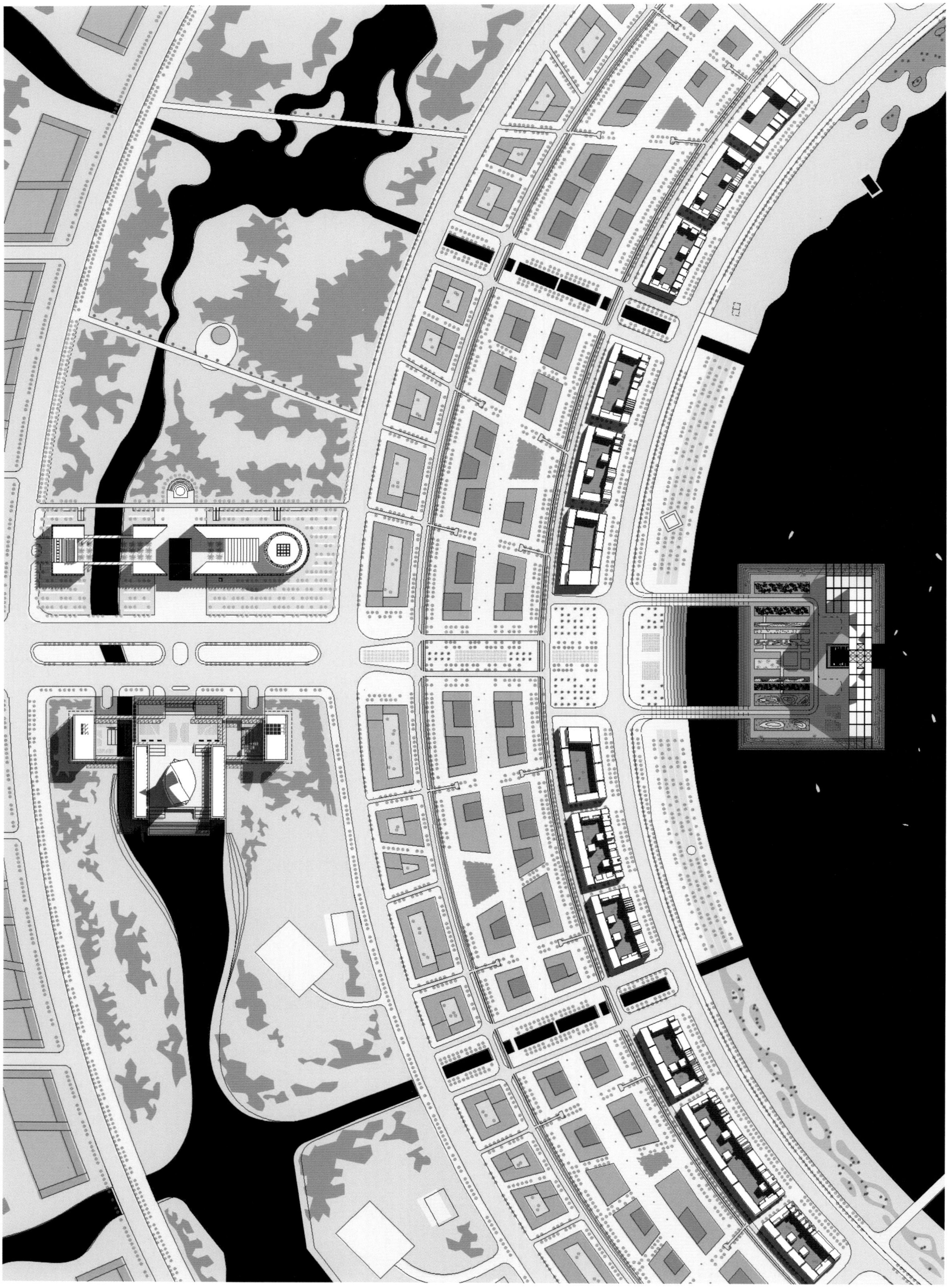

WETTBEWERB: 2002/2003 – 1. Preis
ENTWURF: Meinhard von Gerkan
BAUHERR: Shanghai Urban Planning Administration Bureau
GRÖSSE: 74 km^2
BAUZEIT: 2003–2020

gmp – VON GERKAN, MARG UND PARTNER, HAMBURG

LINGANG NEW CITY – EINE GROSSSTADT IM CHINESISCHEN MEER
LINGANG NEW CITY – A METROPOLIS IN THE EAST CHINA SEA

Um das enorme Bevölkerungs- und Industriewachstum von Shanghai aufzunehmen, lobte das dortige Stadtplanungsamt einen internationalen Wettbewerb zur Planung einer neuen Hafenstadt in Zusammenhang mit dem internationalen Container-Tiefseehafen Yangshan aus. Der erste Preis des mehrstufigen Wettbewerbs ging an das Hamburger Architekturbüro gmp. Die neugeplante Satellitenstadt Lingang New City soll auf ca. 74 km^2 Platz für 800.000 Einwohner bieten und stellt neben Chandighar, Brasilia und Canberra die einzige Stadtneugründung dieser Größenordnung während der letzten hundert Jahre dar.

Das Konzept von Lingang New City greift die Ideale der tradierten europäischen Stadt auf und verbindet sie mit einer „revolutionären" Idee: Den Mittelpunkt bildet – anstelle eines baulich verdichteten Stadtzentrums – ein kreisrunder See von 2,5 km Durchmesser und 8 km Seepromenade mit einem Badestrand a la Copa Cabana im Herzen der Stadt. Kulturbauten und Freizeitangebote sind auf Inseln situiert und per Schiff erreichbar. Die Stadt Alexandria, als eines der sieben Weltwunder, stand Pate für den Entwurf; die Lebensqualität der Nähe zum Wasser bezieht sich auf Referenzen aus Hamburg.

Das Bild konzentrischer Wellen, die durch einen ins Wasser fallenden Tropfen gebildet werden, ist das metaphorische Leitbild der ganzen Stadtstruktur. Dieser Allegorie entsprechend gliedern sich die Nutzungsstrukturen in konzentrischen Ringen von innen nach außen um den zentralen Lake Dishui: von der Promenade über einen Businessdistrikt mit hoher Verdichtung, einen 500 Meter breiten, ringförmigen Stadtpark mit solitär eingelagerten öffentlichen Bauten bis hin zu den blockartigen Wohnquartieren für jeweils 13.000 Menschen.

Der Stadtring zwischen Seepromenade und Grüngürtel, der Businessdistrikt, bildet das Zentrum des städtischen Lebens. Hier befinden sich in Mischnutzung Büros, Geschäfte, Einkaufspassagen, Fußgängerzonen und verdichtetes Wohnen.

Die konzentrische Struktur wird von radialen Strahlen in Form von Straßen und Wegen nach dem

In order to accommodate the huge growth of population and industry in Shanghai, the city-planning department conducted an international competition for the planning of a new harbour city that incorporates the international deep-sea container harbour Yangshan. The first prize of the competition, which took place in several stages, was awarded to the Hamburg architect's office gmp. The newly-planned satellite city Lingang New City is intended to provide space for 800,000 inhabitants in an area of 74 square kilometres and represents, alongside Chandighar, Brasilia and Canberra, the only city of this scale to be founded in the past hundred years.

The concept for Lingang New City takes up the ideals of the traditional European city and combines it with a 'revolutionary' idea: instead of a high-density centre, the focal point will be a circular lake with a diameter of 2.5 km and an 8 km lakeside promenade with a bathing beach a la Copa Cabana in the heart of the city. Cultural buildings and leisure facilities are located on islands, which can be accessed by boat. The design was inspired by the city of Alexandria, one of the Seven Wonders of the World; the quality of life provided by the close proximity to water draws its references from Hamburg.

The whole city structure is based on the metaphor of an image of concentric ripples, formed by a drop falling into water. In line with this allegory, the utility structures are ordered in the form of concentric rings spreading outwards from the central Dishui Lake: from the promenade, through to the extremely dense business district, a circular city park, 500 metres in width which incorporates solitary public buildings, to the block-like living quarters for 13,000 inhabitants respectively.

The city ring between the lakeside promenade and the green belt, the business district, forms the centre of city-life. A mix of offices, shops, arcades, pedestrian precincts and dense living space is located here. The concentric structure is layered following the principle of a compass rose, the streets and pathways radiate out from the centre. These provide the city with a clear, ordered structure and divide the built-up rings

Lingang New City ist der Brückenkopf eines neuen Hafens auf einer Inselgruppe 30 km vor der Küste. Die Hafenlogistik wurde von der Firma Hamburg Port Consulting (HPC) geplant. Linke Seite: Lageplan mit Rathaus, Maritim-Museum und der Western Island.

Lingang New City is the bridgehead of a new harbour on the group of islands located 30 km off the coast. The firm Hamburg Port Consulting (HPC) planned the harbour logistics. Lefthand page: Layout plan with town-hall, Maritime Museum and Western Island.

LINGANG NEW CITY – WESTERN ISLAND
BÜRO- UND HOTELKOMPLEX
GUTACHTEN: 2004
ENTWURF: Meinhard von Gerkan
PARTNER: Nikolaus Goetze
BAUHERR: Shanghai Harbour City Investment Co.
BGF: 135.000 m^2
BAUZEIT: bis 2007

Prinzip einer Windrose überlagert. Sie geben der Stadt ein klares Ordnungsprinzip und unterteilen die bebauten Ringe in einzelne Sektoren. Auf diese Weise entsteht ein ideales Erschließungsnetz, innerhalb dessen sich die Stadt auch über das geplante Maß hinaus erweitern kann. Die Landschaft dringt keilförmig bis zum zweiten Ring vor. Wasserläufe und kleine Seen durchdringen alle Quartiere und thematisieren das „Wohnen am Wasser" in zahlreichen Varianten.

Das öffentliche Verkehrssystem mit Light-Trains auf Straßenniveau funktioniert als Ringbahn mit angehängten Schleifen.

Im Jahr 2006 soll bereits der erste Bauabschnitt der neuen Stadt für 80.000 Einwohner auf dem Gebiet des heutigen Festlandes abgeschlossen sein. Zweiter und dritter Bauabschnitt folgen bis zum Jahr 2020. Das hierfür benötigte Areal wird durch Aufschüttung dem Ozean abgerungen. Im Zuge dieser Landgewinnung entsteht auch der Lake Dishui als Mittelpunkt der neuen Hafenstadt.

into separate sectors. In this way, an ideal network of access is created, within which the city can also expand above and beyond the planned scale. The countryside penetrates like wedges in as far as the second ring. Waterways and small lakes extend into all quarters, underlining the central theme 'waterside living' in a wide variety of forms.

The public transport system with light-trains on street-level functions as a circular railway with adjoining loops.

The first construction phase of the new city for 80,000 inhabitants in the present mainland area should be completed by 2006. The second and third phase of construction will follow until 2020. The area required for this will be dragged up from the ocean by means of aggregation. In the process of obtaining this land, the Dishui Lake will be formed as the central point of the new harbour city.

Lingang New City – Western Island, Büro- und Hotelkomplex

Die Stadtinsel bildet den Schlusspunkt der Ost-West-Achse von Lingang New City. Die exponierte Lage der Grundstücke auf der im Westen des Sees liegenden Insel fordert somit eine ebenso einzigartige architektonische Komposition. Die neuen dominierenden Landmarkgebäude erhalten ihre Identität aus einer konstruktiven Diagonalstruktur, die das Erscheinungsbild zu einer expressiven Skulptur mit unverwechselbarer Einprägsamkeit macht. Der Charakter knüpft an die Tradition der Konstruktivisten des 20. Jahrhunderts an, einer stilistischen Epoche, die viele aufregende Entwürfe, jedoch nur wenige realisierte Bauten hervorgebracht hat.

Lingang New City – Western Island Office and Hotel Complex

The city island forms the termination of the east-west axis of Lingang New City. The exposed location of the plots on the island in the western part of the lake therefore calls for an equally unique architectural composition. The new dominating landmark buildings receive their identity from the diagonal organisation of the structural elements which compose an expressive sculpture of distinctive memorability. The character ties in with the tradition of the constructivists of the 20th century, a stylistic epoch which generated numerous exciting designs but only little realized projects.

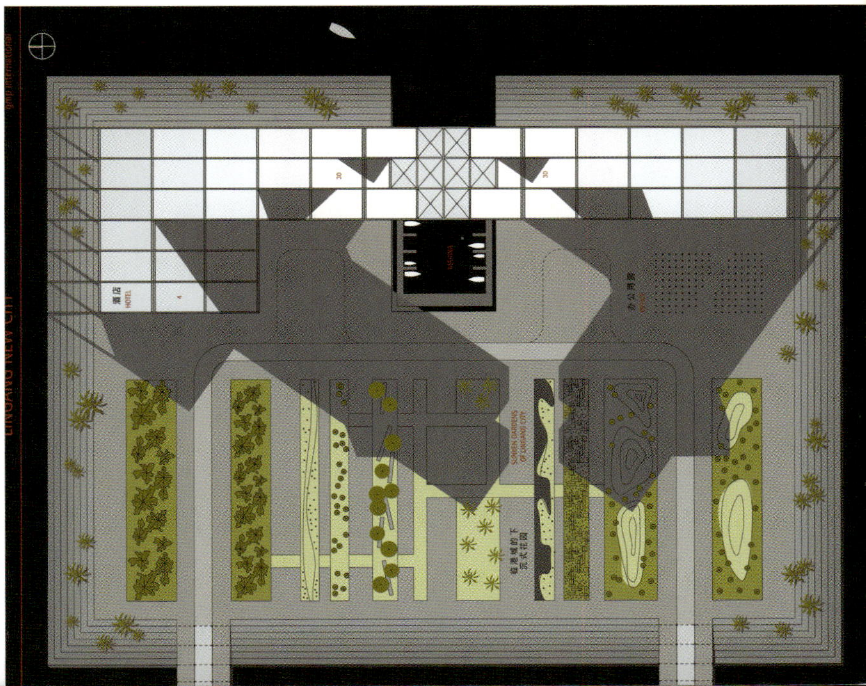

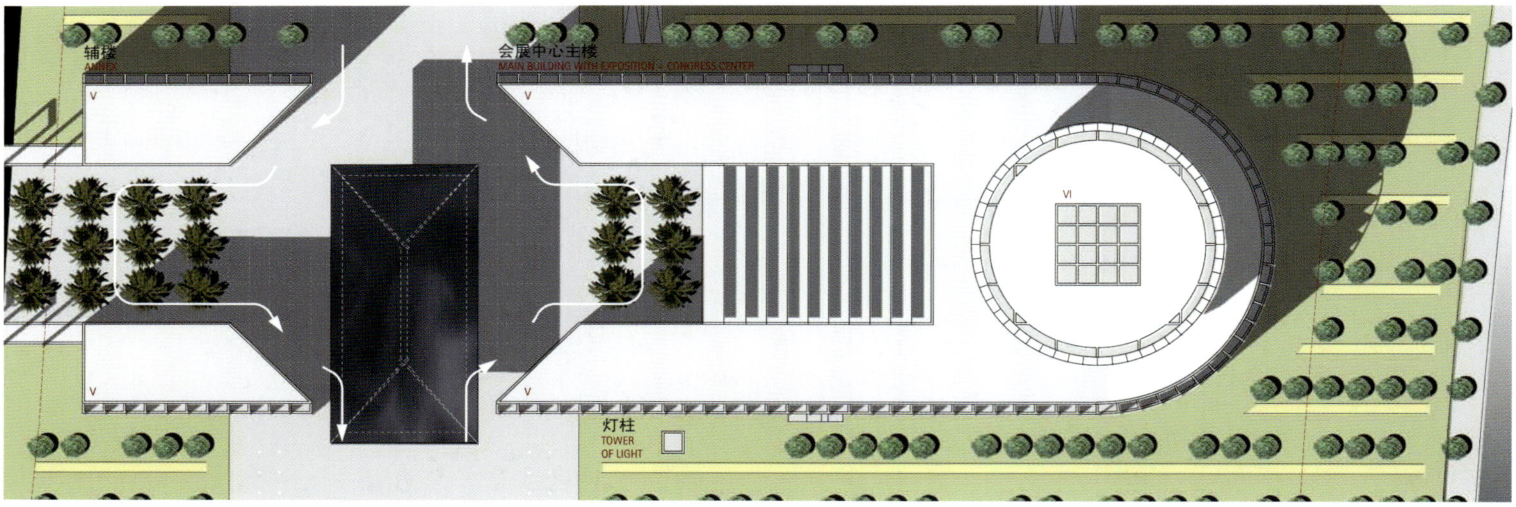
辅楼
ANNEX
会展中心主楼
MAIN BUILDING WITH EXPOSITION + CONGRESS CENTER
V
V
V
V
VI
灯柱
TOWER
OF LIGHT

WETTBEWERB: 2005 – 1. Preis
ENTWURF: Meinhard von Gerkan
PARTNER: Nikolaus Goetze, Wei Wu
BAUHERR: Shanghai Lingang Economic Development Group Co., LTD
BGF: 85.000 m^2

Lingang New City – Bezirksparlament

Lingang New City – Administrative Office Center

Die exponierte Lage des Grundstücks an einer der Haupteinfahrtsstraßen von Lingang New City fordert eine ebenso exponierte wie auch klare architektonische Komposition der einzelnen Haupt- und Nebengebäude des Office Center, die sich zu einem übergeordneten Ensemble gruppieren. Prägender Gedanke der Konzeption ist es, eine Ausgewogenheit zwischen der Einheit der Gesamtanlage und der Vielfalt ihrer unterschiedlichen Einzelgebäude herzustellen.

Zum einen wird die Einheit durch eine großzügige Natursteinfassade erreicht, die je nach Nutzung durch zusätzliche Verschatter oder horizontale Fassadenbänder variiert wird, zum anderen durch die übergeordnete Typologie zweier paralleler Gebäuderiegel, die mittig außen liegende Höfe bzw. Erschließungsfoyers begleiten.

Der zentrale Platz der Anlage wird von einem großen quadratischen Dach überspannt, ein von diesem permanent herunterlaufender Wasservorhang definiert zusätzlich noch den Platz und sorgt für eine angenehme Kühlung und eine hohe Verweilqualität.

Diesem Patio schließen sich im Osten und Westen der Anlage zwei mit Sheddächern überspannte, lichtdurchflutete Eingangshallen an.

Im östlich gelegenen Hauptgebäude gelangt man über kaskadenartig angelegte Treppen in die zentrale Zone, die von einem bis zu 2.500 Personen fassenden Konferenzsaal abgeschlossen wird.

Im Westen der Anlage gruppieren sich die Nebengebäude um den vom Fluss durchbrochenen palmenbestandenen Innenhof.

The exposed position of the plot by one of the main access roads of the Lingang New City demands a similarly exposed as well as distinct architectural composition of the individual main buildings and annexes of the Office Center which will be grouped together to form a super-ordinate ensemble. The distinguishing thought behind the conception is to establish a balance between the unity of the whole complex and the diversity of its various individual buildings.

The unity is assured on the one hand by the super-ordinate theme of the generous natural stone façade that, depending on the use, is varied by additional shading elements or horizontal bands of façade and on the other hand by the super-ordinate typology of two parallel strips of buildings that accompany centrally outlying yards or access foyers.

The central square in the complex is spanned by a large quadratic roof, a curtain of water permanently running down from this lends additional emphasis to the square and ensures pleasant cooling and a high incentive to linger here.

In the east and west of the complex two light-filled entrance halls covered with shed roofs adjoin this patio. In the main building on the east side a cascade-like staircase leads to the central zone that is crowned by a conference hall with capacity for up to 2,500 people.

On the western side of the complex the annexes are grouped around the inner courtyard with its palm trees and the river flowing through it.

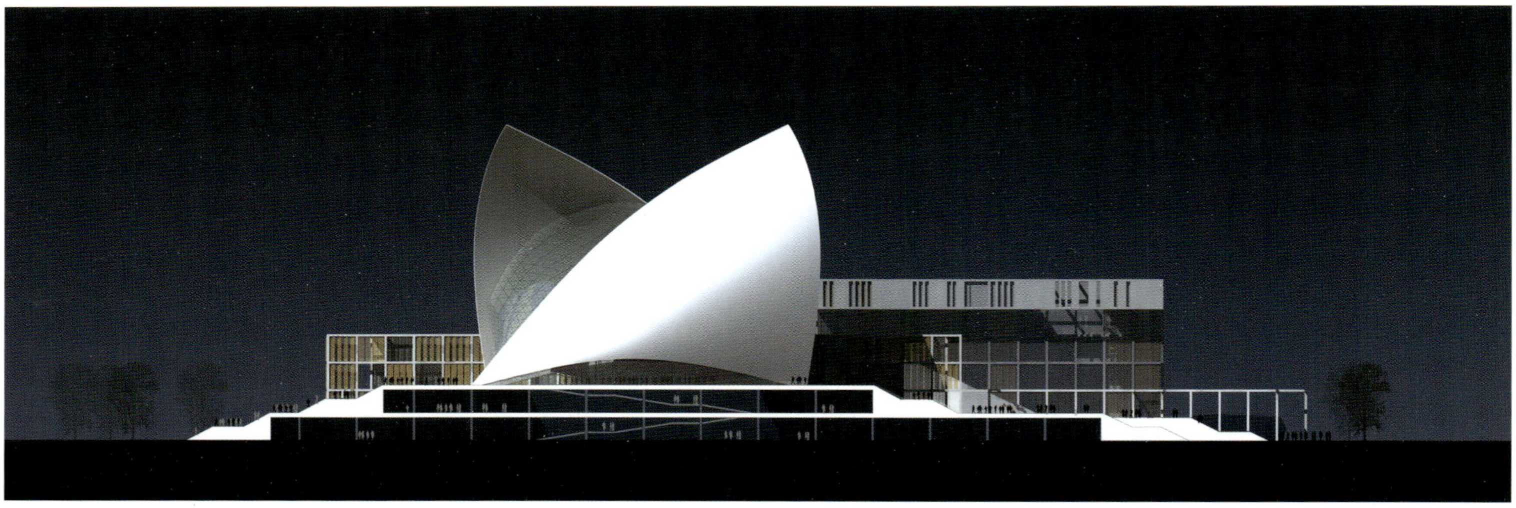

GUTACHTEN: 2004
ENTWURF: Meinhard von Gerkan
BAUHERR: Shanghai Harbour City Investment Co.
BGF: 72.400 m²
BAUZEIT: 2005–2007

Lingang New City – Maritim-Museum, Schifffahrtsmuseum, Jugendzentrum und Bibliothek

Maritime Museum, Youth Centre and Library in Lingang

Die solitärhaften Baukörper des Schifffahrtsmuseums, des Jugendzentrums und der Bibliothek werden mit Hilfe einer einheitlichen Form- und Materialsprache zu einer homogenen Gesamtanlage zusammengeführt. Arkaden, Stege, Brücken und Luftbalken bilden subtile Gestaltungsmittel, die im Gesamtspiel von Licht und Schatten unter Einbindung von Wasser- und Grünflächen dem Komplex der drei unterschiedlichen Funktionen entwurflichen Zusammenhang verleihen.

Aus dieser formalen Gesamtgestalt setzt sich das Schifffahrtsmuseum mit seiner expressiven Dachform deutlich und eigenständig ab. Zwei gegeneinander gesetzte leichte Dachschalen, die im weitesten Sinn die maritime Form und Analogie eines Segels beim Betrachter hervorrufen, bilden das für die Gesamtfigur wichtige und identitätsbildende Leitbild für das Museum. In dem sich unter dieser Dachform spannenden, hallenförmigen Luftraum sollen große, historische Schiffsexponate kulturgeschichtlich gewertet und dem Publikum zugänglich gemacht werden.

Die sich gegeneinander verschränkenden „Segelflächen" stehen frei auf einem Sockel, in dem sämtliche museumsbedingten Funktionen enthalten sind. Großzügige Freitreppen laden zum Verweilen ein und bilden einen unmittelbaren Bezug zu den landschaftlich gestalteten Freianlagen. Die formalen Entwurfselemente des frei zugänglichen Sockels, der über eine Freitreppe erschlossen wird, findet sich auch bei den zwei direkt benachbarten Gebäuden, Bibliothek und Jugendzentrum. Diese beiden formal verwandten Baukörper stehen sich auf einer imaginären Achse vis-a-vis gegenüber und flankieren somit das Schifffahrtsmuseum mit seiner leichten, weithin sichtbaren maritimen Dachform.

The solitaire-type structures of the Maritime Museum, the Youth Centre and the Library are combined to form a homogenous overall complex with the help of the uniform use of shapes and materials. Arcades, footbridges and open beams form subtle design elements that, in an overall play of light and shade and integrating the water and green areas, lend the complex of the three different functions a mutuality in their design.

The Maritime Museum with its expressive roof shape stands out distinctly and independently against this formal overall construction. Two light roof shells, facing each other and overlapping, that in the broadest sense evoke in the observer the idea of a maritime shape and an analogy to a sail, create the identity-forming landmark of the Museum that is so decisive for the overall character of the complex. The large, hall-like space below this roof construction is intended for the exhibition of large, ancient ships that have been assessed as being valuable to cultural history. Here they will be made accessible to the general public.

The entwined 'sails' stand freely on a pedestal in which all the functions of the Museum are accommodated. Spacious open staircases are inviting places to linger and bear an immediate relation to the landscaped open spaces. The formal design elements of the publicly accessible pedestal that can be reached via a generously arranged outside staircase can also be found in the two directly neighbouring buildings, the Library and the Youth Centre. These two formal, structurally related building components stand on an imaginary axis directly opposite to one another and therefore flank the Maritime Museum with its light marine roof construction that is visible from a great distance.

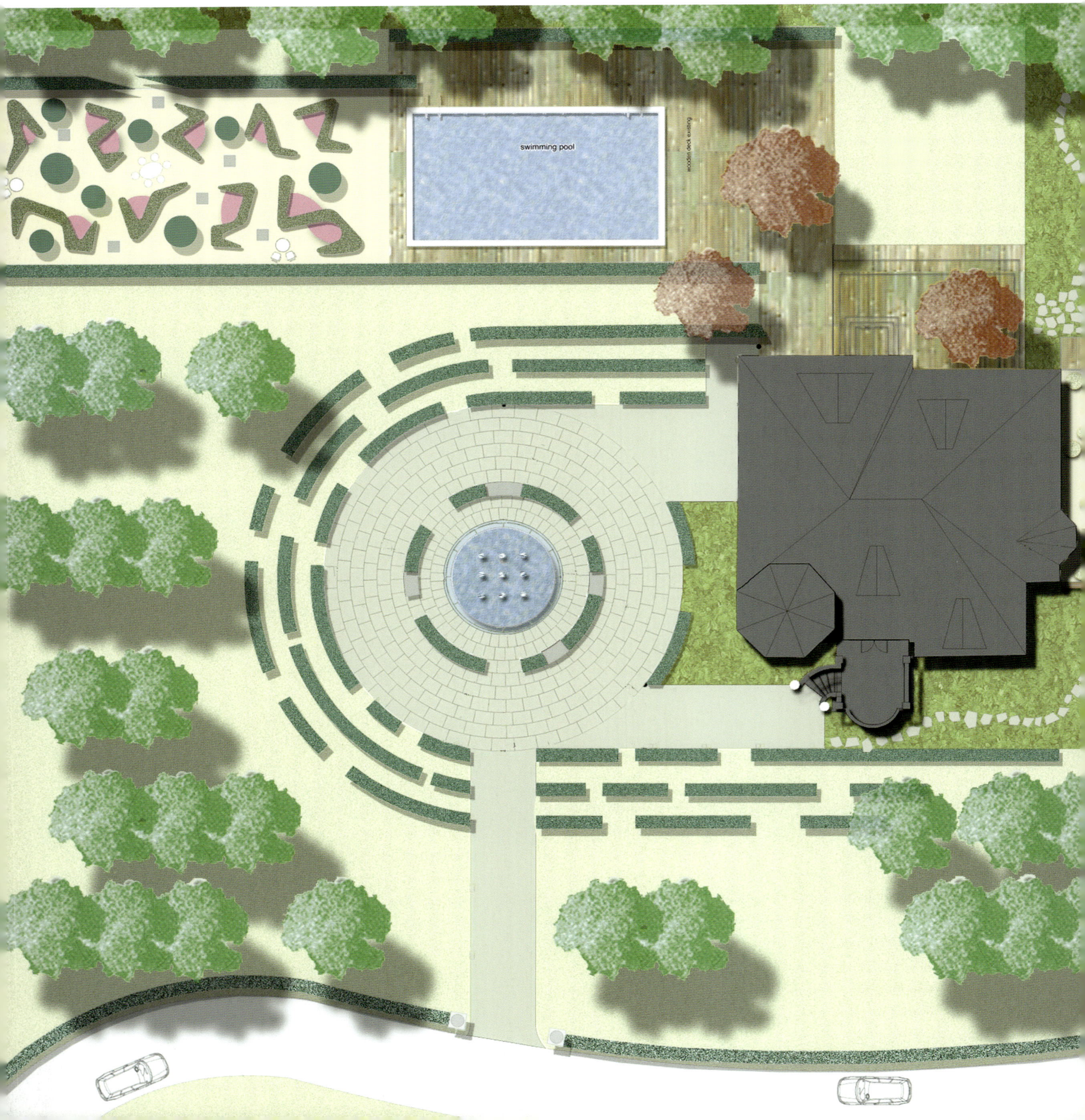
swimming pool
wooden deck existing

DIREKTAUFTRAG, GRÖSSE: 4.200 m²
KOSTEN: ca. 1,45 Mio. RMB

GNÜCHTEL · TRIEBSWETTER LANDSCHAFTSARCHITEKTEN

EIN VILLENGARTEN IN PEKING
GARDEN OF A VILLA, BEIJING

Der hintere Gartenteil inszeniert mit Heckenelementen Raumqualitäten, die aus verschiedenen Blickwinkeln unterschiedliche Raumeindrücke ermöglichen.

The rear section of the garden uses hedges to create garden rooms with different qualities and, depending on the viewing angle, changing aspects.

Idyllisch situiert mit Blick auf einen See in der Peripherie von Peking, umgibt ein 5.000 m² großer Garten den Neubau einer Villa. Die Gestaltung des Gartenraums folgt dem Wunsch des Besitzers, repräsentativ nach außen zu wirken und zugleich private Aufenthaltsbereiche im Freien zu schaffen.

Daher wurde in enger Kooperation mit dem Bauherrn ein Konzept miteinander verwobener Gartenräume erarbeitet, die einer Systematik abgestufter Privatheit folgen. Auf ausdrücklichen Wunsch des Bauherrn greift der Garten stilistisch nicht auf die chinesische Tradition zurück, sondern bedient sich der Formensprache der europäischen Gartentradition. Wesentlicher Grundgedanke ist – neben der Öffnung und Schließung von Räumen entsprechend dem Grad ihrer Repräsentation oder Privatheit – immer wieder überraschende Raumfolgen und Ein- und Ausblicke zu schaffen. Die Baumart wechselt von Reihe zu Reihe zwischen Baummagnolien und Ginkgos ab und sorgt so zu jeder Jahreszeit für deren angemessenen Effekt.

This 5,000 m² garden of a new villa on the outskirts of Beijing is an idyllic spot overlooking a lake. The landscape design complied with the wish of the client for a 'prestigious front' and secluded private garden at the back of the house.

This is why the architects, in constant dialogue with the client, developed a sequence of interwoven garden rooms, each of them more intimate and private than the previous one. As the client expressly did not wish a Chinese garden, the design was based on European garden traditions. The main idea was not only to open or seclude the different garden rooms according to their degree of privacy, but to create unexpected enfilades, views out of and glimpses into these rooms. Tree species alternate between magnolias and gingkos which add interest to the garden in their seasons.

Die Gartenbeleuchtung nutzt die Geometrie des Gartens, um gezielte Lichtakzente zu setzen. Mit den Fontänen im Zentrum des Rondells unterstreicht die Beleuchtung den Kreis des Rondells.

The garden lights represent carefully placed luminous accents in the geometry of the garden. The water spouting from the fountains in the middle of the circular flower bed reflects and enhances the lights installed around the bed.

Der privaten Erschließungsstraße und dem See zugewandt ist der Garten auf der Eingangsseite mit einem lockeren Hain überstellt.

Oriented and open to the private drive and the lake, the garden is screened at the front by a loosely planted cluster of trees.

Die beiden Ausgänge in den Innenhof werden durch einen gedeckten Gang verbunden, ebenfalls ein Motiv aus den klassischen Gärten Suzhous. Die Dachkonstruktion ist eine Anlehnung an die wellenförmige Ausbreitung der Datenströme als Sinnbild der IT-Industrie.

The two doors leading onto the interior patio are linked by a covered passage – a motif from classical Souzhou gardens. The roof structure evokes the image of the data flows of the IT industry spreading in waves.

Eingebettet in eine Modellierung hinter dem Teich und überschirmt von blühenden, Schatten spendenden Bäumen liegt der Parkplatz, der weitestgehend aus dem Blickfeld des eigentlichen Parks verschwindet.

Nestling in the modulated ground behind the pond, and shaded by blossoming trees, is the parking lot which is largely hidden from view from the park itself.

DIREKTAUFTRAG, GRÖSSE: 31.000 m^2
KOSTEN: 9 Mio. RMB

GNÜCHTEL · TRIEBSWETTER LANDSCHAFTSARCHITEKTEN

VERWALTUNGSGEBÄUDE EINES DEUTSCHEN KONZERNS IN SOUZHOU

OFFICE ENVIRONMENT FOR A GERMAN CHIP PRODUCER IN SUZHOU

Vom nördlichen Besucherausgang ausgehend, führt der Fußweg über den See und dann immer näher am Wasser zur Kantine. Deren Außenterrasse inmitten der Lotusblüten ist wie das Erdgeschossniveau der Kantine deutlich unter der Wasseroberfläche gelegen.

Starting at the northern visitor exit, the pedestrian route leads across the pond and then – gradually approaching the water's edge – on to the staff restaurant. This has an outdoor terrace, surrounded by lotus flowers, the floor of which is significantly below the pond surface, as is the ground floor of the canteen.

Inspiriert wurde dieser Entwurf von den berühmten Gärten von Suzhou.

Wenn auch die Anforderungen andere sind, konnten dennoch übertragbare Prinzipien herausgelöst werden, die sich auf die Konzeption eines modernen Verwaltungsbaus übertragen ließen. So entstand das Konzept eines eingeschossigen, um einen offenen Innenhof mäandrierenden Verwaltungsbau und einer ebenfalls eingeschossigen Kantine. Zentrales Herzstück der Anlage ist ein großer Teich, der Distanz zwischen Kantine und Verwaltungsbau schafft.

Die Erdmassen aus dem Fundamentaushub wurden dazu benutzt, Höhenunterschiede im Gelände von bis zu 4 m zu erzeugen, die dazu dienen, Parkplatz und Chipfabrik auszublenden, sowie ein Oben und Unten, ein Innen und Außen zu erzeugen.

Statt hinter Mauern wie bei den klassischen Gärten verbirgt sich die Pavillonarchitektur auf der einen Hälfte des Grundstücks hinter einer großen Bambuspflanzung, auf der anderen hinter einem dichten Laubholzbestand.

This design was inspired by the famous gardens of Souzhou. Even though the programme was different, the classical Chinese garden scheme includes a number of principles that could be applied to the design of a modern administration complex. The result is a one-storey structure meandering around an open interior courtyard, supplemented by a one-storey staff restaurant. The focus of the layout is a large pond that creates distance between the offices and the canteen.

The earth from the excavation pit was used to modulate the grounds with differences in levels of up to 4 m so as to screen the parking lot and the chip factory by earth works and to create upper and lower, interior and exterior spaces.

Instead of standing in a classical walled garden, the pavilion is hidden behind a large bamboo grove on one side and densely planted deciduous trees and shrubs on the other.

北京国际汽车博览中心
Beijing International Automotive Expo

规划总平面图
Masterplan 1:1000

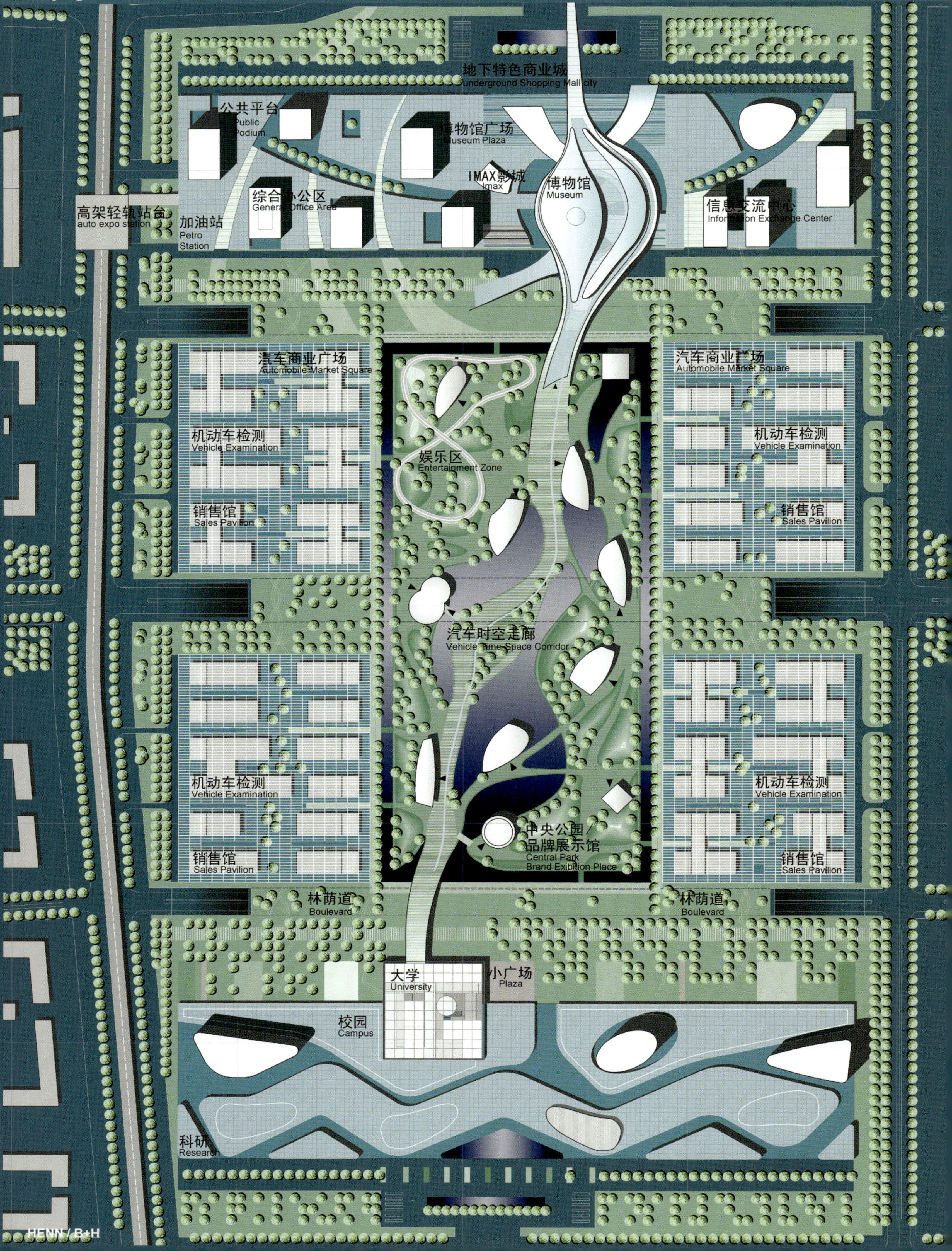

HENN ARCHITEKTEN, MÜNCHEN

INTERNATIONALER WETTBEWERB BEIJING INTERNATIONAL AUTOMOTIVE EXPO

BEIJING INTERNATIONAL AUTOMOTIVE EXPO, INTERNATIONAL COMPETITION

Die Beijing International Automotive Expo ist eines von rund 60 Großprojekten, mit denen sich die Stadt Peking anlässlich der Olympischen Spiele 2008 der Weltöffentlichkeit präsentieren wird.

Die ständige Automobilausstellung wird im Südwesten der Stadt am 4. Ring auf einem 60 ha großen Grundstück entstehen. Alle globalen Automarken werden hier vertreten sein. In einer Zeitreise aus der Vergangenheit durch die Gegenwart bis in die Zukunft erfährt der Besucher die Vielfalt des Automobils. Die Anordnung der Gebäude, ihre Funktion sowie die Topografie des Geländes orientieren sich an dieser Grundidee.

Beijing's International Automotive Expo is one of around 60 large projects through which the city of Beijing will be presenting itself to the global public on the occasion of the 2008 Olympic Games.

The permanent automotive exhibition will be created to the south west of the city on the 4th ring on a 60-ha large property. All global auto brands will be present here. With a journey through time extending from the past over the present through to the future visitors experience the variety of the automobile. The arrangement of the buildings, their function as well as the topography of the premises are oriented toward this underlying idea.

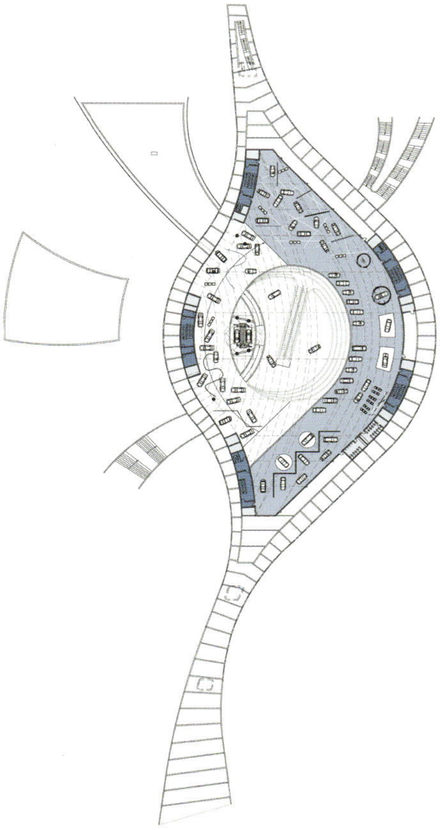

Level 6

HENN ARCHITEKTEN, MÜNCHEN _ **INTERNATIONALER WETTBEWERB BEIJING INTERNATIONAL AUTOMOTIVE EXPO**

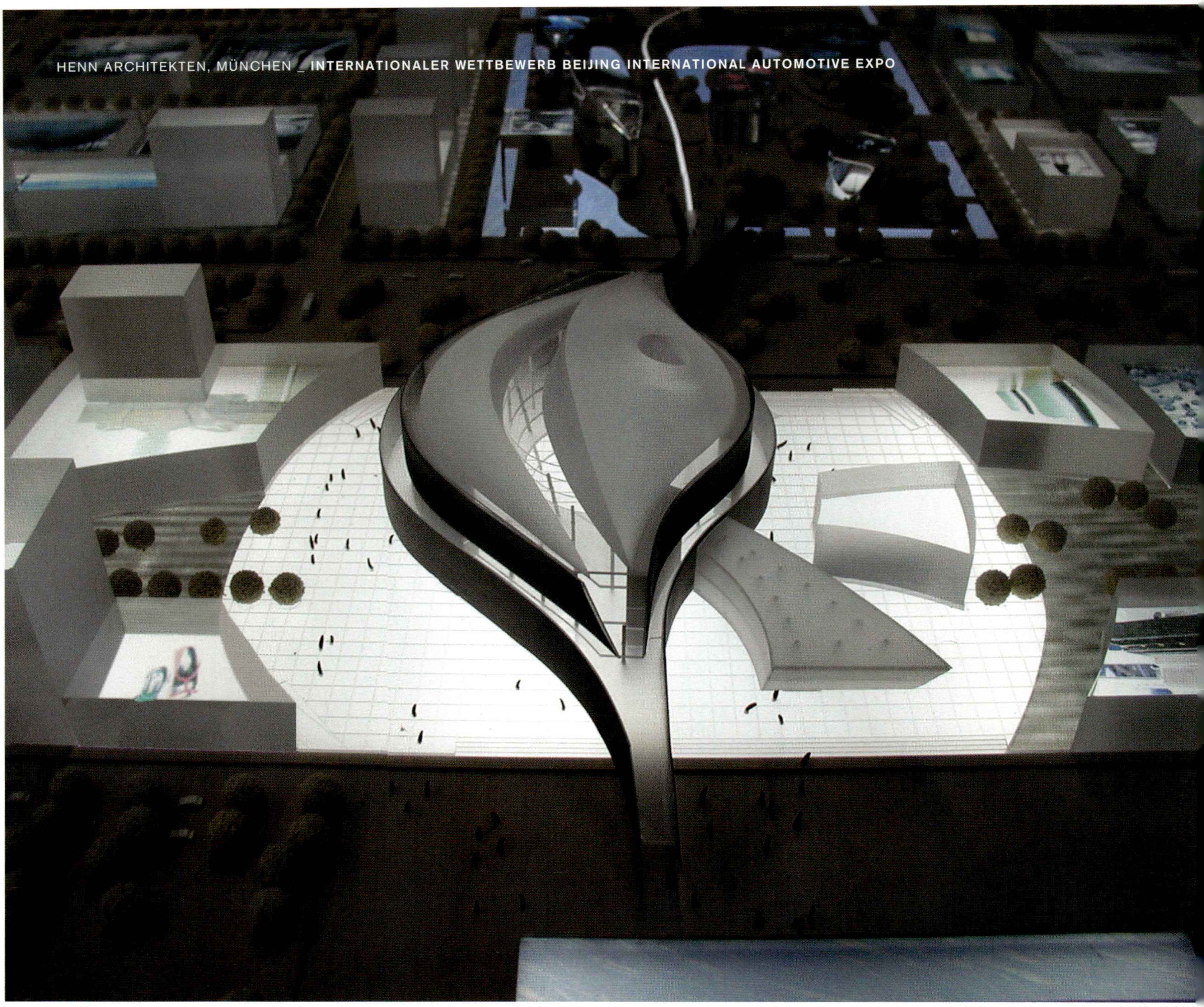

BAUHERR: Construction Office of Beijing, International Vehicle Expo Center
FLÄCHE: Bruttogrundfläche 500.000 m^2
PLANUNGSZEIT: 2003–2007
LAGE: Südwestlich des Stadtzentrums am 4. Ring

Der Parcours wird von einem Automobilmuseum eröffnet und steigert sich – einer dramaturgischen Leitlinie folgend – bis hin zu einer Auto-Universtität. Geplant sind neben dem zentralen Automuseum Dienstleistungsgebäude für die Automobilunternehmen, Niederlassungen der Marken, Autohäuser mit Werkstätten sowie Hotels und Shopping-Malls.

In der Mitte des Ausstellungsgeländes entsteht in geometrischer Analogie zu der Verbotenen Stadt ein rechteckiger Themenpark, in dessen topografischer Landschaft Markenpavillons angeordnet sind.

The course is opened by an automotive museum and increases – following a dramaturgical line – all the way to an automotive university. It is planned that service buildings for the automotive companies, branches of the brands, car dealers with workshops as well as hotels and shopping malls be located next to the central auto museum.

At the centre of the exhibition area, in geometrical analogy to the Forbidden City, is a square theme park whose topographical landscape houses the brand pavilions.

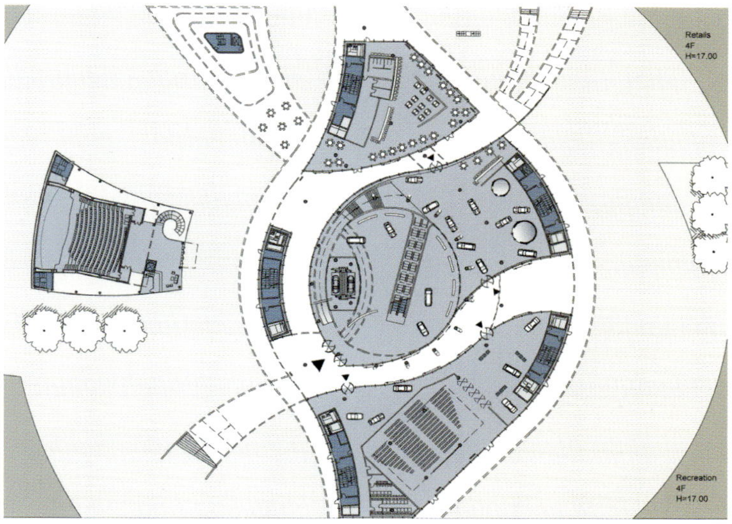

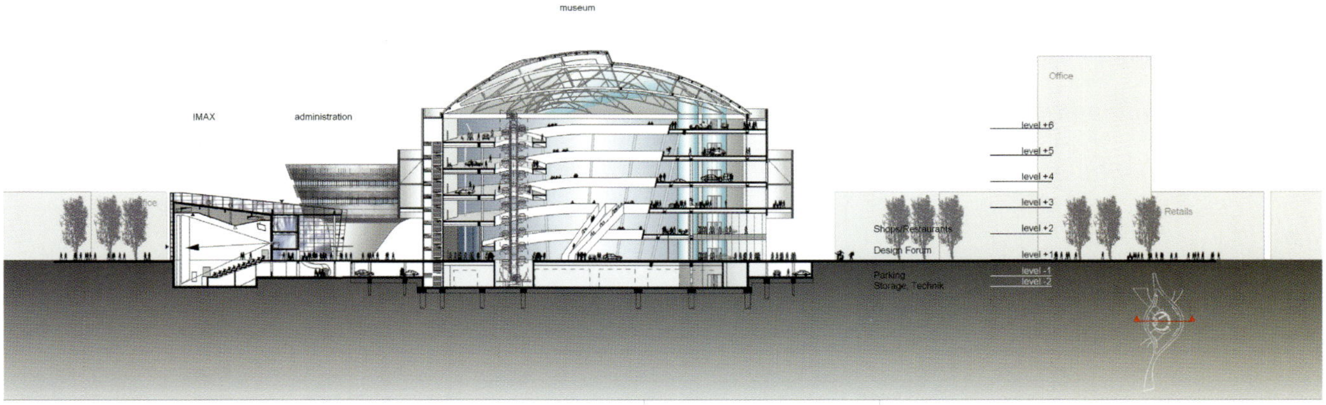

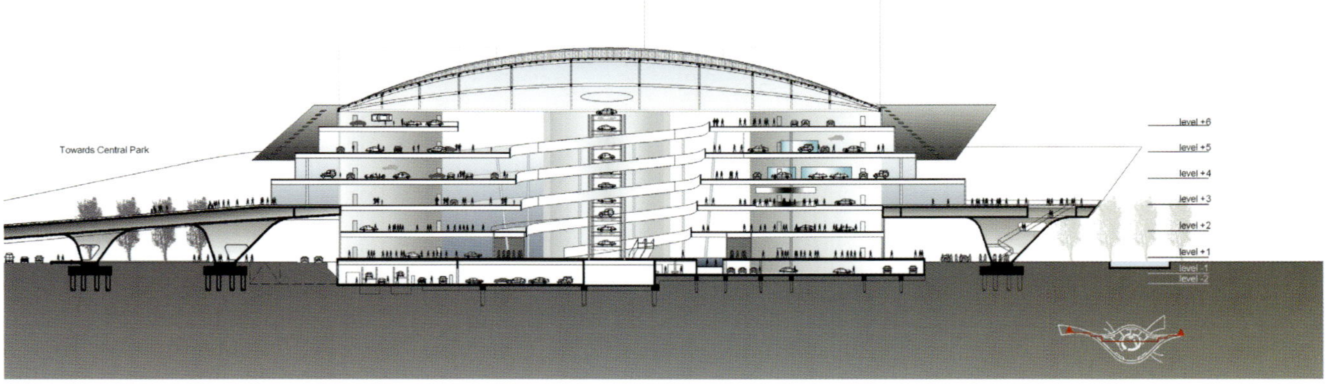

Luftbild
Aerial view

Detail westlicher Mall-Eingang
Western entrance to the mall, detail

Der Entwicklungsschwerpunkt FengJing mit der Zielrichtung der Konzentration der Kompetenz im Bereich Textil verarbeitender Maschinen möchte im Zusammenhang mit seiner urbanen Entwicklung als Mittelzentrum der stark wachsenden Bevölkerung am westlichen Eingang in die Provinz Shanghai an strategisch herausgehobener Lage ein angemessenes Einzelhandels- und Freizeitangebot anbieten. Hierzu wurde ein integratives Nutzungskonzept erarbeitet, das die Funktionen Handel, Gastronomie, Unterhaltung, Hotel, Verwaltung und Parken in einem innovativen Projekt zusammenführt.

The industrial city of Fengjing at the western inroad to Shanghai province is an urban development area with a focus on the production of textile-processing machinery. The city has been developing into a medium-sized urban centre with a fast-growing population and therefore planned adequate new shopping and leisure facilities in a strategic location. The architects developed an integrative occupancy scheme which included retail spaces, catering outlets, entertainment facilities, offices and parking in an innovative structure.

KOHL & FROMME ARCHITEKTEN

FENGJING GATEWAYMALL, SHANGHAI

FENGJING GATEWAY MALL, SHANGHAI

Lageplan
Location plan

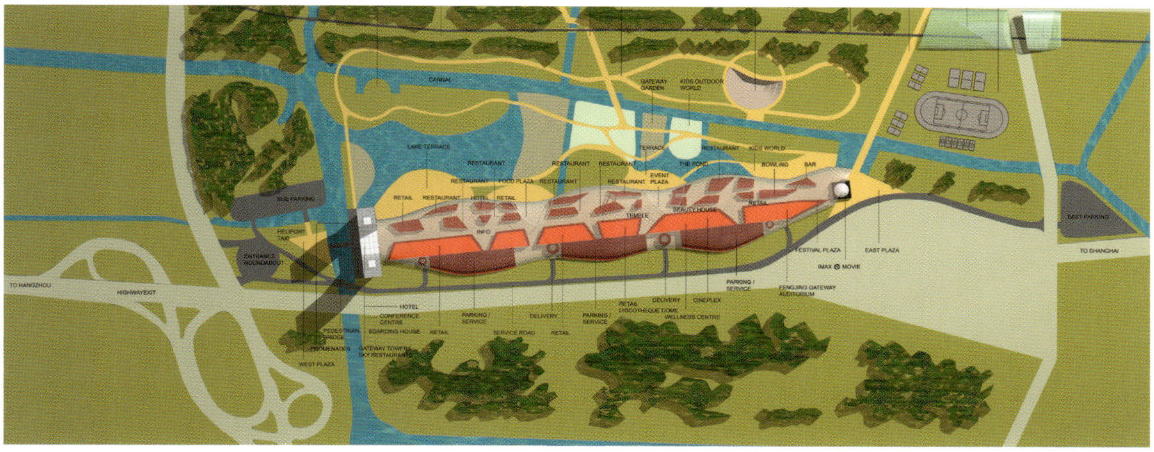

Ein membranüberspannter Raum von 150 m Breite und 900 m Länge umschließt die einzelnen Funktionsbereiche Handel, Gastronomie und Veranstaltungsräume. Die Figur verweist auf die Seidenraupenkokons, die Grundlage der Seidentextilverarbeitung dieser Region. Die transluzente Membran erscheint durch die feingliedrige Konstruktion und die wechselnde Lichtdurchlässigkeit als ein organisch bewegter Körper, der im Wechsel von Tag und Nacht vom angestrahlten Objekt zum selbst leuchtenden Zeichen wird.

Die exponierte Lage entlang der Autobahn und der Provinzgrenze geben dem Projekt eine ausgeprägte Bedeutung als Eingangstor in die Region Shanghai.

A 150 x 900 m hall, spanned by a textile membrane, encloses all the different commercial, restaurant and events facilities. Its construction and shape are reminiscent of silk-worm cocoons – the basis of the local silk industry. The filigree structure is just visible through the diaphanous membrane. This filters the natural light with varying intensity so that the hall appears like a moving organic body – light-flooded from above by day, radiating from within by night.

The exposed location on the motorway and the provincial border give this mall special significance as a gateway to Shanghai province.

Das Projekt befindet sind in einer Parkanlage, die entlang der Autobahn Shanghai – Hangzhou angelegt ist. Der Park und das Projekt bilden den öffentlichen Gemeinschaftsraum zwischen der historischen Kernzelle der Stadt, den Wohngebieten und der Gewerbezone.

The project is situated in a park parallel to the Shanghai-Hangzhou motorway. The park and the mall building form a public place between the historic city centre, the residential quarters and the industrial zone.

So genannte „Torhäuser" sind als städtebauliches Thema wichtig, da Raumfolgen und Sichtbeziehungen geschaffen werden.

So-called 'gateway houses' are an important urban design theme as they create spatial sequences and sight axes.

Blick in einen Blockinnenraum mit den halböffentlichen Freiräumen.

View of the interior of a perimeter block and its semi-private open areas.

AUSLOBER: Shanghai International Automobile City Real Estate Co., LTD
GESAMTFLÄCHE: 50.000 m^2
KOSTEN: 60 Mio. Euro

KRAMM & STRIGL, DARMSTADT

ANTING NEW TOWN

ANTING NEW TOWN

Die Wohnstadt Anting New Town im Nordwesten Shanghais soll nach deutschem Vorbild entstehen. Deutsche Architekten wurden eingeladen, „Anting New Town“ mittels deutscher Architektursprache, deutscher Konstruktionsmethoden und deutscher Technologie zur „German Town“ werden zu lassen.

Der vorliegende Lageplanentwurf im Maßstab 1/1000 wurde grundsätzlich beibehalten. Durch Schließung der vorgegebenen Struktur an wichtigen Stellen entstehen städtische Blöcke. Dadurch wird der Blockinnenraum privater, bleibt aber durchlässig. Kleine Plätze laden zum Verweilen ein, dort sind auch die Spielbereiche für Kleinkinder vorgesehen.

Die Straßen-Wege-Hierarchie wird durch Platzabfolgen gegliedert. Der Boulevard bildet den dominanten Straßenraum, wogegen der ovale Platz und sein gegenüber, der runde Platz, als die prägenden Orte des Stadtteils verstanden werden. Die Platzeinfassung mit dem europäischen Thema der Arkadengänge ermöglicht eine ganzjährige Nutzung der Erdgeschosszone. Die Strenge der Fassadengliederung korrespondiert mit der Dynamik der elliptischen Grundrissform. Die Baukörper sind Kuben mit glatter Oberfläche ohne hervorspringende Bauteile. Ziel ist es eine homogene, moderne und zeitlose Architektursprache zu transportieren.

The residential new suburb of Anting New Town northwest of Shanghai was to be based on German models. German architects were invited to make Anting New Town a ‘German town’ by using ‘German architectural language’ as well as ‘German structural design and technology’.

The existing site layout (scale: 1:1000) was basically retained. Filling gaps in strategic places of the proposed structures produced urban street blocks with buildings enclosing large open areas. These are more private, but still publicly accessible. Small squares welcome residents and visitors, while small children have fun in the playgrounds.

The hierarchy of streets and footpaths was based on the principle of spatial sequence. The dominant street space is the boulevard, while oval or circular public squares were seen as the identity-shaping places in the new suburb. European-style arcades around a square make it possible to use the ground-floor areas all the year round. The austere facade design corresponds to the dynamics of the elliptic floor area. The buildings are cubes with smooth surfaces without any projections. The design aimed to express a homogeneous modern, and timeless, architectural language.

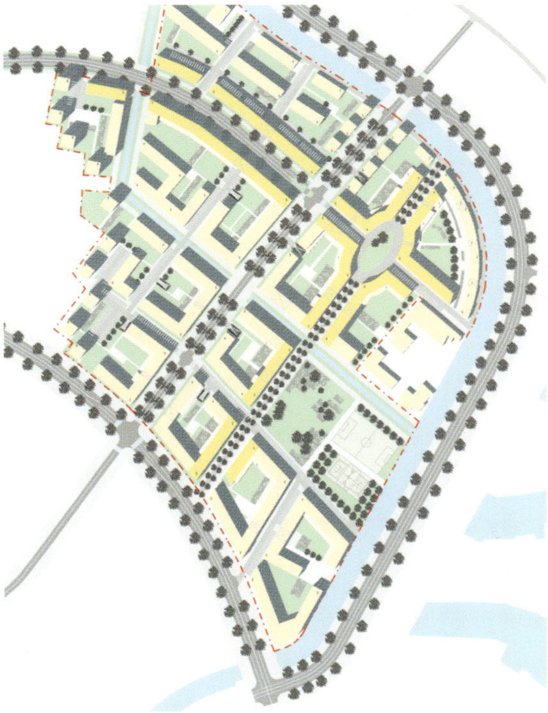

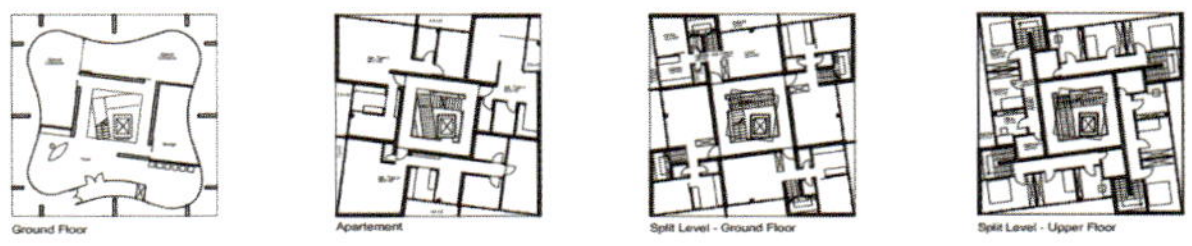

Haus-im-Haus-Konzept: Durch die Drehung der einzelnen Geschosse haben alle Wohnungen ein gleiches Maß an Sonne und Aussicht.

House-in-house design. Due to the staggered rotation of the floors, all the apartments receive sunlight in equal measure and afford lovely views.

Der Sockel des Gebäudes besteht aus einer Stahlbetonstruktur. Die Stützen stehen im Raster 7,50 m mal 7,50 m.

The base is an RC structure with columns placed on a grid of 7.5 x 7.5 m.

Aufgabe ist die Erweiterung der bestehenden Bibliothek um einen zweiten Bauabschnitt mit einer Fläche von 80.000 m² für ca. 12 Mio. Bücher.

Ein wichtiger, zukunftsweisender Bestandteil der Erweiterung der bestehenden Bibliothek ist die „Digitale Bibliothek". Von historisch und kulturell jedoch kaum zu übertreffender Bedeutung ist die über 200 Jahre alte „Si Ku Quan Shu"-Sammlung des Kaisers Quianlong (1736–1795), die ebenfalls im neuen Bau untergebracht werden soll. Sie bewahrt in Kopien alter historischer Schriften das vieltausendjährige Wissen und die Kultur des traditionellen China.

Der Entwurfsbeitrag von KSP Engel und Zimmermann gliedert sich sowohl architektonisch als auch inhaltlich in drei wesentliche Bereiche: den erhöhten Sockel – die klassische Bibliothek mit der historischen Si Ku Quan Shu (Vergangenheit), die Säulen – eine Zone zur Interaktion des Volkes mit dem kulturhistorischen Erbe (Gegenwart) und das schwebende Dach – die Digitale Bibliothek (Zukunft).

The competition was for an extension of the existing national library with a ground floor area of 80,000 m² for approx. 12 million books.

An important, seminal part of the extension is the 'digital library'. More important still is the 200-year-old, historically and culturally unsurpassable Si Ku Quan Shu Collection of Emperor Quianlong (1736–95) that is also to be kept in the new extension. This collection includes copies of historical manuscripts of thousands of years of knowledge and Chinese traditional culture.

In terms of both architecture and function, the design proposed by KSP Engel and Zimmerman consists of three essential sections: the raised base, classical library with historical Si Ku Quan Shu (the past); the columned structure, a place for people to encounter their cultural history (the present) and the 'floating-roof' level containing the digital library (the future).

KSP – ENGEL UND ZIMMERMANN ARCHITEKTEN, FRANKFURT AM MAIN

PARTNER: EAST CHINA ARCHITECTURAL & RESEARCH INSTITUTE CO., LTD., SHANGHAI

CHINESISCHE NATIONALBIBLIOTHEK, PEKING

NATIONAL LIBRARY OF THE REPUBLIC OF CHINA, BEIJING

Ein internationaler Wettbewerb mit neun Teilnehmern aus China, Dänemark, Deutschland, Großbritannien, Japan und den USA

International competition among nine participants from China, Denmark, Germany, Great Britain, Japan and the United States

Lesesaal mit 2.000 Plätzen und 12 Mio. Bänden, Digitale Bibliothek und Konferenzbereich.

The library has a reading room which accommodates 2,000 users; it holds 12 million books, a digital library and a conference area.

BAUHERR: National Library of China, Beijing
BGF (GESAMT): 80.000 m^2
BESUCHER PRO TAG: 8.000
BESTAND: 12 Mio. Bände
FACHPLANER: Weischede, Herrmann u. Partner, Lemon Consult
GRUNDSTÜCKSFLÄCHE: 22.000 m^2
FERTIGSTELLUNG: 2006
STELLPLÄTZE: 370 unter-, 100 oberirdisch

Konzept

Design Concept

Die drei Elemente – der erhöhte Sockel, die Säulen und das Dach – sind auch in der chinesischen Bauhistorie stilistische Elemente, die ursprünglich bedeutenden, meist öffentlichen Bauten vorbehalten waren. So greift der Entwurf diese Elemente in Form einer zeitgenössischen Interpretation bewusst auf und stellt das Gebäude so auch formal in den seiner Funktion angemessenen historischen Zusammenhang.

Analog zum Erscheinungsbild des gesamten Gebäudes gliedert sich die Tragstruktur in zwei Teile. Die beiden unteren der drei Kellergeschosse bilden mit einer Kantenlänge von ca 90 m mal 119 m den Sockel des Gebäudes. Über diesem Sockel schwebt eine zweigeschossige Struktur. Sie ist so steif ausgebildet, dass sie trotz ihrer Kantenlänge von ca. 100 m mal 112 m nur sechs Füße zur Auflagerung auf den Sockel benötigt.

The three building sections – raised base, columned structure and roof level – represent stylistic elements which also in Chinese architectural history were reserved for important, mostly public buildings. The design therefore reinterprets them in a contemporary language, thus also placing the extension in a historical context which matches its historical contents.

In analogy to the appearance of the entire building, the load-bearing structure is two-part. The two bottom of three basement floors – measuring 90 x 119 m – form the 'plinth' of the library from which a two-storey block rises whose extremely rigid structure, despite its area of 100 x 112 m, only needs six bearings supported by the base.

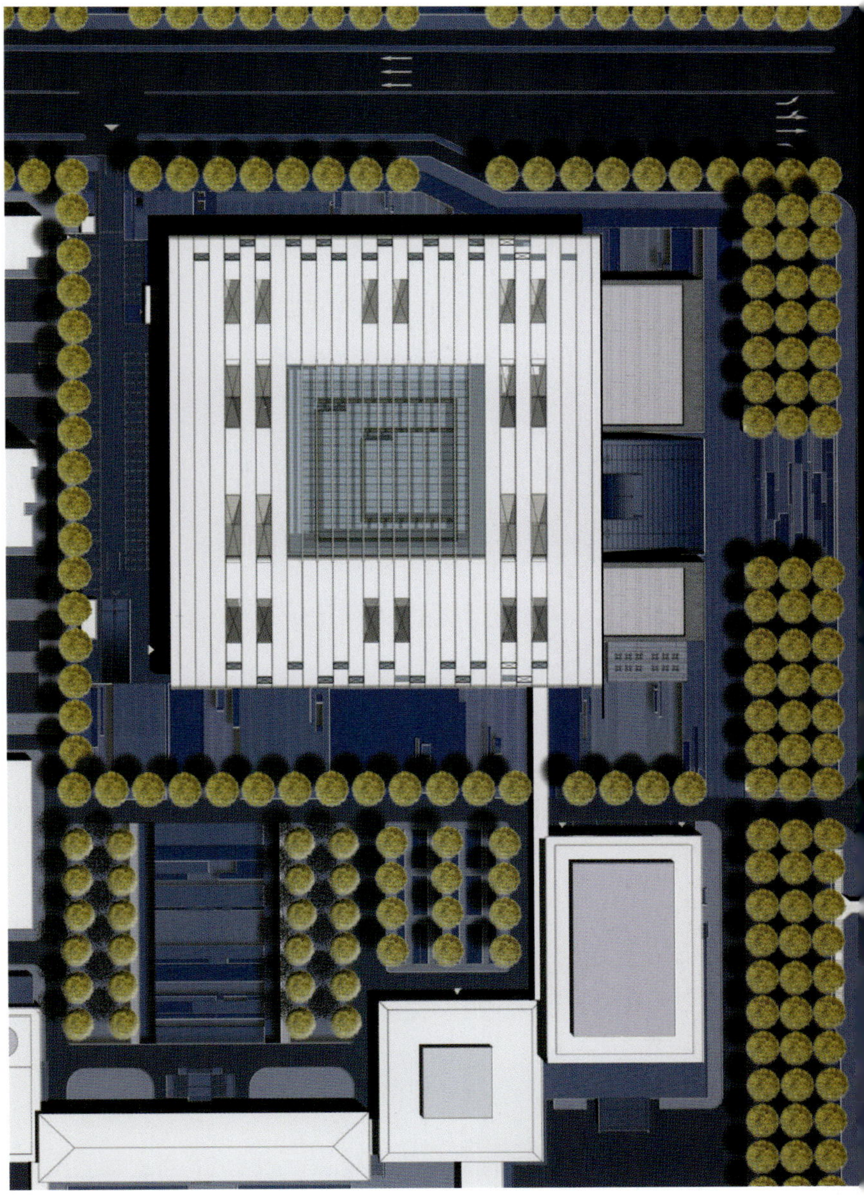

Der über dem Sockel schwebende Gebäudeteil hat einen zentrischen Innenhof von ca. 50 m x 50 m. Als Tragstruktur werden Fachwerkträger in einer Stahlkonstruktion ausgebildet.

The structure that seems to float on top of the base has a central patio of about 50 x 50 m. The steel structure includes a number of space girders.

Der Haupteingang.

View of the main entrance.

KSP – ENGEL UND ZIMMERMANN ARCHITEKTEN, FRANKFURT AM MAIN

CULTURAL SQUARE SHANGHAI: GRÜNE OASE UND KULTURZENTRUM

CULTURAL SQUARE SHANGHAI: GREEN OASIS – CULTURAL VENUE

Dieser neue Gebäudekomplex in Shanghai umfasst ein zentrales Gebäude, in dem sich das Hauptauditorium mit Bühne und Hauptfoyer befindet. Der Bau erhebt sich über zweieinhalb Untergeschosse mit Tiefgarage und Anlieferung (–2) und einer zentralen Einkaufspassage (–1).

Das zentrale Gebäude zeichnet sich durch steile Seitenwände und ein sanft geneigtes, begrüntes Dach aus, das auf der Vorderseite als Baldachin über dem abgesenkten Hof 27 m auskragt. Die darunter liegende Gebäudefassade zum Hof hin steht schräg.

Die Untergeschosse und die wichtigsten tragenden Konstruktionen des zentralen Baus (d.h. die Außenmauern) bestehen aus Stahlbeton, das Tragwerk des grünen Daches und des auskragenden Vordaches aus Raumfachwerkträgern.

The new Shanghai Cultural Square complex consists of a central building, which contains the main theatre with stage area and main foyer. This building rises above two and a half basement levels of underground garage, delivery areas (–2) and a central shopping mall (–1).

This central structure is characterized by sheer sidewalls and a gently sloping green roof whose front end cantilevers approx. 27 m to form a canopy over the sunken courtyard. The courtyard facade underneath the canopy is inclined.

Whereas the levels below ground and the main structures of the central building (i.e. the enclosing walls) are designed as RC structures, the green roof including the cantilever canopy is to have a steel space-frame structure.

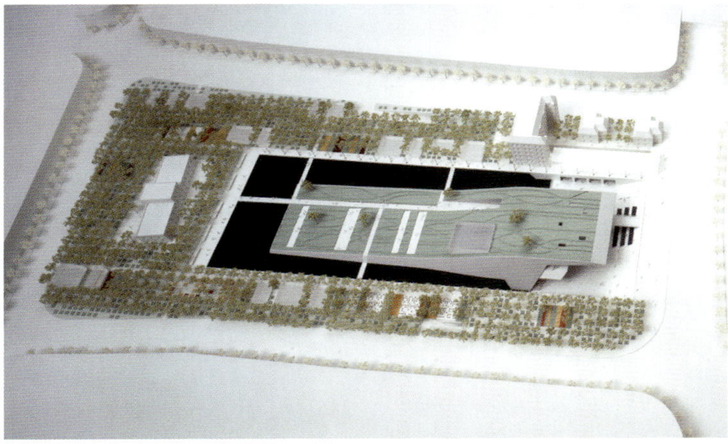

Im Gegensatz zur dicht bebauten heterogenen Umgebung profitiert der Musical Park von einer weiträumigen Parklandschaft. Im südlichen Geländeabschnitt befindet sich ein kleiner Hain, im Norden geht der Park „nahtlos“ in die landschaftliche Umgebung über.

In contrast to its densely built-up heterogeneous neighbourhood, the Musical Park enjoys a spacious country-like setting. To the south, there is a grove of trees, to the north, the grounds blend with the surroundings.

BAUHERR: Shanghai Cultural Square Investment Co. Ltd.
BGF (oberirdisch): 16.450 m^2
BRI: 8.332 m^3
GRUNDSTÜCKSFLÄCHE: 54.000 m^2
WETTBEWERB: 2004

Ventilation und Klimaanlage

Ventilation and AC

Am vorderen Dachrand fungieren die Fachwerkträger als Kragarme, zwischen den Seitenwänden bilden sie ein orthogonales Raumfachwerk.

Die Planung der Ventilationsanlage ist auf den Komfort der Menschen im Zuschauerraum ausgerichtet. Die Architekten wählten ein flexibles System, das entweder entlang der Wände oder unter der Betondecke des Zuschauerraums installiert werden kann. Die Anlage ist den örtlichen Klimaverhältnissen angepasst. Da hier eine sehr hohe Luftfeuchtigkeit herrscht, wird nur ein Minimum an Frischluft über Ventilatoren ins Theater geleitet, um einerseits die Lufthygiene und andererseits Kosteneffizienz zu gewährleisten. Die Klimatisierung (Temperaturregelung) erfolgt daher mittels Luftzirkulation. Die Abluft wird über in den abgehängten Decken integrierte Rohre durch hoch effiziente Wärmerückgewinnungsanlagen geleitet. Selbstverständlich arbeiten diese Systeme gemäß den akustischen Standards für Theater und Konzerthallen geräuscharm.

Die Klimaanlagen werden ausschließlich computergesteuert und gleichen sämtliche klimatischen Schwankungen aus.

At the front end of the roof, the lattice girders act as cantilevers; between the sidewalls they form an orthogonal space frame.

The design of the ventilation equipment is geared to the comfort of the people sitting in the auditorium. The designers chose a flexible system which can be installed either along the walls or underneath the concrete ceiling of the theatre. The layout adapts to local climatic conditions. As the climate is very humid, only a minimum of fresh air will be drawn into the theatre via ventilators to guarantee hygienic air conditions as well as cost-efficiency. Air-conditioning in terms of temperature is therefore effected via air circulation.

The return air will be collected via ducts in the suspended ceiling and conducted through highly efficient energy-recovering systems. It goes without saying that all these systems are noise-reduced to the usual standards for theatres and concert halls. The air-conditioning systems are fully computer-controlled and adaptable to any climatic changes.

KSP – ENGEL UND ZIMMERMANN ARCHITEKTEN, FRANKFURT AM MAIN

EXPO 2010 SHANGHAI

EXPO 2010 SHANGHAI

Die Expo bietet die große Chance, das Ufer des Flusses Huang-p'u-Chiang – der die größte unbebaute Fläche der Stadt bildet – für die Einwohner direkt zugänglich zu machen. Das wird ihr Bewusstsein für die ökologische Bedeutung der Wasserwege und -flächen im Stadtgebiet von Shanghai schärfen.

Die Expo sollte Gelegenheit geben, eine neue Uferanlage für Freizeit- und kulturelle Veranstaltungen zu bauen, ähnlich wie der „Bund" genannte Kai im 19. Jahrhundert.

Das Expo-Projekt will mit Hilfe intelligenter urbaner Strukturen das Verkehrsaufkommen reduzieren, neue Infrastrukturen und ein Stadtquartier mit allen Einrichtungen und Funktionen wie Wohnen, Arbeiten, Information, Kommunikation, Kultur, Unterhaltung und mehr schaffen. Während der Turm der (fakultativen) Seilbahn die Mitte des Expo-Geländes markiert und sichtbar macht, bilden zwei (ebenso fakultative) Türme das Ost- und das Westende der Gesamtanlage.

The Expo offers the great chance to open the city to the river Huang p'u Chiang, which is the largest urban area not covered by buildings. Giving the inhabitants new ways of direct access to the riverside will foster their awareness of the ecological importance of the water system in the urban area of Shanghai.

The Expo should be the opportunity to build a new waterfront and events area in the same way as the quay called 'The Bund' did in the 19th century.

The Expo project aims to reduce traffic volumes by means of an intelligent urban structure, to create new infrastructures and an urban quarter with all the amenities for living, working, information, communication, culture, entertainment and more. While the tower of the (optional) funicular marks the centre of the development and makes it visible, two (equally optional) towers landmark the eastern and western ends of the Expo grounds.

BAUHERR: International Consultation of Planning and Design for World Expostion 2010 in Shanghai
PLANUNGSFLÄCHE: 300 ha
GRUNDSTÜCKSFLÄCHE: 1,2 Mio. m^2
WETTBEWERB: 2004
PROJEKTPARTNER: CAUPD, Beijing

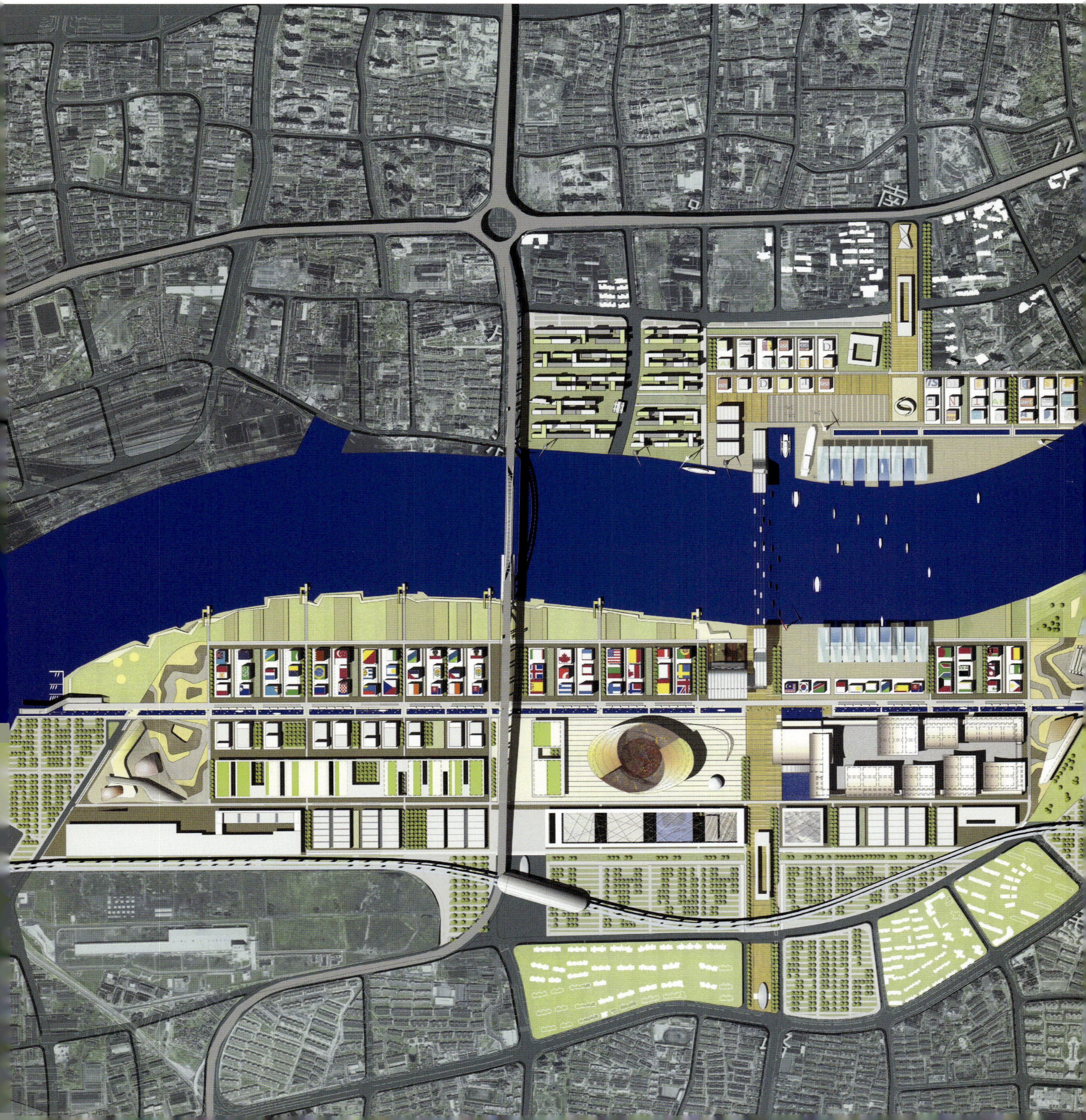

冷藏车

BAUHERR: Mr. Goa, Jing Qiu Lai Tai
GRUNDSTÜCKSFLÄCHE: 125.610 m²
BRI: 473.166 m³
WETTBEWERB: 2004, 1. Preis

KSP – ENGEL UND ZIMMERMANN ARCHITEKTEN, FRANKFURT AM MAIN

JING QIU LAI TAI GEBÄUDEENSEMBLE

JING QIU LAI TAI BUILDING

Das Baugelände des Lai-Tai-Gebäudeensembles befindet sich in der Mitte eines Straßenblocks ohne direkte Anbindung an die Hauptverkehrsstraßen der Stadt. Aus der Ferne wird es aufgrund seiner ungewöhnlichen Form einen starken Eindruck machen. Die einzelnen Gebäudeteile sind so gegliedert, dass sie sich in den Kontext einfügen. Die Anlage basiert auf der Dreiecksform und wirkt wie eine Insel inmitten der Stadt.

Der begrünte Innenhof bildet eine Oase auf dieser Insel. Die hohen Gebäudeabschnitte haben markant dynamische Formen, die einander widerzuspiegeln scheinen und so für das geschlossene Erscheinungsbild des Komplexes sorgen. Die bestehende Einkaufsstraße wird in die Südostecke des Geländes verlängert und führt dort zu einem neuen unterirdischen Einkaufszentrum. Der Haupteingang zu den öffentlichen Einrichtungen befindet sich am Südrand gegenüber dem Garten der US-Botschaft. Der Innenhof ist über Passagen zwischen den Hochhäusern zugänglich.

Die drei Hochhäuser in den nordöstlichen und südwestlichen Ecken des Dreiecks – End- und Höhepunkte des Entwurfs – prägen die räumliche Struktur der Anlage.

The site of the Lai Tai Building project is inside a street block without direct access to the main streets of the city. From further away, the building ensemble is to make a strong impression because of its unusual shape. The building sections are organized to integrate with the surroundings. A triangle serves as the dimensional form of the structure, which is like an island in the city.

The planted patio of the building ensemble forms an oasis on this island. The high buildings have stark dynamic forms, which seem to reflect each other and result in the overall unity of the complex. The existing shopping street is extended to the southeast corner of the site and leads to a new underground shopping mall. The main entrance to the public facilities is placed on the southern edge to face the garden of the US embassy. The entrances to the patio are placed between the high-rise structures.

The three high-rises on the northeast and southwest corners of the triangle – the end points and highlights of the ensemble – define the entire spatial structure of the site.

LÉON WOHLHAGE WERNIK ARCHITEKTEN, BERLIN

„RAY OF CENTURY" FERNSEH- UND AUSSICHTSTURM, GUANGZHOU

RAY OF CENTURY TV- UND SIGHTSEEING TOWER GUANGZHOU

In einem internationalen Wettbewerb für den Bau eines Fernseh- und Sightseeing-Towers in Guangzhou, China errangen Léon Wohlhage Wernik Architekten 2004 einen ersten Preis. Das zukünftig höchste Gebäude der Welt soll nach dem Willen der Auslober kein rein technisches Bauwerk sein, sondern zum neuen Wahrzeichen der aufstrebenden Region im Süden Chinas werden.

Die Architekten sind mit ihrem Entwurf – einer L-förmigen und 660 Meter hohen Konstruktion – neue Wege bei der Formfindung gegangen: Anstelle eines klassischen Fernsehturms mit schlankem Schaft und einem Kopf mit Aussichtsrestaurant und Sendetechnik entwickelten sie für die neue Mitte Guangzhous einen orthogonalen Winkel mit oszillierender Hülle.

In the 2004 international competition for a television and sight-seeing tower in Guangzhou, Léon Wohlhage Wernik Architects won one of several first prizes. The structure is to be the highest building in the world and, according to the clients' wishes, not merely a technical structure, but a new landmark of the booming region in China's south.

With their design of a 600-metre L-shaped high-rise, the architects took a new path in form-giving. Instead of the classical television tower with a slender shaft and a 'head' containing a panorama restaurant as well as the broadcasting station, they developed an 'angle bar' with a shimmering skin.

Der Turm erhält – einem Schlagschatten vergleichbar – einen lang gestreckten, horizontalen Fuß. In diesem Bauteil entwickelt sich auf 500 Metern Länge eine „Promenade der Ideen", die den Besucher über die fünf Feng-Shui-Elemente des Bauens informiert: Holz, Wasser, Erde, Metall und Feuer.

The tower has a flat, elongated 'foot' which appears like its hard shadow. In this structure, a 500-metre 'promenade of ideas' is developed which informs visitors about the five Feng-shui elements: wood, water, earth, metal and fire.

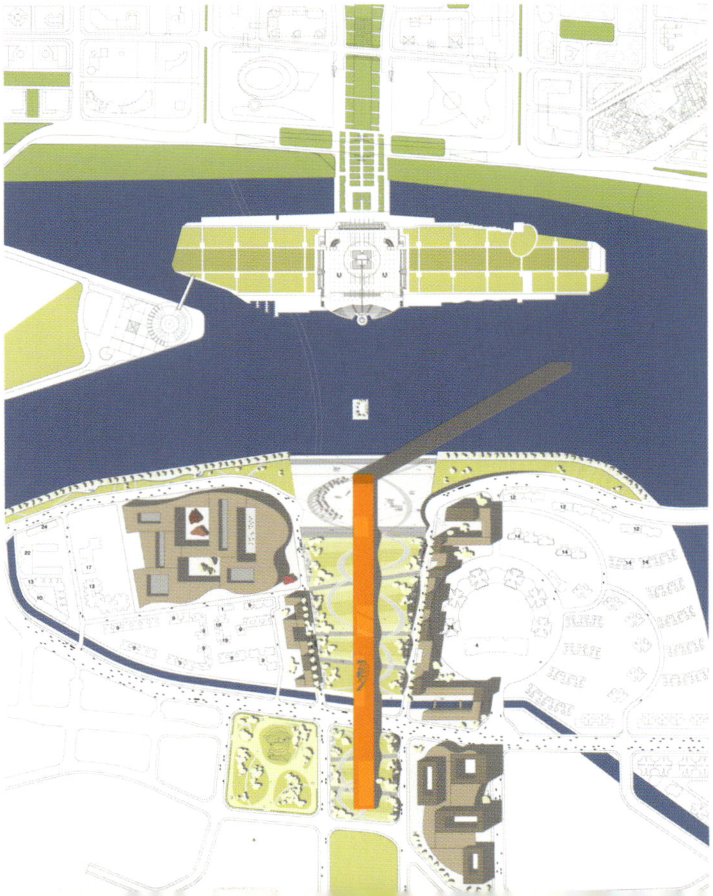

Internationaler Wettbewerb, ein erster Preis 2004

International competition project, a first prize, 2004

Die Tragstruktur besteht aus einem Netz filigraner Elemente, das von einer goldglänzenden Haut aus Metallgewebe umspannt wird. Diese Hülle setzt sich aus Millionen von Glasfaserkabeln zusammen und kann nachts als riesige Projektionsfläche bespielt werden. Gleichzeitig übernimmt sie die komplette Energieversorgung des Gebäudes und so entsteht der erste sich selbst versorgende und ökologisch autarke Fernsehturm der Welt. Das Konzept wurde in enger Zusammenarbeit mit den Stuttgarter Ingenieurbüros von Werner Sobek und Transsolar Energietechnik entwickelt.

The load-bearing structure consists of a web of filigree members covered by a shimmering gold-coloured metal-mesh skin. This consists of millions of glass fibre cables and can be used as a huge projection screen after dark. At the same time it is the solar power plant of the building which makes this the first ecologically self-sufficient television tower in the world in terms of energy supplies. This concept was developed in close co-operation with the Stuttgart-based engineering firms of Werner Sobek and Transsolar Energietechnik.

AUSLOBER: Guangzhou Municipal Construction Commission and Guangzhou Urban Planning Bureau
BGF: 96.800 m^2
HÖHE: Turm 509 m, Antenne 155 m (gesamt: 664 m)
WETTBEWERB: Juli / August 2004 – ein 1. Preis

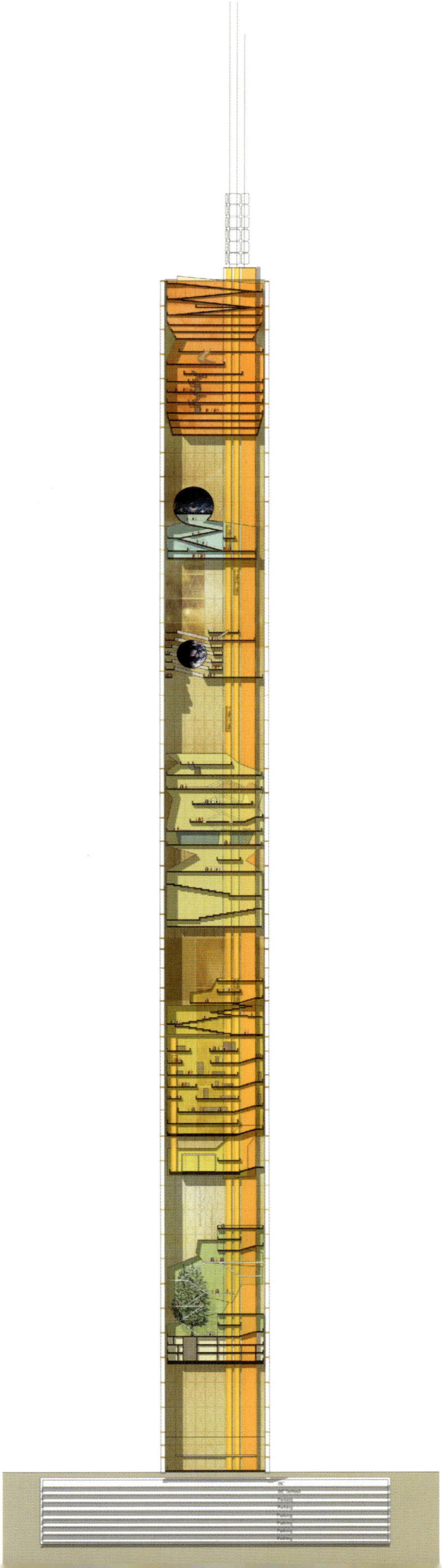

Der vertikale Bauteil wächst auf einer Grundfläche von 22 mal 40 Metern in die Höhe. Auf dem Weg zum Sky-Deck, der letzten Station 450 Meter über dem Boden, passieren die Besucher verschiedene „Activity Zones“. Diese frei in die Konstruktion eingehängten Raumskulpturen bieten Platz für Ausstellungen, Kongresse und Entertainment-Nutzung.

The vertical building section rises from a ground floor area of 22 x 40 m. On the way to the sky deck, their final destination 450 m above ground, visitors pass different 'activity zones'. These room sculptures, freely suspended from the tower structure, offer space for exhibitions, symposia and entertainment.

Shenyang ist die Hauptstadt der Provinz Liaoning im Nordosten Chinas. Der Flughafenentwurf sah einen ersten Bauabschnitt für ein Passagieraufkommen von 6 Millionen pro Jahr vor; in einem zweiten Bauabschnitt soll der Flughafen für eine Kapazität von 12 Millionen erweitert werden. Die Flughafengebäude umfassen das Terminal und einen lang gestreckten Flugsteig. Die beiden konkaven Dächer des Abfertigungsgebäudes wurden in Anlehnung an den chinesischen Stil gestaltet. Die großen verglasten Fassadenflächen geben ein Bild von Durchsichtigkeit und Leichtigkeit ab und beziehen sich auf das Element „Luft". Die übersichtliche Gliederung der Verkehrsflächen und Funktionsbereiche und das geschickte Verkehrskonzept auf der Landseite des Flughafens überzeugten die Jury. Im Wettbewerb mit elf weiteren Projekten erhielt OBERMEYERS Entwurf den ersten Preis. Der Bau wurde 2002 fertig gestellt.

Shenyang is the capital of the Liaoning province in North East China. The airport was designed in a first stage capacity of 6 million passengers per year, which can be extended to about 12 million in a second stage.

The airport consists of a central passenger terminal and a linear pier. The two concave roofs of the terminal are designed similar to the Chinese style. The large glazed areas of the façade provide an impression of transparency and lightness,which refer to the element „air ". The clear layout of the ways and well arranged functions as well as the clever traffic concept on the landside of the airport convinced the jury.

Among 11 competitors OBERMEYER won the first prize. The construction was completed in 2002.

INTERNATIONALER WETTBEWERB: 1. Preis (realisiertes Projekt)
BGF (PHASE 1): 80,000 m^2
KAPAZITÄT NACH FERTIGSTELLUNG: 12 Mio. Passagiere
FLUGGASTAUFKOMMEN: 6 Mio. Passagiere (pro Jahr)
KOSTEN: 50 Mio. Euro

OBERMEYER PLANEN + BERATEN GMBH
INTERNATIONALER FLUGHAFEN SHENYANG TAOXIAN
SHENYANG TAOXIAN INTERNATIONAL AIRPORT

Terminal Landseite

Landside of the terminal

Leistungen: Architektonischer Entwurf und Tragwerksplanung, haustechnische und elektrische Anlagen.
Beschreibung: Wettbewerb für Shenyang International Airport; Entwurf von Abfertigungsgebäude und Gestaltung von Vorfeldbereich sowie landseitigen Freiflächen.

Scope of services: schematic design in architecture, structure, HVAC and electrical engineering.
Description: competition for Shenyang International Airport; design of passenger terminal, airside and landside developments.

Oben: Querschnitt
Unten: Lageplan

Above: cross section
Below: site plan

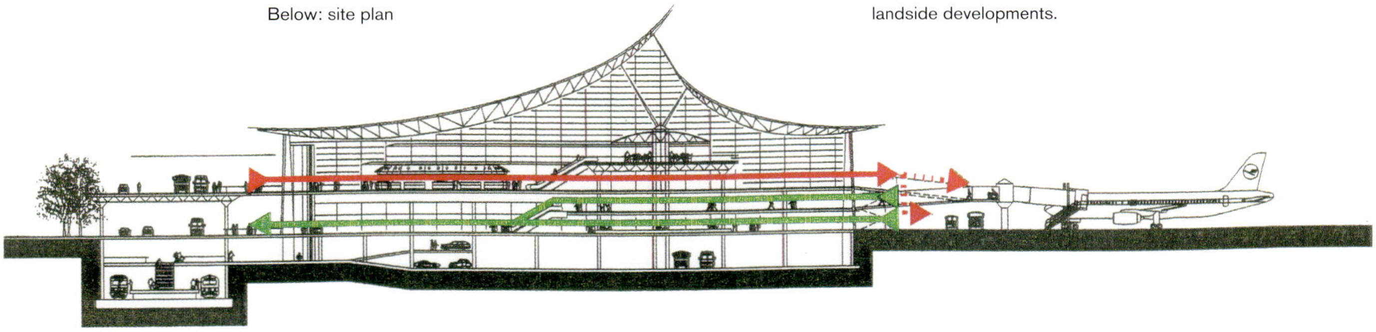

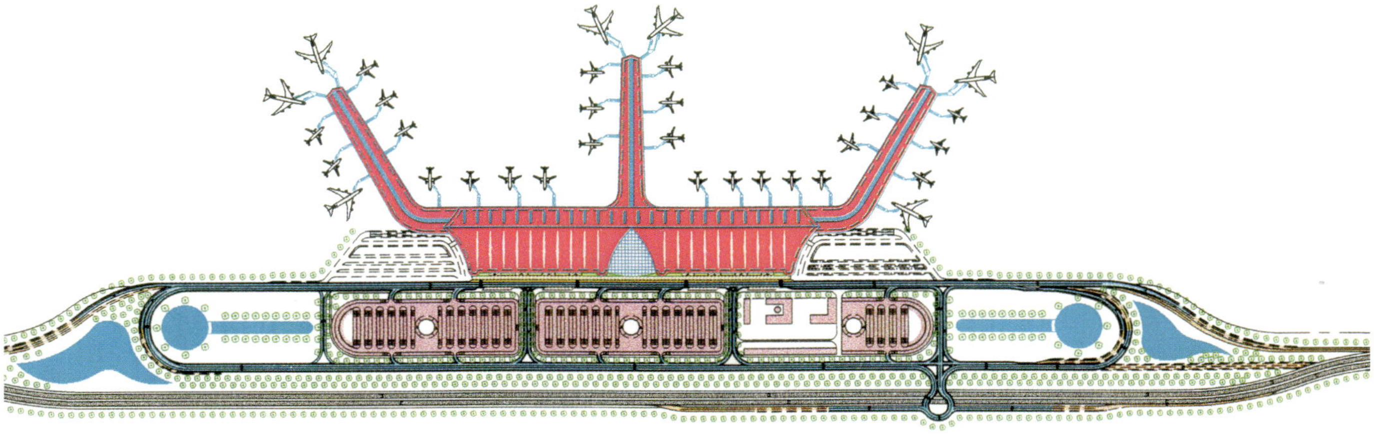

Abflughalle

Departures hall

Wohnhochhaus für gehobene Ansprüche in Pekings neuem zentralen Geschäftsviertel (CBD) mit Einzelhandelsflächen (Erd- und Untergeschoss), Fitness-Club und Schwimmbecken (Dachebene), 332 Wohnungen (57 bis 195 m^2 groß), Dienstleistungsbetrieben und Gewerbe (ca. 7.000 m^2), Büros (ca. 4.250 m^2) sowie Tiefgarage für ca. 672 Fahrzeuge.

First-class residential high-rise in Beijing's new CBD with retail facilities (ground floor and basement); fitness club and rooftop swimming pool; 332 flats (ranging in size from 57 m^2 to 195 m^2); commercial areas (approx. 7,000 m^2); offices (approx. 4,250 m^2); underground car parks for approx. 672 vehicles.

REALISIERTES PROJEKT
BGF: ca. 95,000 m^2
BRI: ca. 330,000 m^3
KOSTEN: 100 Mio. Euro

OBERMEYER PLANEN + BERATEN GMBH
TIANYA GARDEN (VAN PALACE), CBD PEKING
TIANYA GARDEN (VAN PALACE), CBD BEIJING

Das Baugelände des Van Palace befindet sich im neuen Geschäftsviertel Central Business District, einem der vielversprechendsten Stadtentwicklungsgebiete im Zentrum von Peking. Der Van Palace ist ein klassisches Doppelturm-Hochhaus mit einem niedrigeren Verbindungsbau. Die Türme erreichen eine Höhe von rund 125 m, der Verbindungsbau ist etwa 70 m hoch. Eine dreigeschossige Halle mit linsenförmigem Atrium auf der Südseite bildet optisch den Sockel des gewaltigen Hochhausgebildes. An diesen öffentlichen Bereich schließt sich außen ein Hof an, ein Ort der Stille. Indem die Architekten dem Gebäude eine zweite Glashaut gaben, die als Lärm-, Staub- und Wetterschutzwand für alle Wohnungen fungiert und an einigen Stellen der Fassade wie ein Schutzschild vorgelagert ist, schufen sie einen eleganten „Kristallpalast".

The Van Palace Site is situated in the CBD area, one of the developing zones in Beijing city centre with the most promising future. The Van Palace itself is a classical double-wing tower building with a joining lower building between. The wing towers reach a height of approx. 125 m, the lower building approx. 70 m. The three level public area with a convex lens-shaped atrium in the south gives a necessary optical foundation to the big, high-rise construction and is combined with a unique silencing homeliness yard zone. By the use of the second glass skin serving as a noise-, dust and climate protection in all living areas, sometimes as glass shield before the perforated façade, an elegant crystal palace has been erected.

Grundriss

Ground plan

GRUNDSTÜCKSFLÄCHE: 20.000 m^2
BGF: 66.000 m^2 (einschließlich Untergeschosse) mit Wohnungen, Laden- und Büroflächen, einem Kindergarten für zwölf Gruppen, 392 Autostellplätzen in der Tiefgarage und einer Grundschule für achtzehn Klassen

OBERMEYER PLANEN + BERATEN GMBH
CLD FORUM HOUSING (PHASE III), PEKING
CLD FORUM HOUSING (PHASE III), BEIJING

Die Doppeltürme mit angrenzendem Kindergarten- und Schulgebäude bilden ein Gebäudeensemble im modernen internationalen Architekturstil, in Form und Farbe futuristisch anmutend und mit allen technischen Raffinessen ausgestattet. Stromlinienförmig gebogene Bauteile reichen von innen nach außen und lassen den Bau sich öffnen und entfalten. Die Doppeltürme bilden die Landmarke des Bezirks und scheinen sich zu umarmen. Dieser Eindruck der Verbundenheit wird dadurch betont, dass eines der Hochhäuser höher ist als das andere. Die Schule und der Kindergarten sind geräumig und hell und strahlen Lebendigkeit und Optimismus aus. Die Gestaltung fördert die Kreativität und geistig-seelische Entwicklung der Kinder. Wie eine voll aufgeblühte Blume geformt, findet das Gebäude bei ihnen großen Anklang.

This twin tower together with the adjacent primary school forms an ensemble in a modern international architecture style,futuristic in shape and colour and equipped with Hi-Technology. Streamlined curves have been used from indoors to outdoors to make the whole environment unfolded and free. The twin towers, acting as the district's landmark, virtually hug each other, an association of intimateness which is supported by the image of one high and one short.

The design of the school and kindergarten, spacious and bright,expresses an active and optimistic image,supporting creativity and the development of a healthy psychology of the children. Shaped like a flower in full bloom, it easily wins the children's admiration.

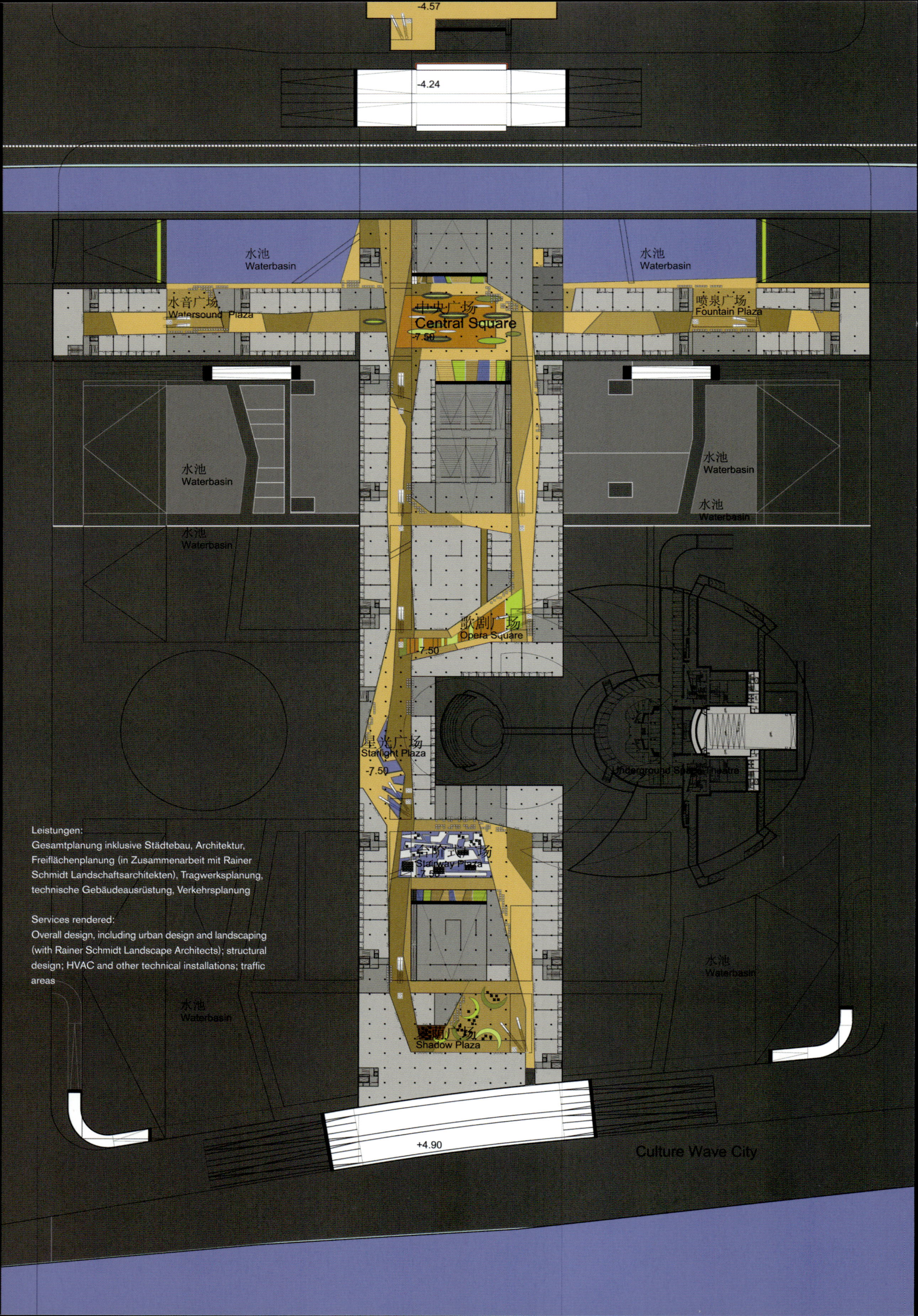

Leistungen:
Gesamtplanung inklusive Städtebau, Architektur, Freiflächenplanung (in Zusammenarbeit mit Rainer Schmidt Landschaftsarchitekten), Tragwerksplanung, technische Gebäudeausrüstung, Verkehrsplanung

Services rendered:
Overall design, including urban design and landscaping (with Rainer Schmidt Landscape Architects); structural design; HVAC and other technical installations; traffic areas

EINGELADENER INTERNATIONALER WETTBEWERB: 1.Preis
REALISIERUNG: 2005
UMBAUTER RAUM: 1.2 Mio m^3
BGF: 180.000 m^2
KOSTEN: 150 Mio. Euro

OBERMEYER PLANEN + BERATEN GMBH

UNTERSTADT DES NEUEN CENTRAL BUSINESS DISTRICT VON HANGZHOU UND RIVER MUSEUM
UNDERGROUND SPACE OF THE NEW CBD AREA OF HANGZHOU AND RIVER MUSEUM

Das Planungsgebiet der unterirdischen „Stadt" umfasst eine Länge von ca. 1.200 m und eine Breite von 400 bis 1.000 m. Ziel der Planung ist es, ein unterirdisches Netz aus Mallflächen, öffentlichen Passagen und Plätzen zu schaffen, um die einzelnen CBD-Büroblocks und die wichtigen städtischen Funktionen wie das Municipal Citizen Center, das Theater und das Kongresszentrum untereinander zu verbinden.

Der 115 m breite und ca. 700 m lange Streifen zwischen Municipal City Center und Fluss wird zum eigentlichen Schwerpunkt der Unterstadt auf Level −1 ausgebaut. Das gesamte Areal bildet mit einem System von Rampen, Plätzen, Kultur-, Verkaufs- und Multifunktionsflächen die Culture Wave City. Diese mündet im City Balcony, das Bindeglied zwischen Stadt und Fluss, der sich über 300 m Breite bis zu 70 m in den Fluss hineinschiebt und als River Museum genutzt wird. Die Culture Wave City mit dem City Balcony schafft einen städtebaulichen Ausgangs- und Endpunkt für die Kulturachse der Stadt Hangzhou.

The project area of the underground 'city' is roughly 1200 m long and 400 to 1000 m wide. The plan was to create a network of shopping malls, public passages and squares below ground which would also form underground links between the office blocks and most important public buildings such as the civic centre, the theatre and the congress centre rising above them.

The corridor between the civic centre, approximately 115 m wide and 700 m long, is the main focus of the underground structure (level −1). It comprises the system of ramps, squares, spaces for cultural events, retail and other functions of the so-called Culture Wave City.This extends to the City Balcony, which links the city to the river. This 'pier' is 300 m wide and stretches over 70 m out into the river; it houses the River Museum. The Culture Wave City and the City Balcony form the end of the urban axis of cultural buildings of the city of Hangzhou.

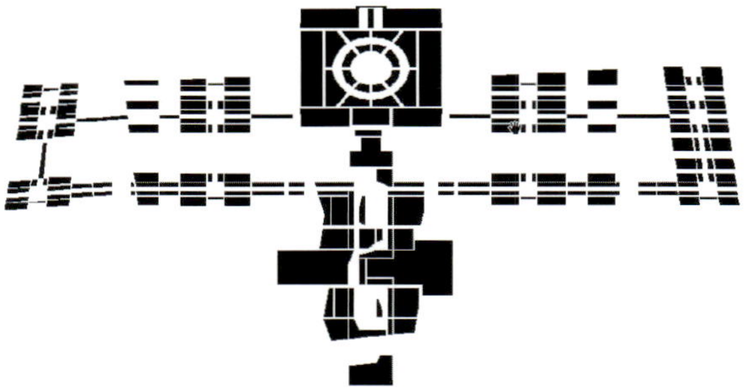

Leistungen: STÄDTEBAU: Flächennutzungsplan, Gestaltungsplan, Gebäudehöhenplan, Parzellierung / LANDSCHAFT (in Zusammenarbeit mit Rainer Schmidt Landschaftsarchitekten): Grünsystem, Landschaftsstruktur, Freiflächengestaltung, Gestaltung der Parklandschaft / VERKEHR: Verkehrssystem, Straßenplanung / INFRASTRUKTUR: Systemzeichnungen für die verschiedenen Sparten

Services rendered:
Urban design: zoning; urban layout, structural heights, parcelling-out, Landscaping (with Rainer Schmidt Landscape Architects): green system, topographical structuring, design of open areas and landscape park
Traffic: layout of traffic areas and street alignments
Infrastructure: drafting plans/maps for the abovementioned works

EINGELADENER INTERNATIONALER STÄDTEBAULICHER WETTBEWERB: 1. Preisgruppe
PLANUNGSUMGRIFF: 25,13 km^2
BGF: 5,28 Mio. m^2

OBERMEYER PLANEN + BERATEN GMBH

SOFTWARE PARK DALIAN

SOFTWARE PARK DALIAN

Die Hafenstadt Dalian liegt im Nordosten Chinas, ca. 600 km östlich von Peking, am Gelben Meer. Die Nähe zum Pazifischen Raum, insbesondere zu Japan und Südkorea, führte zu einer rasanten Entwicklung der Softwareindustrie. Das Planungsgebiet zieht sich vom südwestlichen Stadtrand in das hügelige Hinterland. Parallel zum Haupttal verläuft die Lushun Nan Road. Entlang derer sieht der Entwurf vier eigenständige Bereiche vor: Maritime Harbour City im Osten, Fünf Seitentäler, Park City im zentralen Bereich und Water Delta im Süden. Die Bebauung orientiert sich an der Topografie und dem harmonischen Zusammenspiel der Landschaftselemente „Berge und Meer“.

The harbour city of Dalian is situated in north-eastern China, about 600 km east of Beijing, at the Yellow Sea. Its proximity to the Pacific region, in particular to South Korea and Japan, promoted the 'explosive' development of Dalian's software industry. The project area stretches from the city's south-western periphery into the hilly hinterland. The design proposes four separate structures along Lushun Nan Road which runs parallel to the main valley: the Maritime Harbour City to the east; five side valleys; the Park City with a central public square and the Water Delta to the south. The design followed the natural topography and the harmonious interplay of hills and ocean.

BAUHERR: Stadt Guangzhou
BGF: 33.000 m^2
NUTZFLÄCHE: 16.500 m^2
WETTBEWERB: 2002, 1.Preis

RKW ARCHITEKTUR UND STÄDTEBAU
SONNTAGSSCHULE GUANGZHOU
GUANGZHOU CHILDREN'S PALACE

Im Jahre 2002 folgte RKW der Einladung der südchinesischen Millionenstadt Guangzhou an einem internationalen Wettbewerb zur Erstellung einer Sonntagsschule, Children's Palace, teilzunehmen. Gleichwertig neben zwei anderen renommierten Büros wurde RKW der erste Preis zuerkannt.

In exponierter zentraler Lage, lässt die Stadt Guangzhou ihren besonderen Beitrag zur Ausbildung der Kinder planen. Diesem Rechnung tragend entwarf RKW ein Gebäude gleich einer Skulptur mit poetischem Anspruch. Wie ein alter weiser Mann ein junges Kind unterrichtet, das ihm gegenübersitzt, so erfährt man die geometrische Umsetzung dieser Szene in den beiden keilförmigen Baukörpern. Dazwischen spannt sich der zentrale Platz der Schule, der die Bühne des Lebens der Kinder repräsentiert.

Umgeben wird er von Galerien mit angrenzenden Klassenräumen und von dem kleinen Keil, der das so genannte Performance-Center aufnimmt und gleichzeitig als Tribüne zum Platz hin fungiert.

Innovative Aspekte zur Klimatechnik findet man in der Ausbildung eines Membrandaches ebenso wie in dem Wasserfall an einer großen Glasscheibe, der zur Kühlung des inneren Platzes beiträgt.

In 2002 the city of Guangzhou invited RKW to participate to the international competition on architectural design for No.2 Children's Palace. Among two other international design offices also the design of RKW succeeded.

Along the new central axis of the city in exposed position the new building should represent the effort of Guangzhou to support their youths education. Due to this RKW designed a remarkable sculpture with an poetic statement.

Like an old wise man teaching a child while sitting face to face the geometrical transformation of its intellectual content can be experienced through the two wedges. The open space in-between the wedges represents the stage of children's life. This square is surrounded by galleries , classrooms and the performance center inside the little wedge as a grandstand. Innovative aspects on climate concepts are represented by the membran roof and the waterfall cooling the inner square.

BAUHERR: Stadt Shanghai
WETTBEWERBSFLÄCHE: 1,6 km^2
UMBAUTER RAUM: 900.000 m^3
WETTBEWERB: 2005, 1. Preis

RKW ARCHITEKTUR UND STÄDTEBAU

ZHENRU VICE CENTER, SHANGHAI
ZHENRU VICE-CENTER SHANGHAI

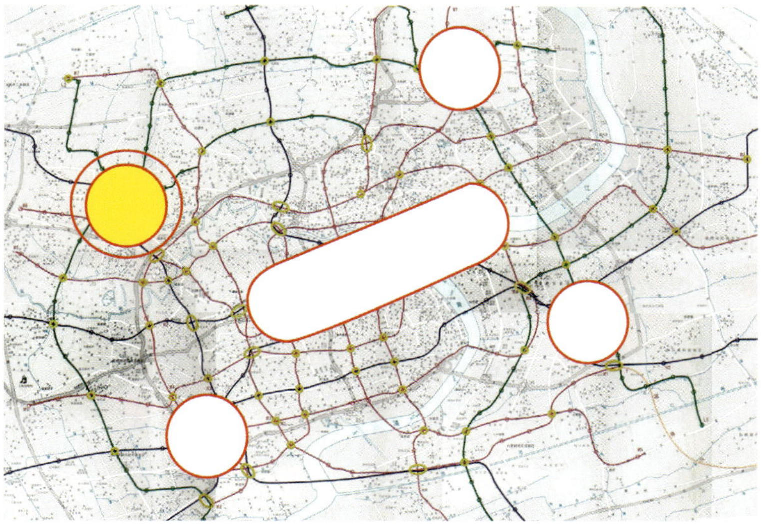

Das enorme Wirtschaftswachstum Chinas hat einen sehr starken Bevölkerungszuwachs der chinesischen Metropolen verursacht. Um den daraus resultierenden Versorgungsbedarf zu befriedigen, hat die Stadt Shanghai mit der Entwicklung von vier Subzentren in einer Entfernung von ca. 5 km rund um die Innenstadt begonnen.

Für das nordwestliche Subzentrum in Putuo hat die Stadtverwaltung einen Wettbewerb mit internationaler Beteiligung ausgelobt, den RKW Architektur und Städtebau und GTL Landschaftsarchitekten für sich entscheiden konnten.

Die zentrale Idee des erfolgreichen Konzeptes war es, die zentrale Nord-Süd-Achse des Planungsgebietes, die Cao Yang Lu, zu einem lebendigen Boulevard zu entwickeln. Einzelhandel, Büros und Wohnen finden hier eine gute Adresse an einem aufwändig gestalteten öffentlichen Raum mit hoher Aufenthaltsqualität.

Because of its enormous growth the government of Shanghai is in the need to develop 4 Vice Centers in a distance of at about 5 km around downtown. The development of the Vice Center in Putuo, Zhenru, started with an international architectural competition that RKW and GTL won.

The central idea in the successful concept was to develop a fully integrated, lively shopping, working and living district around Cao Yang Lu, the main axis to Putuo railway station. High level public space, well designed streets and places and especially Cao Yang Lu as an international boulevard will give Zhenru a unique identity in the melting pot of Shanghai.

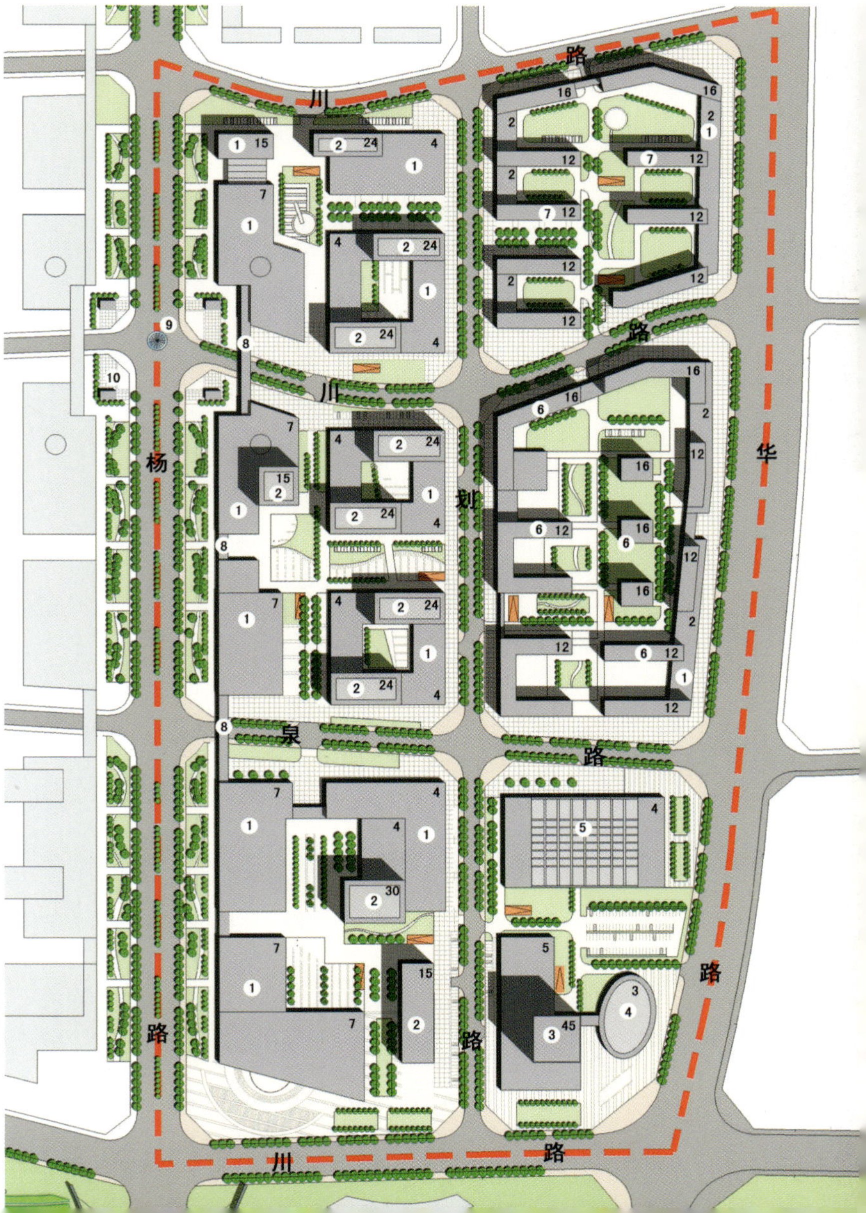

INTERNATIONALER WETTBEWERB: in Zusammenarbeit mit Obermeyer Planen + Beraten
PLANUNGSGEBIET: 180 ha

RAINER SCHMIDT LANDSCHAFTSARCHITEKTEN

INTERNATIONALER WETTBEWERB MASTERPLAN OLYMPISCHE SPIELE 2008, PEKING
MASTERPLAN OF OLYMPIC GAMES 2008 COMPLEX, BEIJING INTERNATIONAL COMPETITION

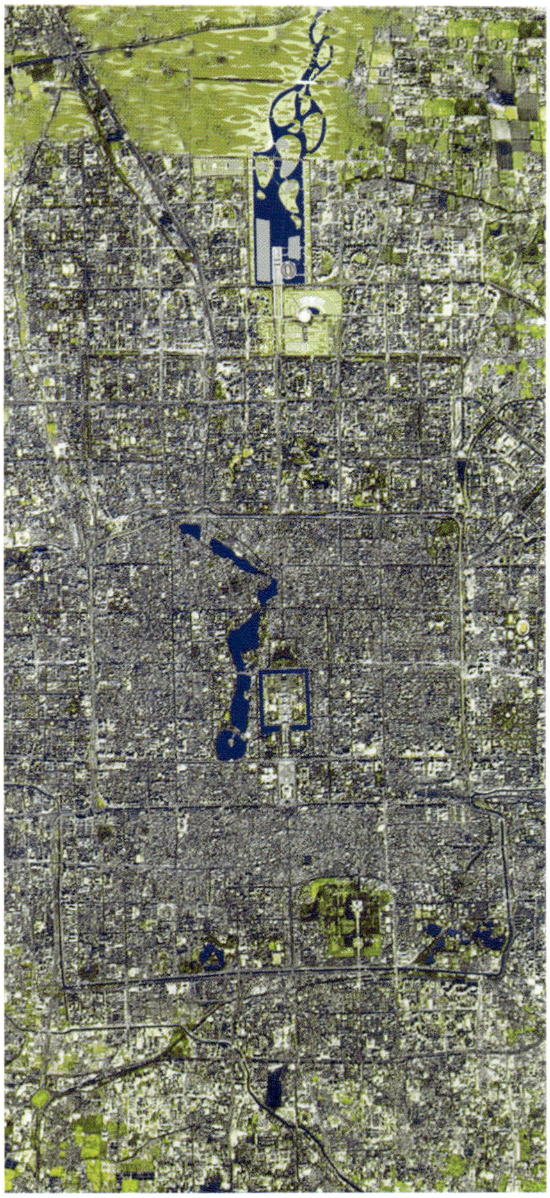

Der Entwurf nimmt mit der Schaffung eines großen Wasserbeckens die Merkmale der weiter südlich auf der zentralen Achse gelegenen Verbotenen Stadt auf.

Die steinerne, städtische Achse endet als Pier im Olympischen See mit dem Olympic Plaza, an dem die Sportbauten wie Schiffe angedockt sind. Der nördlich angrenzende Olympic Forest Park ist Teil des Grünen Ringes um Peking und führt die Landschaft in Form von organischen Inseln bis in das Olympische Becken hinein.

Dieser Bereich dient der Naherholung und der Wasserrückhaltung und -klärung. Die Inseln im Olympischen Becken mit ihren in die Landschaft integrierten Freizeit- und kommerziellen Bauten sind über den gläsernen People Mover an den Sportbereich im Süden angebunden. Der Olympische See wird zu beiden Seiten von Promenaden und Hochhausreihen gefasst.

Durch seine Dimension und Prägnanz schafft der Entwurf ein starkes städtebauliches Merkzeichen als Markierung des städtischen Endpunktes der zentralen Nord-Süd-Achse Pekings im 21. Jahrhundert.

The design reflects a characteristic feature of the Forbidden City further south of the central urban axis by proposing an artificial lake on the Olympic site.

The urban axis of stone extends in a pier, i.e. the Olympic Plaza at the lake, where the sports structures are 'moored' like ships. The Olympic Forest adjoining to the north is part of the green belt around Beijing and continues the landscape into the complex, finally to form organically shaped 'islands' in the Olympic Valley. These serve recreational purposes as well as ground water retention and purification. The 'green islands' in the Olympic Valley, with leisure and commercial buildings integrated into their landscapes, are connected to the sports compound to the south via glazed people movers. Both banks of the Olympic Lake are lined by esplanades and rows of high-rises.

With its dimensions and clarity, the design proposes a strong 21st-century urban landmark to form the end of Beijing's central north-south axis.

Uferparkterrassen vor neuer Stadtkulisse mit Blick über den Qiantang-Fluss

Riverside park terraces against the background of the new city skyline, with a view across the river Qiantang

Die Stadt Hangzhou erweitert sich vom traditionellen am Westsee gelegenen Zentrum bis zum Qiantang-Fluss, an dem das moderne wirtschaftliche und kulturelle Zentrum der Stadt mit Rathaus und zentralen kulturellen Einrichtungen entstehen soll.

Der Entwurf schlägt eine städtische Entwicklungsachse als Parklandschaft vor, in die besondere Funktionen eingebettet sind. Den Endpunkt dieser Achse am Fluss bildet ein großer städtischer Platz mit Rathaus, Verwaltungszentrum, Oper sowie Museen und einem in den Fluss hineinragenden Stadtbalkon.

Den freiraumplanerischen Höhepunkt stellen die rund 100 m breiten Uferparkterrassen mit Uferpromenade dar, die eine bestehende Uferstraße überdeckeln.

The city of Hangzhou is developing from its historic centre at the western lake up to the river Quiantang on the banks of which the new business and cultural city centre is to be built, including a new town hall and central cultural facilities. The design proposes an urban development axis in the form of a strip of parkland in which special functional buildings are embedded. This axis ends at the river with a large urban square surrounded by the town hall, an administrative centre, an opera house, several museums and a 'city balcony' jutting out towards the river. The riverside park terraces, including the esplanade, are roughly 100 m wide and constitute the highlight of the design. The terraces will cover an existing riverside road.

AUFGABE: Internationale Beratung in Zusammenarbeit mit Obermeyer Planen + Beraten – 1. Preis
GESAMTGESCHOSSFLÄCHE: 13 km²
LANDFLÄCHE: 3,8 m²

RAINER SCHMIDT LANDSCHAFTSARCHITEKTEN

NEW CENTRAL BUSINESS DISTRICT HANGZHOU

NEW CENTRAL BUSINESS DISTRICT HANGZHOU

INTERNATIONALER WETTBEWERB: in Zusammenarbeit mit Obermeyer Planen + Beraten – 1. Preis
PLANUNGSGEBIET: 256 ha

RAINER SCHMIDT LANDSCHAFTSARCHITEKTEN

LANDSCHAFTSPLANUNG, GENERALPLAN FÜR DAS ZENTRUM DES NEUEN CBD VON QIANJIANG, HANGZHOU

LANDSCAPE MASTERPLAN FOR THE CENTRE OF THE NEW CBD OF QIANJIANG, HANGZHOU

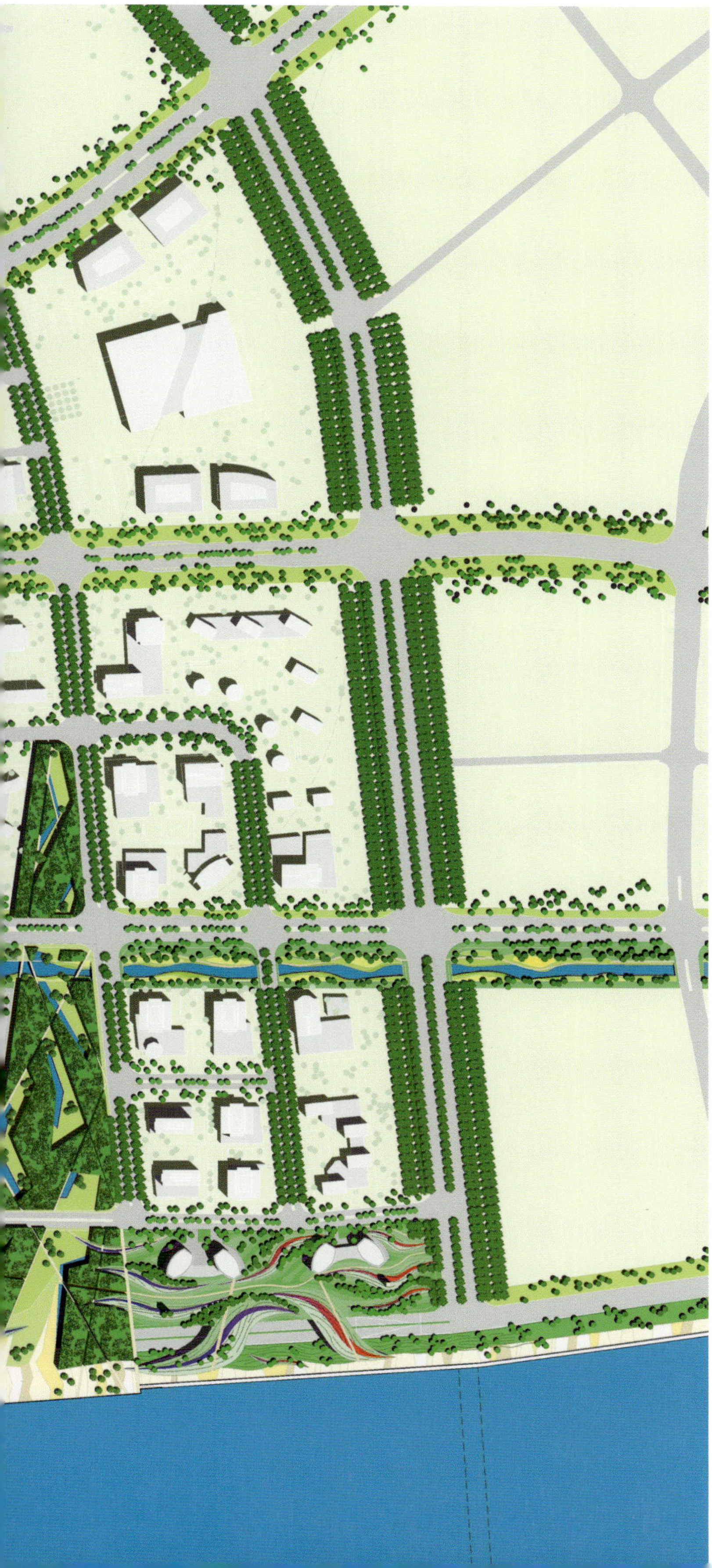

Ziel der Erarbeitung des Masterplans ist es, eine zusammenhängende Landschaftsstruktur entlang des Qiantangjiang River und der New CBD zu entwickeln. Diese Landschaft sollte neben ihrer verbindenden und raumprägenden Wirkung eine hohe Flexibilität und Variabilität besitzen, damit sie auf sich ändernde städtebauliche oder verkehrsplanerische Belange reagieren kann. Grundidee ist das Zusammenspiel von Wasser und Landschaft, von fließend-linearer und landschaftlich-raumgreifender Bewegung.

Das Thema einer bewegenden und sich verändernden Flusslandschaft zieht sich durch den gesamten Entwurf. Mäandrierende Wegeachsen, Baumhaine und Wasseradern durchziehen das Zentrum des New CBD von Norden nach Süden Richtung Qiantangjiang River. Der Fluss mit seiner Promenade und dem Riverside Park bildet den räumlichen Abschluss des New CBD.

The masterplan was required to create a contiguous landscaped area along Qiantang-jiang River and the new Central Business District (CBD). This park was to function as a connecting and space-defining element in the city and to be highly flexible in use, so that it could adapt to changing urban design or traffic-planning interests. The basic design idea was the interplay of water and land, of linear flow and landscape area.

The theme of a moving and changing riverside determined all aspects of the landscape design. The centre of the new CBD is dotted by groves of trees, and traversed by meandering path axes and water courses which lead from north to south to the Qiantang-jiang, to the promenade in Riverside Park which forms the southern border of the CBD.

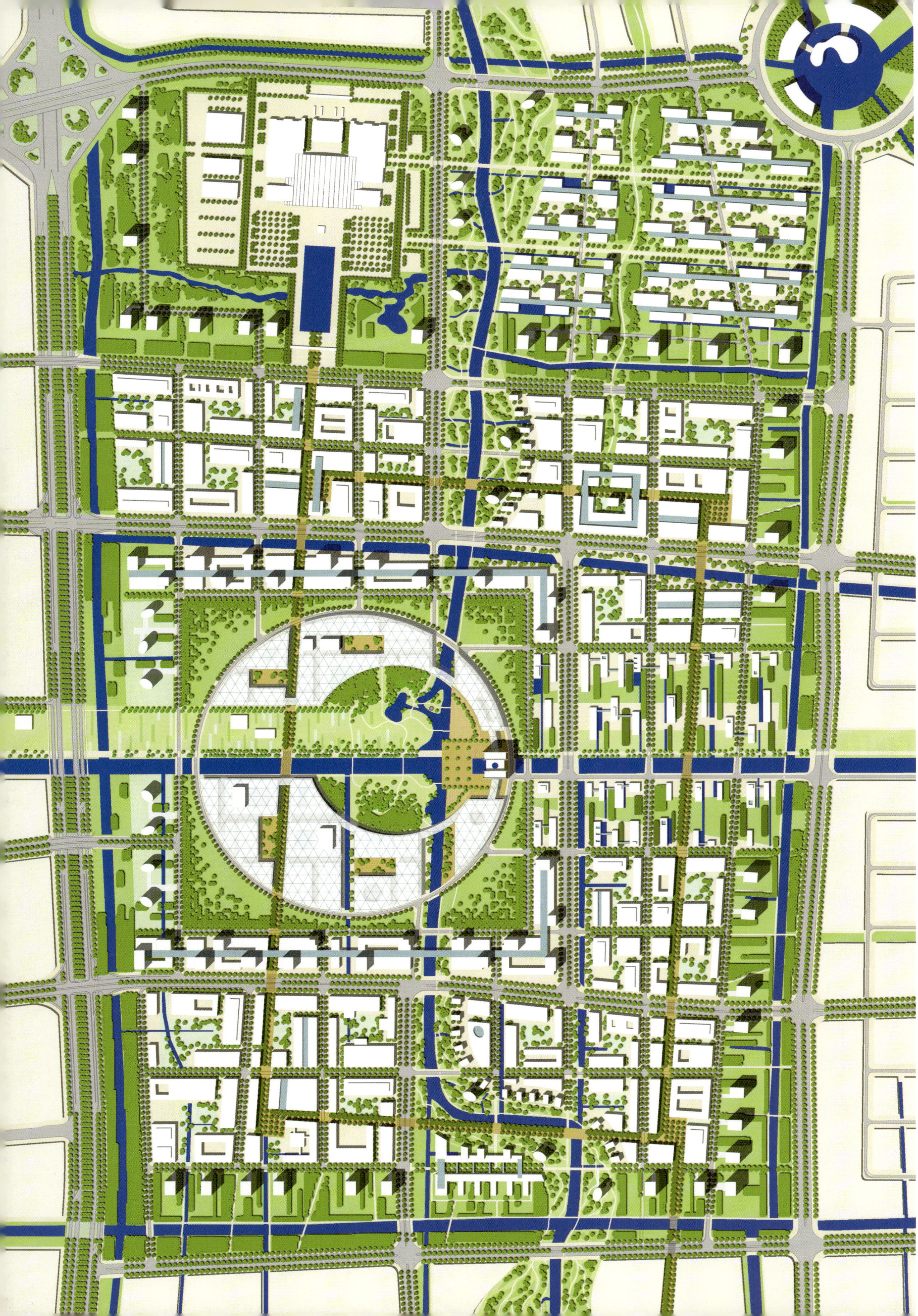

AUFGABE: Internationaler Beratungsauftrag in Zusammenarbeit mit Obermeyer Planen + Beraten – Preisgruppe
PLANUNGSGEBIET: 40 km^2
ZENTRALBEREICH: 17 km^2

RAINER SCHMIDT LANDSCHAFTSARCHITEKTEN

NEW DISTRICT EAST NINGBO

NEW DISTRICT EAST NINGBO

Städtebauliches und freiraumplanerisches Konzept für ein neues Stadtzentrum

Urban and landscaping design for a new city centre

Die Stadt Ningbo plant ihr Stadtgebiet um vierzig Prozent zu vergrößern und ihr Verwaltungszentrum in den neuen östlichen Bezirk zu verlagern. Das alte Stadtzentrum am Gabelpunkt der drei Flüsse soll mit dem neuen östlichen Zentrumsbezirk durch einen Kanal mit begleitendem Grünkorridor verbunden werden.

Ein weiterer Kanal und übergeordneter Grünzug verbinden die Naherholungsgebiete des Yong-Flusses im Norden des neuen Stadtgebietes und den Dongqiang-See im Süden der Stadt. Wege durchziehen eine Landschaft aus künstlichen Hügeln, die immer wieder neue Ausblicke bietet. Die rasterförmige Struktur des neuen Stadtbezirks wird durch ein System von Grünzügen und Parks gegliedert und von einem grünen Rahmen eingefasst. Der kreisrunde Park im Zentrum befindet sich am Kreuzungspunkt der beiden Hauptachsen. Er wird von der städtebaulichen Großform eines Daches eingefasst, unter dem kommerzielle und kulturelle Nutzungen Platz finden. Das Rathaus als wichtigstes Element erhält eine exponierte Stellung.

The city of Ningo plans to extend its area by forty per cent and to shift its administrative centre to the new eastern city district. A canal and accompanying green belt is to connect the old city centre at the confluence of three rivers with the new district.

Another canal and strip of parkland connects the urban recreational areas on the Yong river north of the new district with the Dongquiang Lake in the southern urban area. Paths run through a landscape of artificial hills which afford constantly changing views. The grid structure of the new urban development is livened up by a system of narrow green areas and gardens and framed in greenery. The circular park in the middle marks the crossing of the two main axes. It is covered by a large canopy which protects commercial and cultural functions. The town hall – as the most important single urban element – is placed in a prominent position.

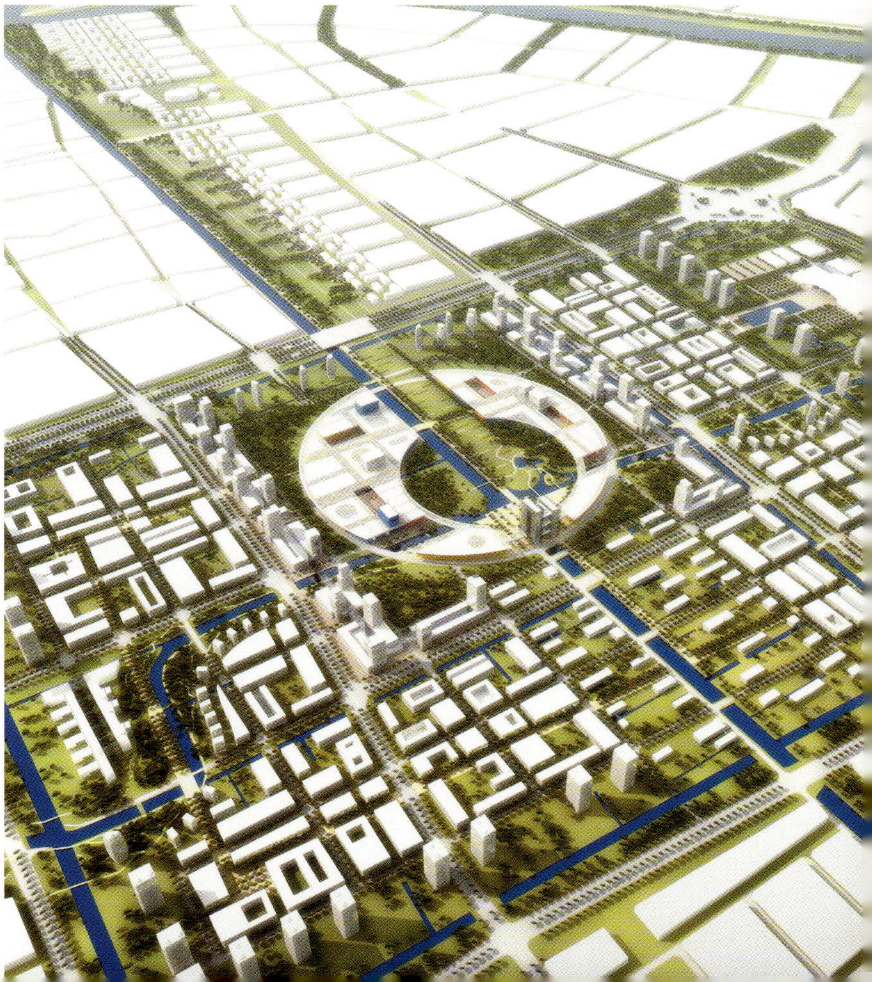

INTERNATIONALER WETTBEWERB: in Zusammenarbeit mit Turenscape, Peking, 1. Preisgruppe
PLANUNGSGEBIET: 180 ha

RAINER SCHMIDT LANDSCHAFTSARCHITEKTEN

INTERNATIONALER WETTBEWERB OLYMPIAPARK PEKING, 1. PREISGRUPPE

OLYMPIC PARK, BEIJING – INTERNATIONAL COMPETITION, 1ST PRIZE GROUP

Landschaftsarchitektur für den Forest Park und Zentralbereich des Olympic Greens

Landscaping design of the Forest Park and the central area of the Olympic Green

Ein Höhensprung von 10 m prägt den Olympischen Park. Die Höhenlinien werden in Form von Terrassen herausgearbeitet, die den Park strukturieren und ihn in differenzierte Landschaftsstreifen gliedern. Vorbild der gewählten Landschaften sind die charakteristischen Landnutzungsformen des agrarischen China. Innerhalb der Parklandschaft bleiben die Strukturen ehemaliger Dörfer sowie alte Tempel und Grabstätten bestehen.

Die zentrale olympische Achse wird durch ein Baumdach beschattet, das durch eine Folge von Plätzen mit Wasserspielen einen Rhythmus erhält. Nach Osten wird der großformatige Plattenbelag zunehmend von Pflanzflächen und Hecken durchsetzt. Ein Äquadukt bildet eine räumliche Begrenzung und stellt den Übergang der befestigten Achse zu den Gärten Chinas her. Fünf typische Landschaften Chinas mit fünf Farben liegen den Gartengestaltungen thematisch zu Grunde.

The ground of the Olympic park rises over 10 m. Its contours are marked by terraces which structure the parkland surface as varied strips of greenery, modelled on the characteristic types of land use of agricultural China. The parkland preserves the structures of former villages as well as of old temples and tombs.

The central Olympic axis is shaded by a tree-top canopy interrupted in rhythmical succession by squares with fountains. Towards the east, the large paving slabs increasingly alternate with flower beds and hedges. An aquaeduct forms a barrier and at the same time the transition from the paved axis to the Chinese gardens. These consist of 'reproductions' of five typical Chinese landscapes in five main colours.

INTERNATIONALER WETTBEWERB: Preisgruppe
PLANUNGSGEBIET: 50 ha

RAINER SCHMIDT LANDSCHAFTSARCHITEKTEN

CHANGZOU – STADT DES DRACHENS – PARK DES 120. ÖSTLICHEN LÄNGENGRADES

CHANGZHOU, THE CITY OF THE DRAGON – 120th DEGREE OF LONGITUDE PARK

Der Park des 120. Längengrades in Changzhou soll Impulse setzen für eine neue inovative und nachhaltige Stadtentwicklung in Changzhou – der „Stadt des Drachens“. Es entsteht ein neuer Grünraum, der zugleich Attraktion für Anwohner, Changzhouer und Touristen ist. Der Park soll bilden und Erholung bieten, soll einladen zum spazieren gehen, bewegen und Sport treiben, aber auch zum Verweilen und Kraft schöpfen.

Die Grundidee ist die Verbindung von Changzhou, der Heimat, mit der weiten Welt. Eine Reise in die Ferne und doch zu Hause bleiben. Die Entdeckung von fernen Ländern und Galaxien und das Erkennen der Schönheit des Landes direkt vor der Haustür.

Die Neuplanung legt großen Wert auf eine nachhaltige und rücksichtsichtsvolle Entwicklung der Fläche. Dabei steht der sensible Umgang mit der Natur im Vordergrund.

The Park of the 120th Degree of Longitude in Changzhou is to set the signal for the sustainable redevelopment of this ‘City of the Dragon’. The new public park is to be an attraction for both citizens and tourists, a place of beauty and recreation where they can walk and play sports, or just rest and gain new strength.

The basic design idea was to connect Changzhou – as the home of its citizens – with the big wide world, to give people the opportunity of experiencing foreign lands while remaining in their home city, of discovering far-away countries and galaxies as well as the beauties of their ownland at their own doorsteps. The new landscape design places great value on sustainability and a careful intervention which respects nature.

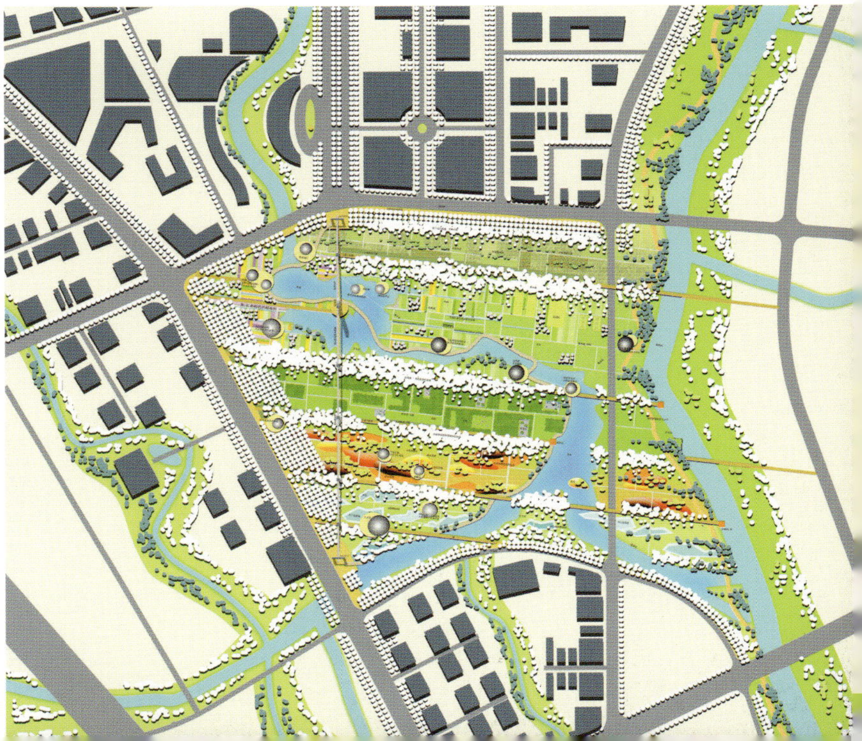

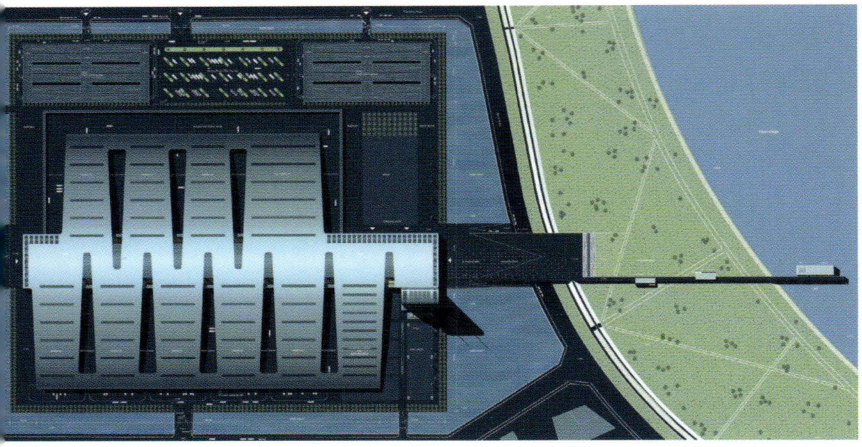

INTERNATIONALER WETTBEWERB: in Zusammenarbeit mit Auer + Weber Architekten – 1. Preis

RAINER SCHMIDT LANDSCHAFTSARCHITEKTEN

MESSE SHENYANG – FREIANLAGEN

TRADE-FAIR GROUNDS, SHENYANG – LANDSCAPING DESIGN

Die Messe liegt auf einer Insel, umgeben von neu angelegten Wassergräben. Eine zweireihige Pappelallee und eine steinerne, 2 Meter hohe Mauer am Rand stärken die besondere Lage dieser Anlage.

Die Gartenhöfe im Inneren des Gebäudes bilden gemeinsam mit der weitläufigen, begehbaren Rasenlandschaft auf dem Dach ein grünes Band, das die gesamte Messe durchdringt und die einzelnen Teilbereiche miteinander vernetzt. Eine lang gestreckte Platzfläche vor dem Haupteingang schafft den Brückenschlag zwischen der Messe und der Flussauenlandschaft.

Zwischen Haupteingang und Parkdeck erstreckt sich der Messeplatz aus großformatigen Steinplatten. Die Mitte bildet ein Teppich aus Pflastersteinen, begrenzt von einem Platanenhain. Diese großzügige Platzfläche dient als Entree für die Messe und bietet ausreichend Fläche für die unterschiedlichsten Veranstaltungen.

The trade-fair site is on an island surrounded by newly built canals. Two rows of poplars and a 2-metre-high stone wall at the edges enhance the island character of the project.

The garden patios inside the complex join the vast walk-on roof turf in weaving a green ribbon through the entire grounds which interconnects its various sections. A long and narrow square in front of the main entrance links the trade-fair complex to the riverside.

The main square of the complex, situated between main entrance and parking, is paved with large stone slabs and, in the middle, with paving stones surrounded by plane trees. This vast square is the introduction to the exhibition pavilions and offers space for various activities and events.

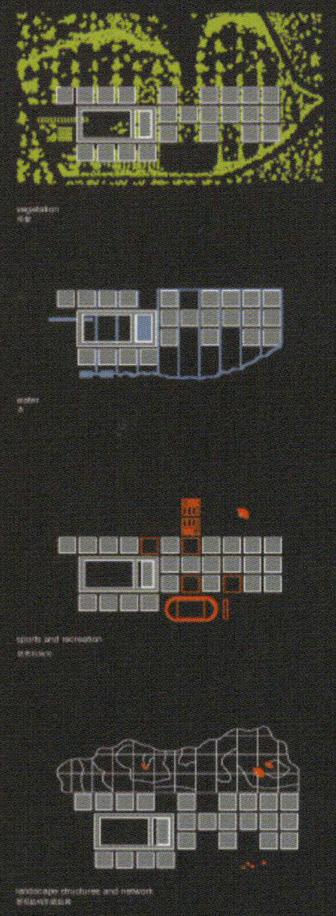

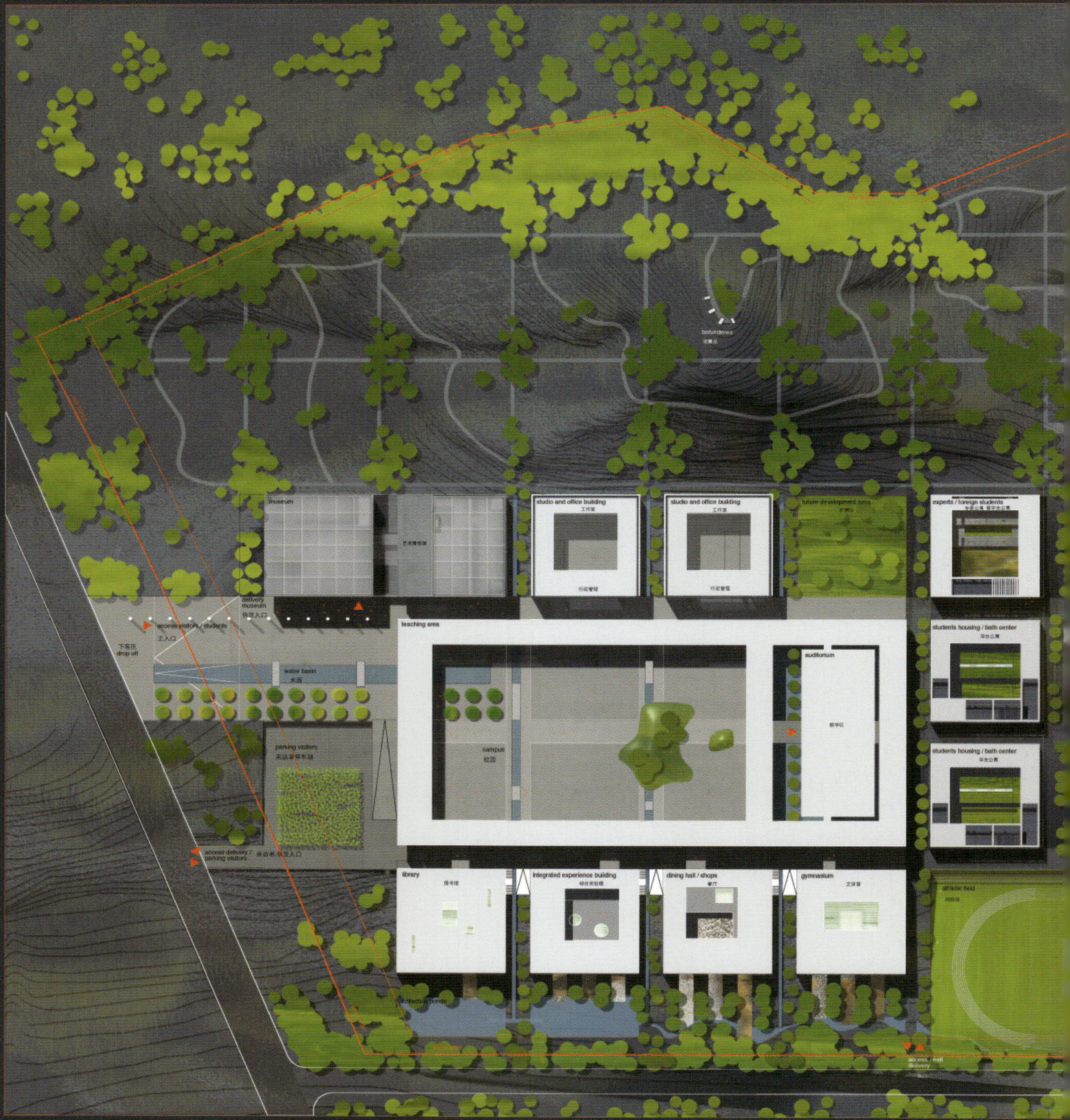
museum
studio and office building
studio and office building
experts / foreign students
delivery museum
access visitors / students
drop off
water basin
teaching area
students housing / bath center
students housing / bath center
auditorium
campus
parking visitors
access delivery / parking visitors
library
integrated experience building
dining hall / shops
gymnasium
athletic field

INTERNATIONALER WETTBEWERB: in Zusammenarbeit mit Auer + Weber Architekten – 1. Preis
PLANUNGSGEBIET: 38,2 ha

RAINER SCHMIDT LANDSCHAFTSARCHITEKTEN
CAMPUS DER LUXUN KUNSTAKADEMIE DALIAN
LUXUN ACADEMY OF ART CAMPUS, DALIAN

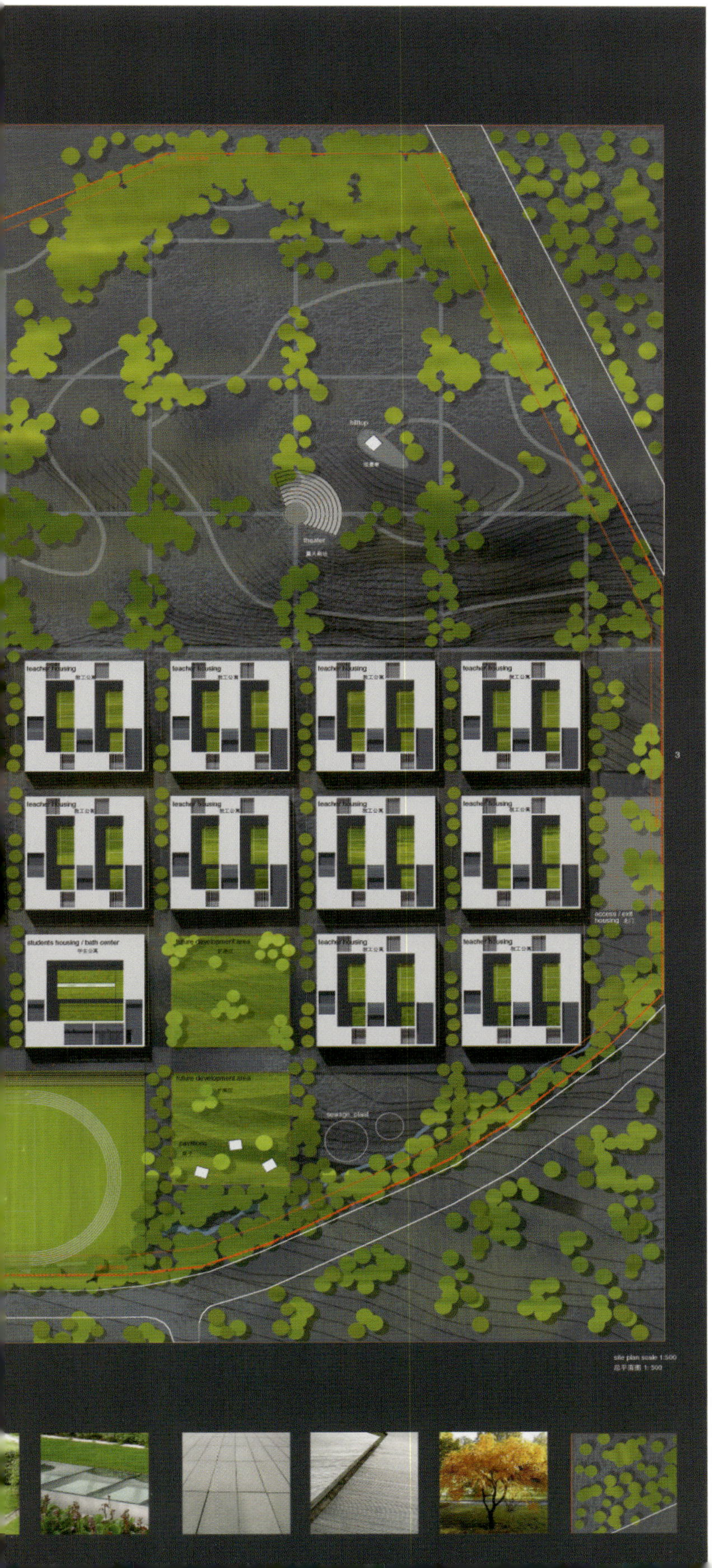

Das Planungsgebiet für den neuen Standort der Luxun Kunstakademie Dalian liegt in hügeliger Landschaft unweit vom Meer.

Der Entwurf basiert auf der Verzahnung von Stadt und Landschaft. Über das bewegte Gelände wurde ein strenges Raster als Ordnungssystem gelegt, worin die verschiedenen Gebäude wie Lehr- und Wohngebäude, Bibliothek und ein Museum sowie Sportanlagen und Freiräume eingepasst sind. Ergänzt und kontrastiert wird das Raster durch aus dem englischen Landschaftsgarten entliehene Gestaltungselemente: grüne Hügel, Aussichtspunkte (Belvedere) und geschwungene Pfade. Ein Wasserbecken verläuft vom Eingangsbereich bis in den Innenhof und ist in Teilbereichen als umspülter Wasserkörper ausgebildet. Die Innenhöfe der anderen Gebäudekomplexe sind artifiziell gestaltet und schaffen ein eigenes Mikroklima für die jeweilige Gebäudeeinheit.

The site of the new Luxun Academy of Art in Dalian is situated in a hilly land-scape not far from the sea.

The design idea was to interlock the city with its natural surroundings. The architects overlaid the uneven terrain with a strict ordering grid into which the different teaching and residential buildings, the library, a museum as well as sports grounds and recreational open areas were fitted. The grid was supplemented and offset by elements borrowed from the English landscape garden, i.e. green hills, viewpoints (belvedere) and meandering paths. A reflective pool stretches from the entrance to the interior courtyard and includes washed-over elements. The artistically designed patios of the other buildings have pleasant microclimates which benefit the interiors.

„Mein Entwurf für 'Peking Image', von mir 'Peking Drachen' genannt, stellt den Versuch dar, mehrere Aspekte der Tradition und des Fortschritts zu integrieren: die Tradition des Raumes und der Südausrichtung, die Zuordnung zum Hof, die starke Form- und Symbolfreude.

Die Figur des 'Drachens' wechselt zwischen der Anordnung von Wohnhöfen und weiträumigen Gärten. Jedes Haus hat Anteil an beidem. Die südseitigen Wohnbereiche der Höfe sind vier- bis fünf-, die nordseitigen sieben- bis elfgeschossig.

So vermitteln die Gebäude die unterschiedlichen Maßstäbe und Situationen. Eine alle Einheiten verbindende 'Diagonale' (zweigeschossige Arkade) erschließt das gesamte Quartier. Die Farbigkeit (durchgehender dunkelroter Sockel) und unterschiedliche obere Bereiche akzentuieren und charakterisieren die einzelnen 'Häuser'."

Otto Steidle

'My design for Beijing Image, which I myself call Beijing Dragon, represents the attempt to integrate several aspects of Chinese tradition and of progress – the attempt to fuse the traditional spatial dimensions and south-orientation, their arrangement around courtyards and strong sense of form and symbolism with modern architecture.

The figure of the 'dragon' alternates between the arrangement of residential courts and spacious gardens. Every house has a part of both courtyard and garden. The residential buildings on the south sides of the courts have four to five storeys, the ones on the north side have seven to eleven floors.

Thus the buildings offer different scales and environments. A unifying 'diagonal' in the form of a two-level shopping arcade interconnects all areas of the new neighbourhood. The colour scheme (continuous dark red base courses) and the changing upper facade designs accentuate every house and make it identifiable.'

Otto Steidle

STEIDLE + PARTNER, MÜNCHEN

BEIJING IMAGE, PEKING

BEIJING IMAGE, BEIJING

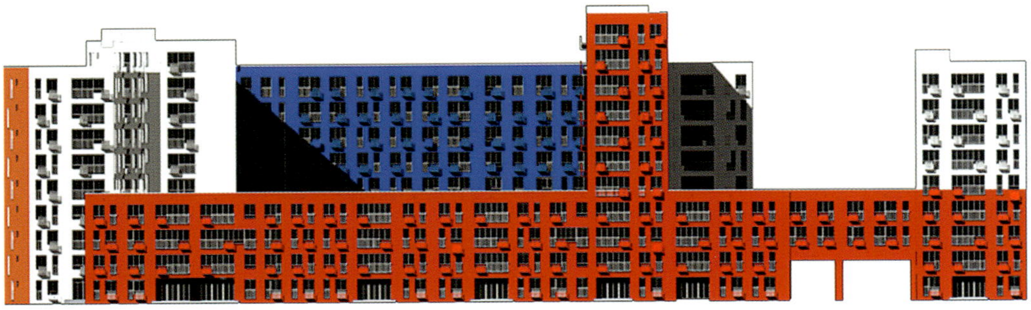

ARCHITEKTEN: Steidle + Partner, München und Strategy Architectural Design Co. Ltd., Peking – Prof. Otto Steidle mit Qiu Zhi sowie Yang Nan, Chen Jinsong, Ma Sen
BAUHERR: Beijing Grand Golden Capital Real Estate Co. Ltd.
BGF: 170.000 m² (991 Wohnungen, 35–160 m² Größe, durchschnittlich 90 m²), 40.000 m² Tiefgarage (845 Stellplätze)
FACHPLANER: Oriental Landscape, Beijing
PLANUNGSZEIT: 2000–2001
BAUZEIT: 2001–2003
FERTIGSTELLUNG: 2003
WETTBEWERB: 2000, 1. Preis

Projektbeschreibung

Project Description

Die Wohnanlage entsteht an der westlichen 4. Ringstraße auf dem Grundstück einer ehemaligen Textilfabrik. Im Gegensatz zu den Entwürfen der anderen Wettbewerbsteilnehmer wurde die geforderte hohe Dichte nicht durch einzelne Turmbauten, sondern durch vier- bis neungeschossige Zeilen, die durch höhere Quergebäude miteinander verbunden sind, erreicht.

So entsteht eine lebendige, urbane Siedlung mit Wegen, Höfen und Plätzen. Die Wohnanlage erschließt sich für Fußgänger und Radfahrer über die zentrale Nord-Süd-Achse. Autofahrer gelangen über die Tiefgarage zu ihren Wohnungen. Durch die bauliche Komplexität und die kräftige Farbgebung wird die Wohnanlage zu einem neuen Wahrzeichen und Orientierungspunkt im Westen Pekings.

The residential development is situated on the western 4th Ring Road on the site of a former textile factory. Unlike the other competition designs, this one does not create the required density with free-standing high-rises, but with four to nine-storey ribbon blocks linked by transverse structures.

The result is a lively and livable urban neighbourhood with footpaths, courtyards and open areas. Pedestrians and cyclists reach it from the central north-south axis. Motorists drive their cars into the underground garage to walk to their flats from there. Structural complexity and strong colours make this housing estate a new landmark and point of orientation in Beijing's west.

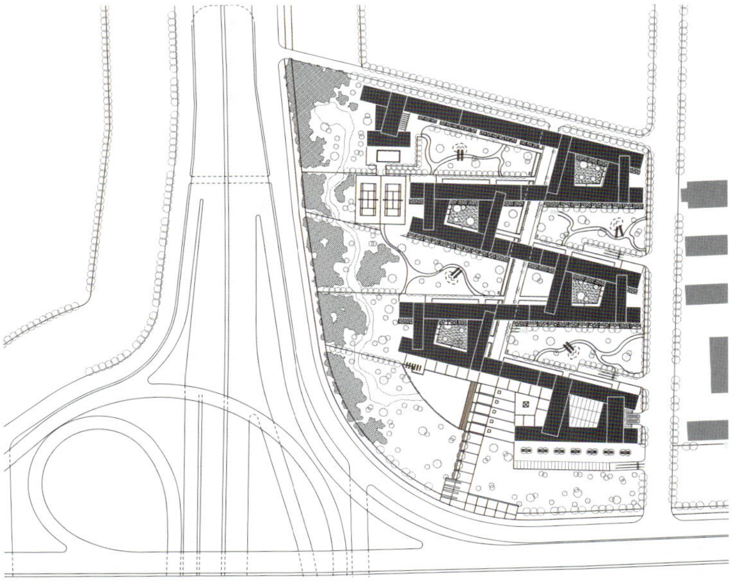

财贸中心
至尊经典
停车

STEIDLE + PARTNER, MÜNCHEN

CHAO WAI MEN, PEKING

CHAO WAI MEN, BEIJING

Projektbeschreibung

Project Description

„Die neueren Bauten der großen Banken, Hotels, Kaufhäuser und Bürohäuser, aber auch manche Wohnhäuser und Wohntürme vermitteln etwas von dem ungeheueren Potenzial Chinas, das die soziale und ökonomische Geschichte erahnen lässt. Auch wenn es noch nicht zu einer eigenen architektonischen Kultur gefunden hat, schafft es einen Eindruck von der ökonomischen Entwicklung, von dem sozialen Gefüge und von dem Wunsch nach Schönheit und Pracht dieses Landes und dieser Städte.

Oft sind es eigenwillige Mischlinge aus westlichem Fortschrittsgeist und chinesischer Zeichenhaftigkeit. Beeindruckt hat mich die Direktheit, mit der große Straßenzüge von großen Bauten gefasst sind und so neue großstädtische Räume entstehen lassen."

Otto Steidle

'The buildings of major banks, hotels and department stores as well as large office structures, some residential blocks and high-rises convey a sense of China's enormous potential evident in its social and economic history. Even though they have not yet found its own contemporary architectural culture, they convey an impression of the economic development, the social fabric, and the longing for beauty and glamour that live in this nation and its cities.

Many new buildings are hybrids of a western spirit of progress and Chinese symbolism. I have been impressed by the directness with which wide avenues have been framed by large buildings and new metropolitan spaces created in this way.'

Otto Steidle

朝外MEN
TAXI

ARCHITEKTEN: Steidle + Partner, München und Strategy Architectural Design Co. Ltd., Peking – Prof. Otto Steidle, Martin Klain, Yang Nan, Chen Min, Qiu Zhi
BAUHERR: Beijing Glory Real Estate Development Co. Ltd.
BGF: 107.000 m²
GRUNDSTÜCKSFLÄCHE: 13.680 m²
PLANUNGSZEIT: 2000
BAUZEIT: 2002–2004
FERTIGSTELLUNG: 2004

Städtebauliche Situation

Urban Situation

Dieser Bau in der Nähe der Chao Yang Men Road befindet sich im zentralen Geschäftsviertel (CBD) von Peking. In architektonischer Hinsicht ist die Umgebung heterogen.

Das Thema „Einheit in Vielfalt" stellte daher in diesem architektonischen und städtischen Kontext eine besondere Herausforderung dar. Die Wahl fiel auf einen Doppelturmbau, der den Straßenblock vervollständigt und einen Gartenhof umschließt. Der Architekt gestaltete diesen als Gemeinschaftsraum mit Holzterrassen, welche die Bewohner einlädt, hier zu sitzen und Tee zu trinken. Darunter befinden sich Ladenflächen.

Das Gebäude ist ein Mehrzweckbau mit Büros, Wohnungen, Geschäften etc. Die Grundrisse der kommerziellen Flächen hat der Architekt bewusst so gegliedert, dass sich diese Räume später ohne großen Aufwand zu Wohnungen umbauen lassen.

This building near Chao Yang Men Road is located in the CBD in downtown Beijing. In terms of architecture, the urban environment of the site is heterogeneous.

The theme of 'unity and diversity' therefore represents a particular challenge in this architectural and urban context. A twin tower was chosen to make up the city block and form the inner garden patio. The architect designed it as a 'common room' with wooden decks which invite residents to sit here and have tea on the roof of the commercial spaces below.

The building complex houses multiple functions: offices, apartments and shops. The floor plan follows the architect's intention to organize these functional areas in such a way that they can easily be converted

CAROUSEL
COURT

STEIDLE + PARTNER, MÜNCHEN

PLA ART BUILDING, PEKING

PLA ART BUILDING, BEIJING

„Die zweite Bauaufgabe, der 'Turmplatz', bezieht sich noch direkter auf eine Strategie einer Bündelung der neuen Aktivitäten entlang einer großstädtischen Straße.

Eine im Masterplan vorgesehene lapidare Ansammlung von drei Hochhäusern wurde zu einem geöffneten Platz-Hof mit vier höhengestaffelten Häusern verändert. Die vier Häuser beinhalten die Maßstäbe der Straße und des Quartiers in einem Ensemble: Ein circa 35 Meter hohes straßenbegleitendes Gebäude, das die Straßenflucht stärkt, ein 60 Meter hoher oder ein von 60 bis zu 75 Meter Höhe gestaffelter Bereich und schließlich ein 90 Meter hoher Turm umschließen einen neuen Platz-Hof-Raum.

So entsteht nicht einfach ein solitäres unzugängliches Gebäude mit entsprechender leerer Vorzone, sondern ein einladender öffentlicher Raum für Geschäfte und Restaurants, ein öffentlicher Ort, von denen das neue Peking wenig bietet."

Otto Steidle

'The second building commission, the 'Tower Square', follows the strategy of concentrating the new commercial and service activities along a wide inner-city street even more directly.

While the masterplan simply envisaged a group of three high-rises, we created four buildings with stepped profiles of different heights around an open area, or wide courtyard. The buildings fit the scale of the street and the surrounding architectural structures: one about 35 m high fronts the street and strengthens the line of existing buildings; another one is 60 m high, the one with a stepped profile 60 to 75 m high, and the fourth is a 90-metre tower. All of them enclose the new large open courtyard.

The result is not simply an inhospitable solitary high-rise with a vast empty forecourt, but an inviting public space lined with shops and restaurants, the likes of which are few and far between in Beijing.

Otto Steidle

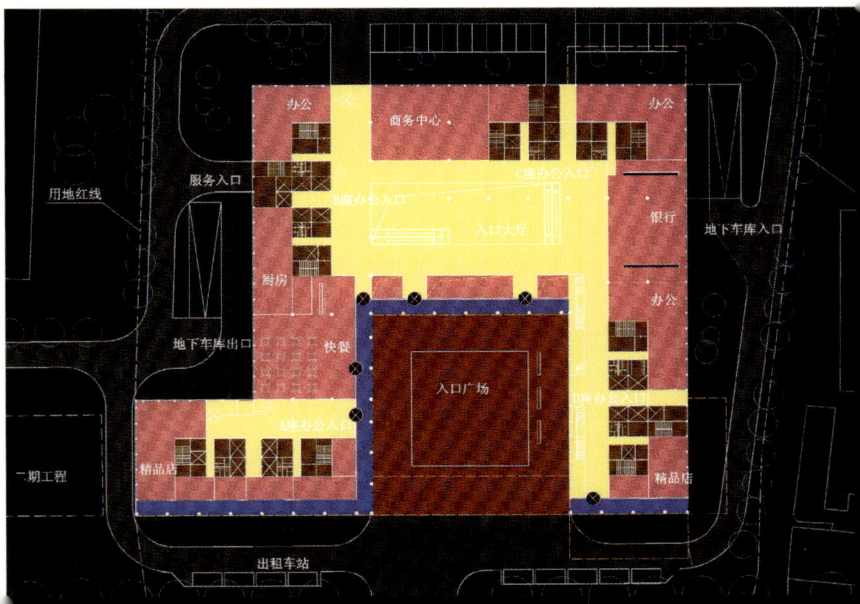

STEIDLE + PARTNER, MÜNCHEN _ **PLA ART BUILDING, BUILDING**

ARCHITEKTEN: Steidle + Partner, München und Strategy Architectural Design Co. Ltd., Peking – Prof. Otto Steidle mit Qiu Zhi, Martin Klein sowie Xu Dan Yi, Yang Nan, Ma Sen
BAUHERR: Beijing Grand Golden Capital Real Estate Co. Ltd.
BGF (GESAMT): 124.000 m² (davon unterirdisch 35.000m²)
GRUNDSTÜCKSFLÄCHE: 12.428 m²
PLANUNGSZEIT: 2001
BAUBEGINN: 2003
FERTIGSTELLUNG: 2006

PLA Art Building

PLA Art Building

Dieser Bürokomplex mit Ladenflächen im Erdgeschoss und auf den darüber liegenden zwei Geschossen befindet sich im Hightech-Industriepark Zhong Guan Cun Nan Dajie im Pekinger Bezirk Haidian.

Der Entwurfsgedanke war, dem Gewerbegebiet Zhong Guan Cun eine „Bauskulptur" zu geben und damit auch Anstöße für die städtebauliche Gestaltung des Kontexts. Der Komplex besteht aus vier verschieden hohen Hochhäusern. Das niedrigste steht an der Straße und setzt die Baufluchten der Nachbarbauten und der dahinter stehenden Gebäude fort. Die Türme werden durch vier Gebäudebrücken miteinander verbunden.

Die Fassaden bestehen aus 1,35 m breiten Modulen, die nicht nur die funktionalen und klimatischen Anforderungen an einen Bürokomplex erfüllen, sondern ihm auch ästhetische Ausdruckskraft verleihen.

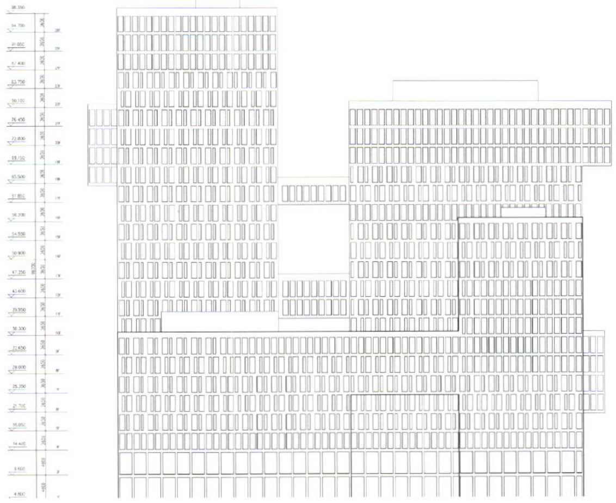

This office complex with three-storey commercial spaces above street level is located in Zhong Guan Cun Nan Dajie, a high-tech industrial estate in Beijing's Haidian district.

The basic design idea was to create an 'urban architectural sculpture' for the Zhong Guan Cun district and at the same time to give a lead to the urban fabric of its surroundings. The building complex consists of four towers of different heights. The lowest fronts the street so that it integrates with the neighbouring buildings next to it and the higher ones behind. Four bridges interconnect the towers.

The facades are composed of 1.35-metre modules which not only meet the functional and climatic requirements of an office complex, but also lend it powerful aesthetic expression.

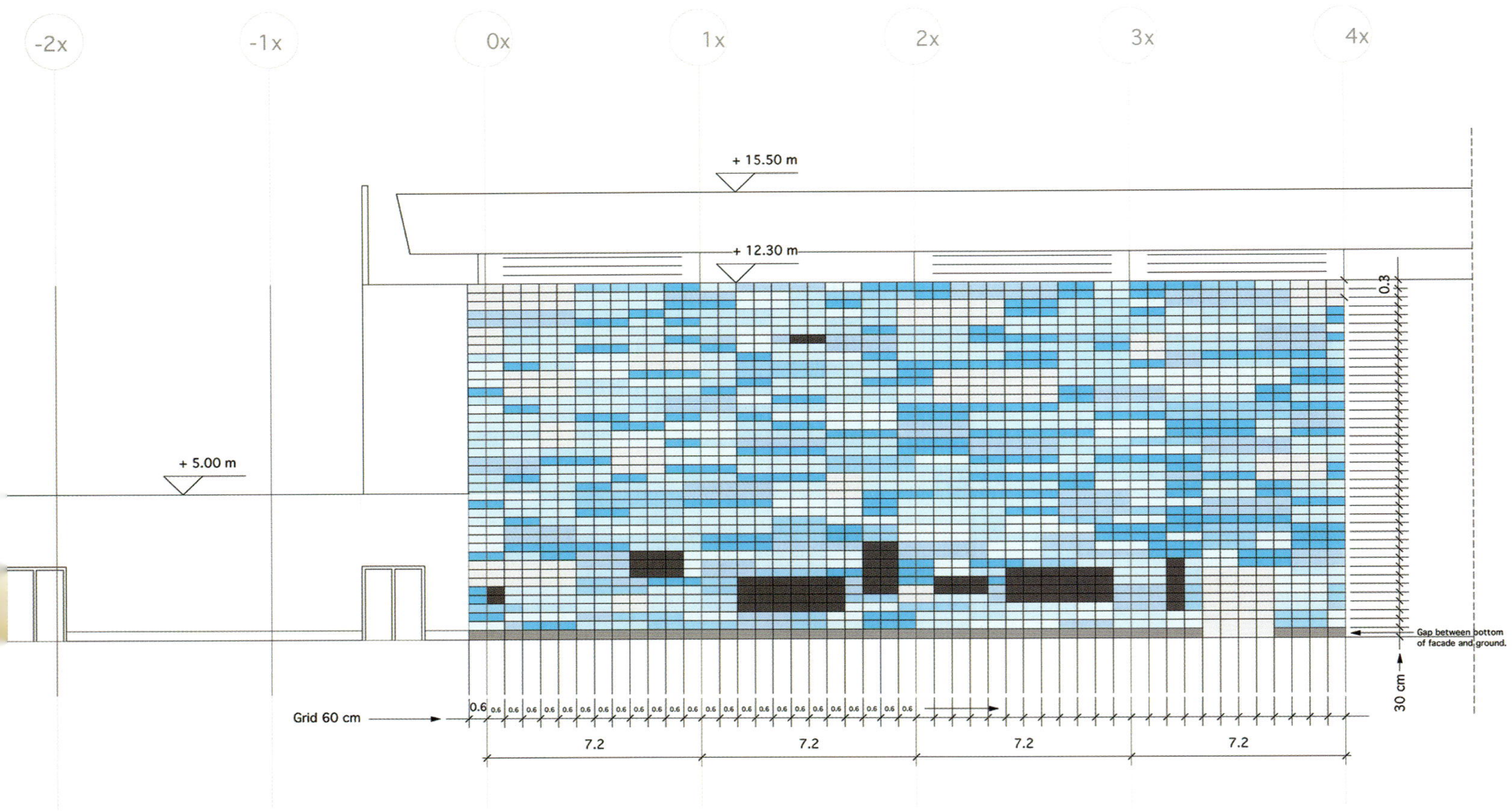

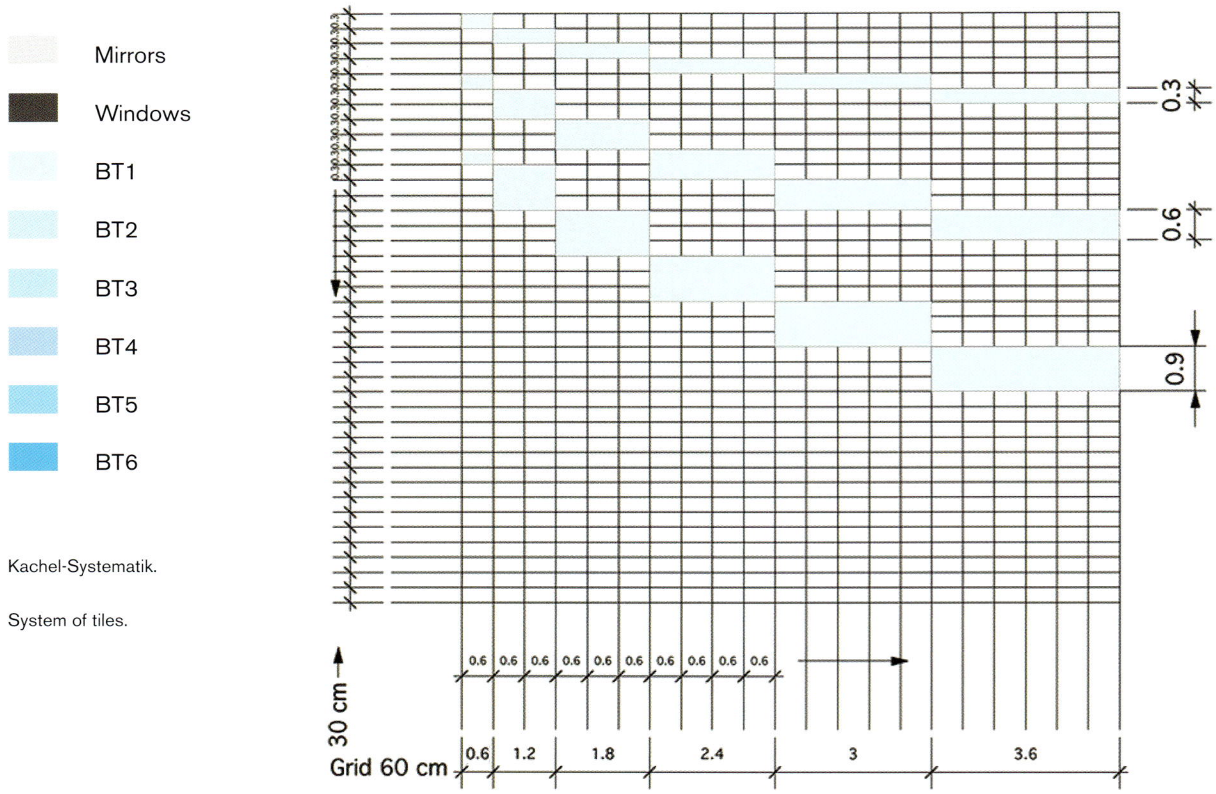

Kachel-Systematik.

System of tiles.

tec ARCHITECTURE – LOS ANGELES, MÜNCHEN, SINGAPORE, TÄGERWILEN (CH)

PARTNER: M + W ZANDER, SHANGHAI & GTL-LANDSCHAFTSARCHITEKTEN, KASSEL

UNTERNEHMENSZENTRALE UND FABRIK, SUZHOU, CHINA
CORPORATE HEADQUARTERS AND FACTORY, SUZHOU, CHINA

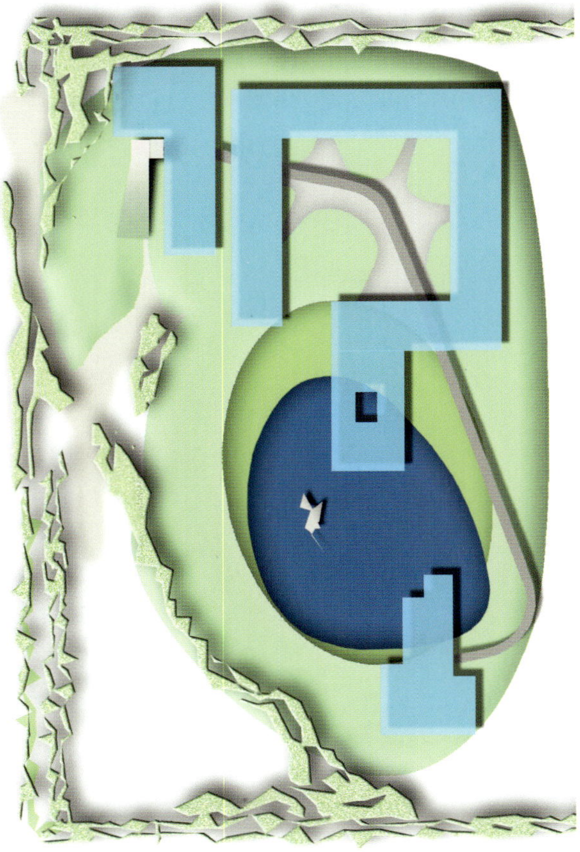

Das Suzhou-Projekt schlägt ein Bürokonzept vor, das einer neuen Auffassung des Begriffs „Arbeit“ folgt.

Viel Hingabe fordernd, lädt die Arbeitswelt heute zu einer Verschmelzung von beruflichen und persönlichen Erwartungen ein, um so einen neuen Typ Arbeitskultur zu formen, der „Arbeit“ und „Leben“ immer mehr zusammenführt. Dieser Abbau von Grenzen erlaubt räumliche Strategien, die soziale Nachbarschaften fördern und Kommunikation als Schlüsselelement zu anregendem, kreativem Denken betonen.

Beim Suzhou-Projekt erreicht man diese Zielsetzung, indem man die Mitarbeiter innerhalb eines einzigartigen Garten-Campus platziert, der Ruhe auf die Arbeitsstätte ausstrahlt. Dieser Dialog zwischen Struktur und Natur beschreibt eine Arbeitsumgebung voller Inspiration, die einer Auffassung von Büroarbeit folgt, die sehr emotional, ja sogar romantisch geprägt ist.

This design for Suzhou proposes an office concept based on a new interpretation of the term 'work'.

Today's world of labour demands much dedication and calls for the merging of professional and private expectations in order to form a new type of working culture that will increasingly unite working and living. This lifting of departmentalization made it possible to follow spatial strategies that promote social neighbourhoods and communication as the keys to creative thinking.

The Suzhou project achieves this by placing offices and factory halls on a unique garden-like campus which furthers quiet concentration at work. This dialogue between architectural structure and nature characterizes a working environment full of incentive and inspiration, based on an emotional, perhaps even romantic, approach to office design.

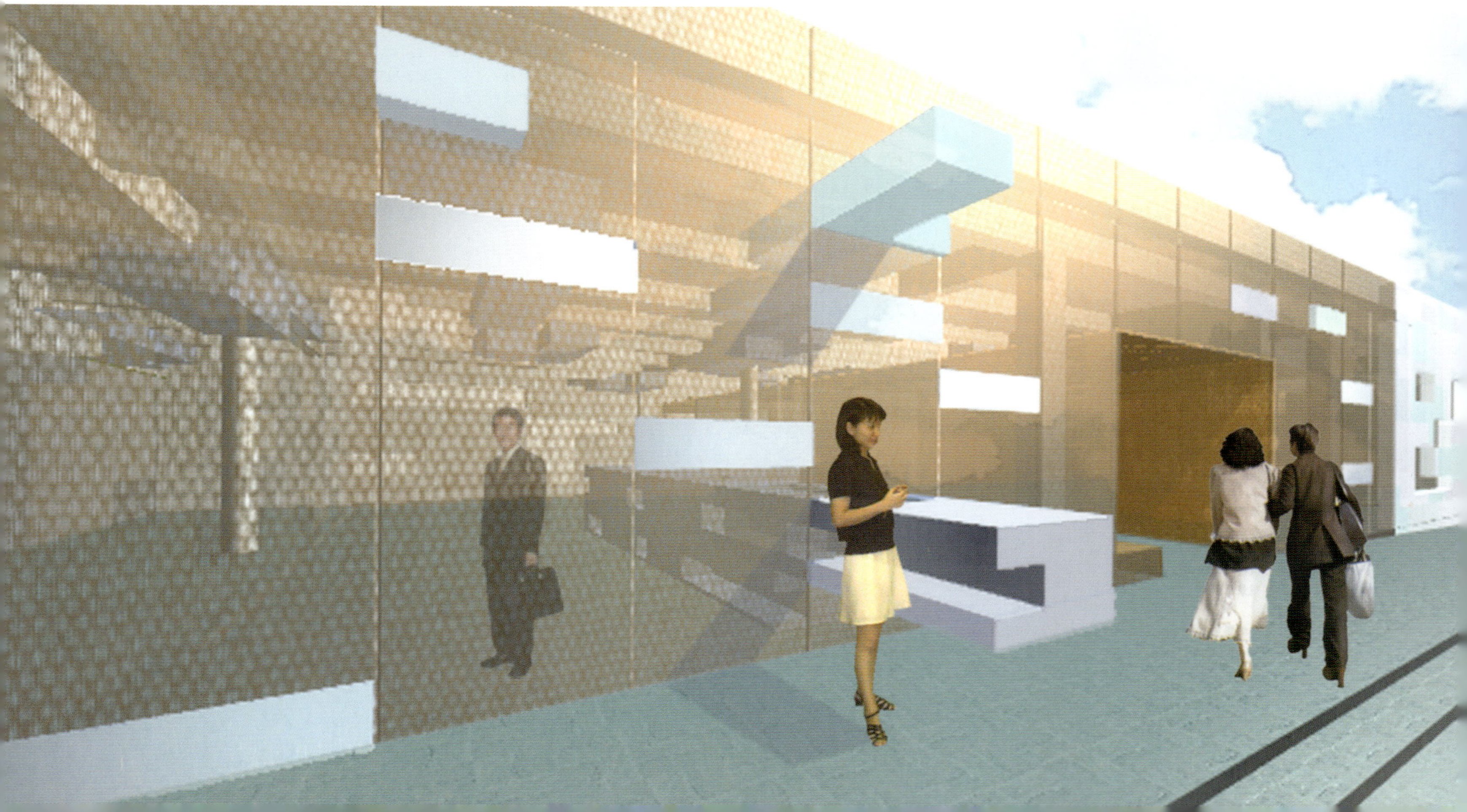

BGF (GESAMT): 29.000 m²
FERTIGSTELLUNG: 2004

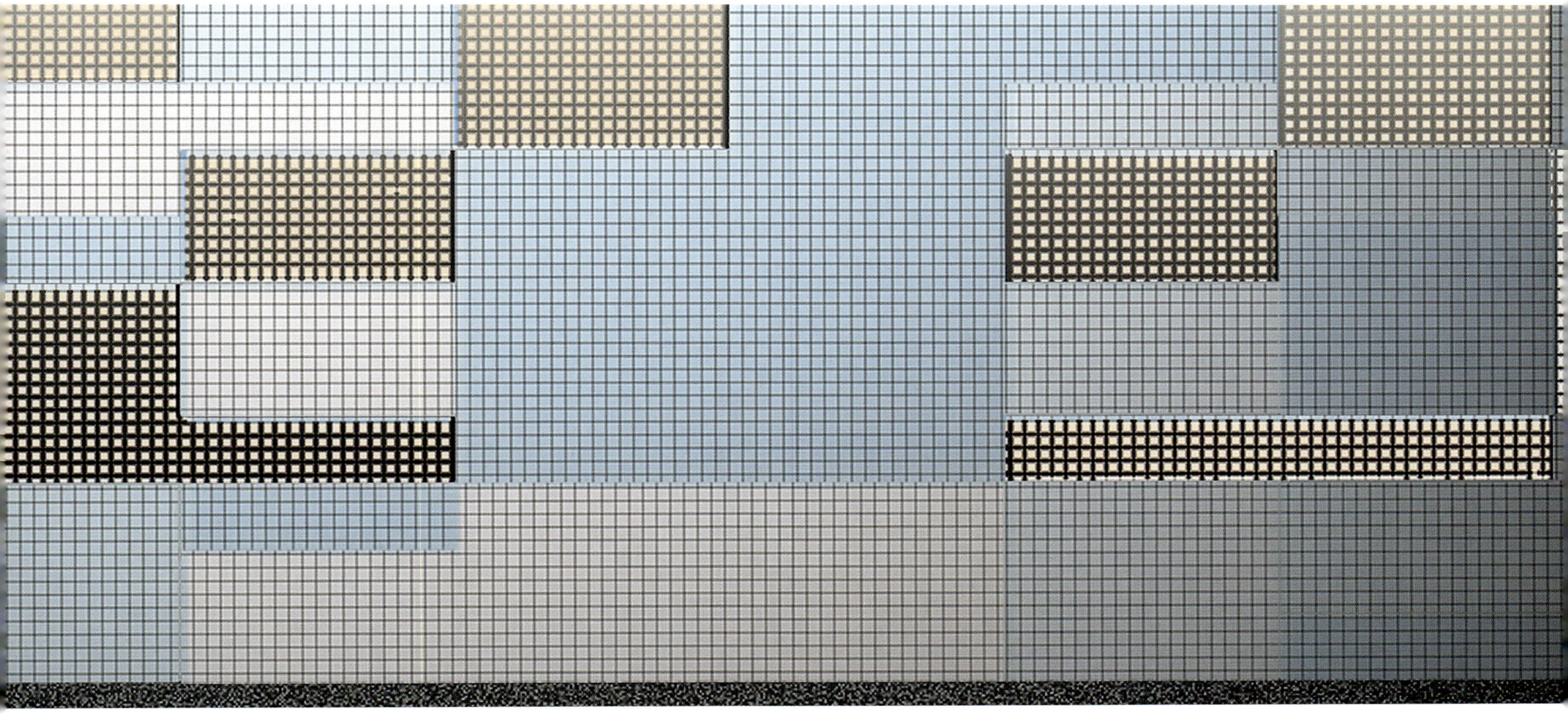

Dem ursprünglich flachen Baugelände wird ein detailliertes Profil verliehen, um so einen zentralen See, der von Bäumen gesäumt wird, zu schaffen – eine Referenz an die berühmten Gärten von Suzhou und eine Hommage an die Bedeutung einer naturgeprägten Umgebung auf einen kreativen Geist.

Die Fassaden verfremden die Themen Himmel und Wasser durch vielfach schattierte Blautöne und sind eher impressionistische Malerei als Funktionsbau. Die Einzigartigkeit des Projektes schafft einen hohen Grad an Identifikation. Ziel des Entwurfs ist die Förderung von Motivation, Kreativität und Kommunikation.

The originally flat construction site is modulated to create a central lake lined by trees – a reference to the famous gardens of Suzhou, and a celebration of the significance of a natural environment for creative spirits. The unique character of this project furthers a high degree of staff identification with the workplace. The design aimed to motivate them and to promote creativity and communication.

Die Abstraktion der Themen Himmel und Wasser wird durch eine komplexe Form- und Farbgestaltung der Fassade erreicht – vielfach schattierte Blautöne, Lichtreflexe und unendliche Spiegelungen.

The facade colours abstract the design themes 'sky' and 'water' with many shades of blue, different shapes, light reflexes and reflections, so that the buildings appear more like Impressionist paintings than functional architecture.

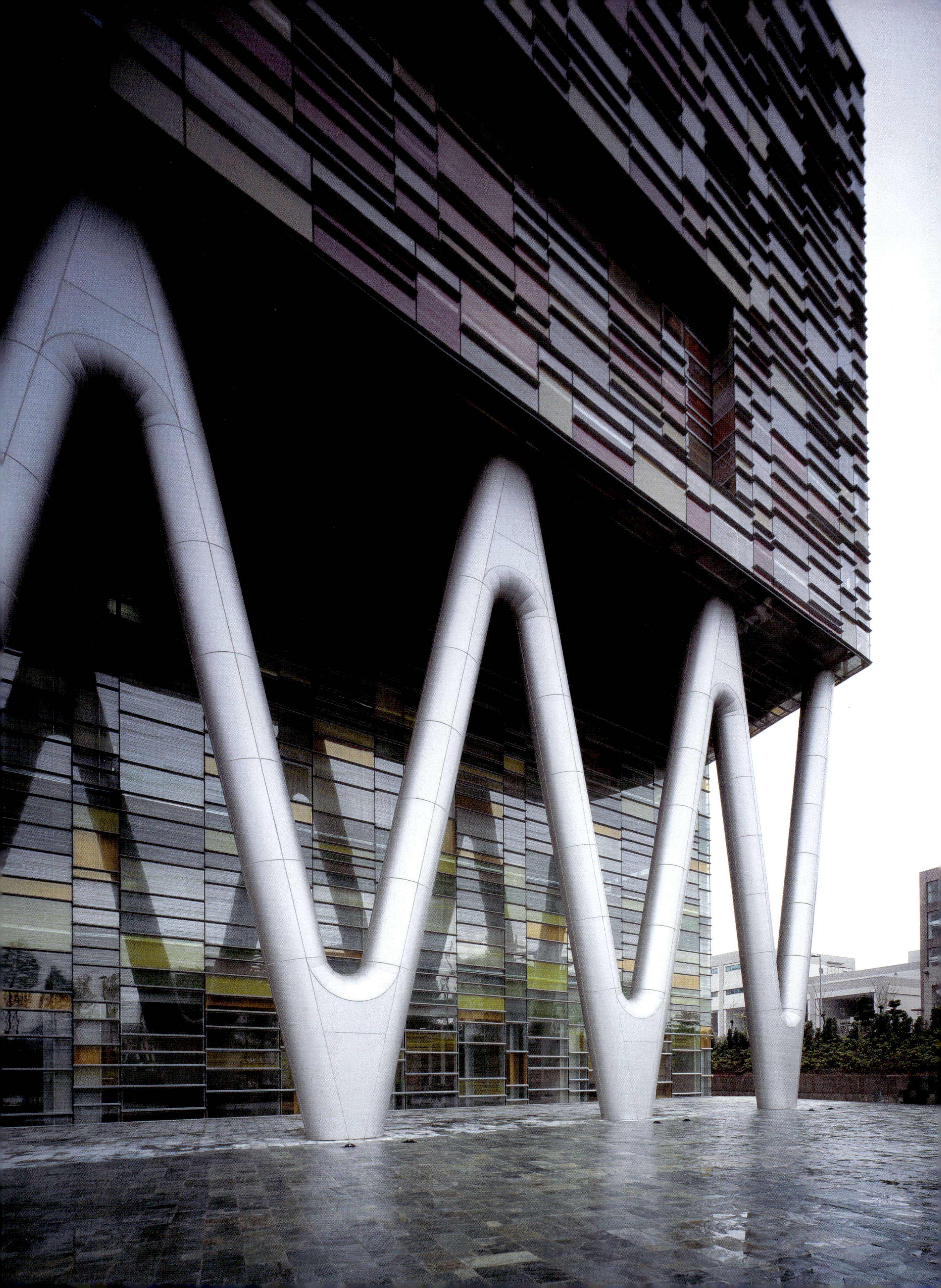

tec ARCHITECTURE – LOS ANGELES, MÜNCHEN, SINGAPORE, TÄGERWILEN (CH)

PARTNER: PHILIP T. C. FEI, FEI & CHENG ASSOCIATES, TAIPEH & GTL-LANDSCHAFTSARCHITEKTEN, KASSEL

INOTERA UNTERNEHMENSZENTRALE, BÜROGEBÄUDE UND MICROCHIP- PRODUKTIONSSTÄTTE INOTERA MEMORIES INC., TAIPEH, TAIWAN

INOTERA CORPORATE HEADQUARTERS, OFFICE BLOCK AND MICROCHIP PLANT INOTERA MEMORIES INC., TAIPEH, TAIWAN

Die Asien-Pazifik-Region, ein wichtiger Entwicklungsstandort für zukunftsweisende Technologien und kreative Intelligenz, profitiert von einer einzigartigen Kombination aus Hightech-Entwicklung und natürlichem Umfeld. Dieses Potenzial wird genutzt, um mit neuen Strategien diese beiden Grundelemente zu integrieren und den Menschen wieder in den Mittelpunkt aller Überlegungen zu stellen.

Die Inotera Unternehmenszentrale verfolgt eine emotionale, fast romantische Auffassung von Büroarbeit. Wie die Blätter eines Baumes oder die Wellen des Wassers spiegeln Hunderte von Farben und Formen eine formale Interpretation der komplexen Natur wider. Dabei erlauben innovative Technologien eine Fassadengestaltung, die durch Mikrochip-Entwicklung, wie sie Inotera betreibt, erst ermöglicht wird. Die Technologie wird dafür eingesetzt, kulturelle Werte und umweltfspezifische Aspekte innerhalb eines zeitgenössischen Kontextes zusammenzubringen.

The Asia-Pacific region benefits from a unique juxtaposition of high-tech developments and nature. This potential is utilized for integrating these two basic elements, pursuing new design strategies, and for reinstating man as the centre of every design consideration.

The design of the Inotera corporate headquarters building is based on an emotional, almost romantic notion of office work. Like tree leaves or ocean waves, hundreds of different colours and shapes represent a formal interpretation of the complex natural world. Innovative micro-chip technology – as developed by Inotera – made it possible to design a facade which shows a combination of cultural values and environmental aspects in a contemporary architectural context.

Innovative Technologien ermöglichen die serielle Herstellung einer Fassade, die sich aus Hunderten von Farben und Formen zusammenstellt.

Innovative technologies made it possible to prefabricate a façade of hundreds of different shapes and colours.

BAUHERR: Inotera Memories Inc. Taipeh, Taiwan
BGF GESAMT: 49.000 m²
BÜROFLÄCHE: 29.000 m²
REINRAUMFLÄCHE: 20.000 m²
FERTIGSTELLUNG: 2004

Durch das Fehlen bestehender ikonografischer „Gestalt“ Konzepte für Hightech-Gebäude diesen Maßstabs verfolgt das Bürogebäude deshalb eine eigenständige Aussage, während die angebundene Fabrik durch seine Fassadengestaltung, eine Komposition aus gekachelten perspektivischen Geometrien, einen fantastischen Hintergrund für eine dadaeske Auflösung des Maßstabs bietet.

Das Grundpotenzial der Technologie, einen Beitrag zu einer wirtschaftlichen und ästhetischen Verbesserung unseres Lebens zu leisten, wird durch eine solche Verwendung veranschaulicht. Sie bildet den Kern einer komplexen architektonischen Herangehensweise, die nicht nur technologische Innovation anwendet, sondern sie auch verinnerlicht.

As there are no generally accepted iconographic or morphological concepts for high-tech buildings of this size, the design of the office building aimed for original expression while the design of the factory annex facade – a composition of tiled perspective geometries – forms a fantastic background to a Dada-type dissolution of scale.

The design demonstrates the basic potential of technology, i.e. of contributing to improving the economics and aesthetics of human life. Technology is at the heart of a complex architectural approach that does not only apply technical innovation, but internalizes it.

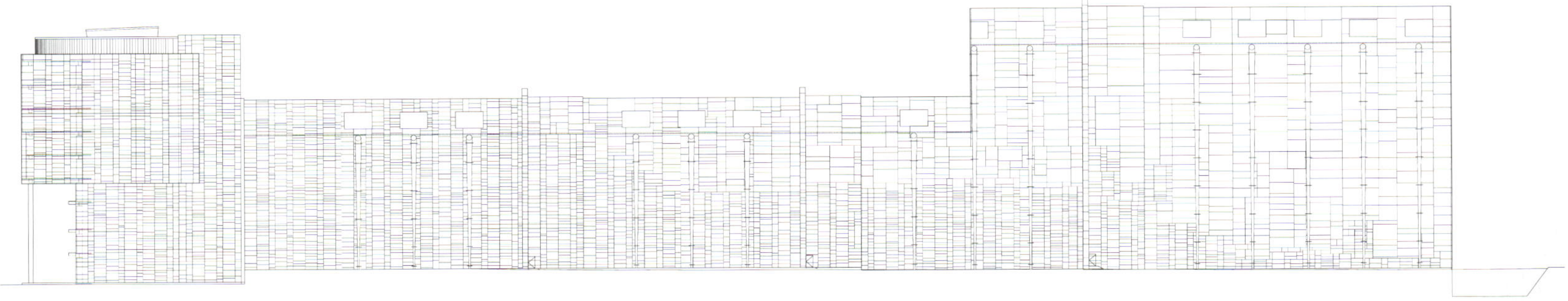

Dynamisch schweben Pressezentrum und Restaurant flügelähnlich über der Rennstrecke. Die Materialwahl (glänzendes Aluminium, Glas und Edelstahl) betont besonders den technischen Charakter.

The press centre and the restaurant seem like wings projecting over the race track. The materials (shimmering aluminium, glass and stainless steel) emphasize their technoid character.

TILKE INGENIEURE UND ARCHITEKTEN

INTERNATIONALE RENNSTRECKE SHANGHAI

INTERNATIONAL RACING COURSE, SHANGHAI

上 „Shang“, das chinesische Zeichen für „hoch“, „oben“ bildet die Aufsicht der neuen Internationalen Rennstrecke in Shanghai, die im September 2004 erstmalig in China die Formel1 ausrichtete.

Die Anlage wurde auf über 40.000 Stahlbetonpfählen und mehr als 340.000m^3 Styropor gegründet. So konnte trotz der sehr schwierigen Gründungsverhältnissen im Yangtse-Delta eine Rennstrecke mit imposanten Gebäuden und herausfordernden Kurven und Steigungen realisiert werden.

Seen from above, the international race track in Shanghai, which in September 2004 hosted the Formula 1 races premiere in China, forms the Chinese character for 'shang' (meaning 'high', or 'above').

The complex was founded on 40,000 RC piles and more than 340,000 m^3 of styrofoam. This made it possible to build a race track with challenging curves and gradients, as well as impressive buildings, despite the problematic soil conditions on this Yangtse delta site.

Die Team Buildings, die als Pavillons in einem See angeordnet sind, erinnern an den antiken Yu-Garden in Shanghai und verheißen Ruhe und Entspannung.

The team buildings – pavilions in a small lake – are reminiscent of Shanghai's ancient Yu Gardens and promise peace and relaxation.

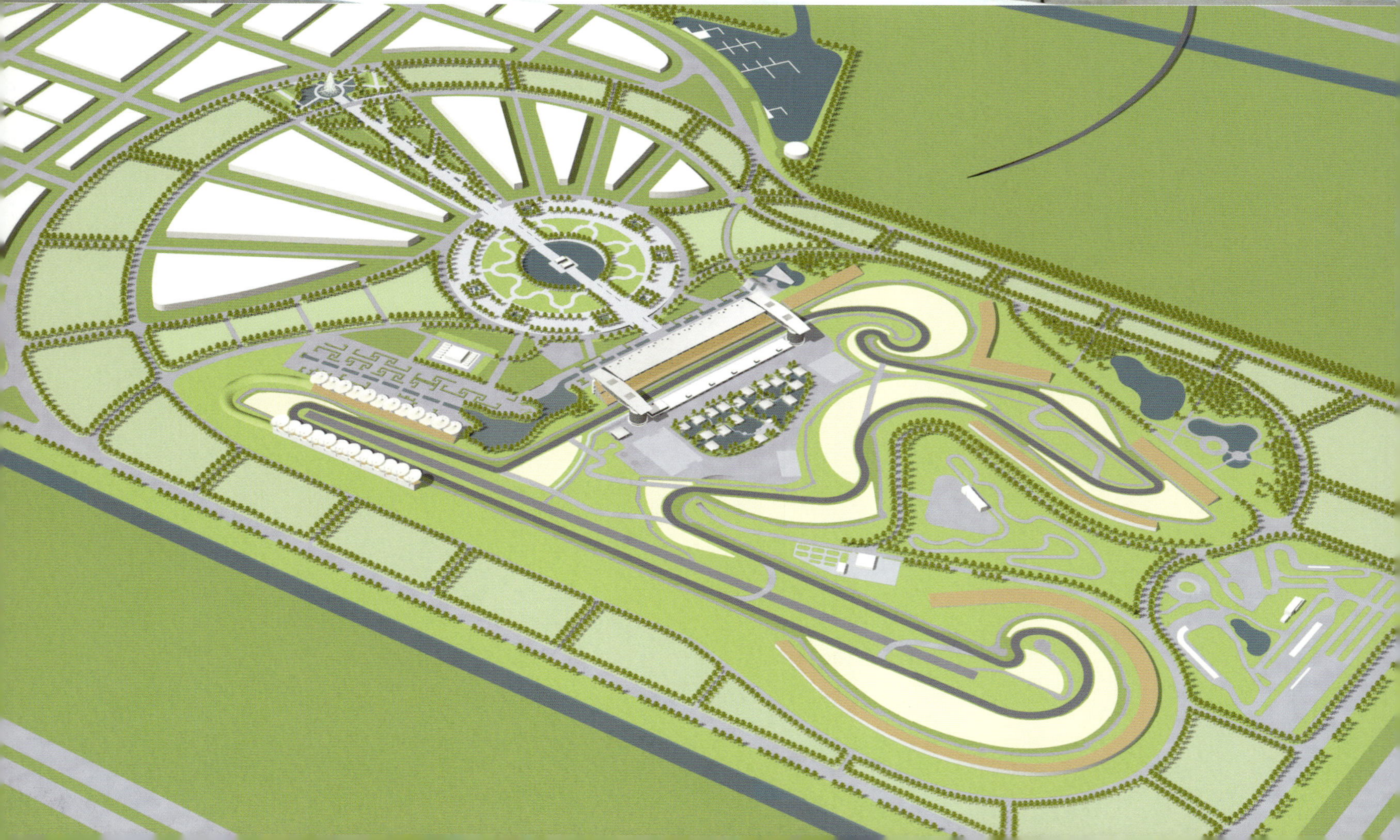

Die Membrandach-Schirme der Arena-Tribünen sind Lotusblättern nachempfunden.

The canopies of the arena stands are modeled on lotus leaves.

BAUHERR: Shanghai International Circuit Ltd.
ENTWURF: Tilke Ingenieure und Architekten

Die Architektur verbindet den Hightech-Charakter der Formel1 mit Symbolen aus der chinesischen Geschichte und Natur, die sich in Formen, Farben und Materialien widerspiegeln. 200.000 Zuschauer finden auf den verschieden Tribünen Platz; vor allem die Haupttribüne bietet einen spektakulären Blick auf fast 80% der 5,4 km langen Strecke.

Die traditionellen Farben Rot und Gold in den zylindrischen Dachausschnitten der Haupttribüne, die wie natürliche Lampions das Sonnenlicht als Lichtquelle nutzen, symbolisieren Glück und Macht. Und „wenn Glück und Macht zusammenkommen", heißt es in China, „ist der Erfolg nicht aufzuhalten."

The architecture combines the high-tech character of the Formula 1 races with symbols from Chinese history and nature reflected in forms, colours and materials. 200,000 spectators can be seated on the different stands. The main stand, in particular, offers a spectacular view over almost 80 per cent of the 5.4-km track.

The cylindrical roof lanterns function like lampions, using the sun as luminant, and appear in the traditional Chinese colours red and gold, symbolizing good luck and power. And if good luck and power come together, say the Chinese, there is no stopping success.

Die Tribünen-Rückseiten sind mit Edelstahl-Gewebe verkleidet.

The backs of the stands are clad with stainless steel mesh.

AUFGABE: Parkentwurf
LANDSCHAFTSARCHITEKTEN: Shanghai Jinyuan Landscape, Christoph Valentien, Dietmar Straub

VALENTIEN + VALENTIEN

BING-HAI-PARK SHANGHAI

BING HAI PARK, SHANGHAI

Auf einem 300 ha großen küstennahen Gelände südlich von Shanghai war ein Park geplant, dessen Muster in einer westlichen Teilfläche schon realisiert wurde. Die Aufgabe war, eine Alternative für die Weiterentwicklung der größeren, östlich gelegenen Fläche zu entwerfen.

Bei der Weiterentwicklung bleibt die existierende Graslandschaft unangetastet. An drei Stellen auf dem Gelände wird eine intensive Neulandgewinnung vorgeschlagen. Punktuell und in sehr bestimmten Grenzen werden Inseln aufgeschüttet, eine Akupunktur in der Landschaft. Wir nennen sie „Terrasse", „Gartenkarussell" und „Botanikum"

Auf der Terrasse befindet sich Wohnen am Wasser. Den Häusern vorgelagert ist eine intensive Zone für Sport und Freizeit. Spielfelder für Fußball, Basketball, Tennis, Volleyball und anderes liegen leicht erhöht über dem wilden Teil der Landschaft.

Das Gartenkarussell bietet in der Mitte einen Wald, umgeben von zwei Ringen aus Gärten und Wasser. Hier könnten Gartenfestivals stattfinden.

Das Botanikum besteht in der Mitte aus einer sanften Rasenfläche mit einem Teich, umgeben von einem Waldsaum. Hier werden Pflanzen gesammelt, bezeichnet und ausgestellt. Ein Ring von Bäumen fasst einen geschützten Innenraum, hier wächst und blüht, was außerhalb nicht vorkommt. Gewächshaus, Besuchergastronomie, Seminarräume, Arbeitsräume für Forschung ergänzen das Programm.

In sanftem Bogen schwebt ein langer Steg über der Landschaft – er verbindet die drei Inseln. Auf der „unteren Ebene" der Salzwiesen werden durch Pfade vorgegebene Zonen erschlossen.

The project was for a 300-hectare area near the coast south of Shanghai. Its western section had already been laid out. The brief demanded an alternative design for landscaping the remaining, larger area to the east.

The design leaves the existing grassland intact, but proposes three areas of reclaimed land, artificial islands that 'acupuncture' the landscape. We have called these islands 'terrace', 'garden roundabout' and 'botanicum'.

The 'terrace' is built up with waterside residences, separated from the shore by a zone of sports and leisure facilities. Areas with football, basket ball, tennis, volleyball and other sports fields are situated on ground that is slightly higher than the natural grassland level.

The 'garden roundabout' has a wood at its centre, surrounded by two rings of gardens and water. This is a place for garden parties and festivals.

The middle of the 'botanicum' is formed by a lawn and a pond, lined by trees. In this area, plants are collected, determined and exhibited. A ring of trees frames a protected interior space where plants thrive and blossom which do not grow locally. A greenhouse, a visitor restaurant, seminar rooms as well as spaces for research complete the programme.

In a wide curve, a long bridge spans the landscape, interconnecting the three islands. At the 'lower level', i.e. that of the salt marshes, pedestrian paths give access to the different programme zones.

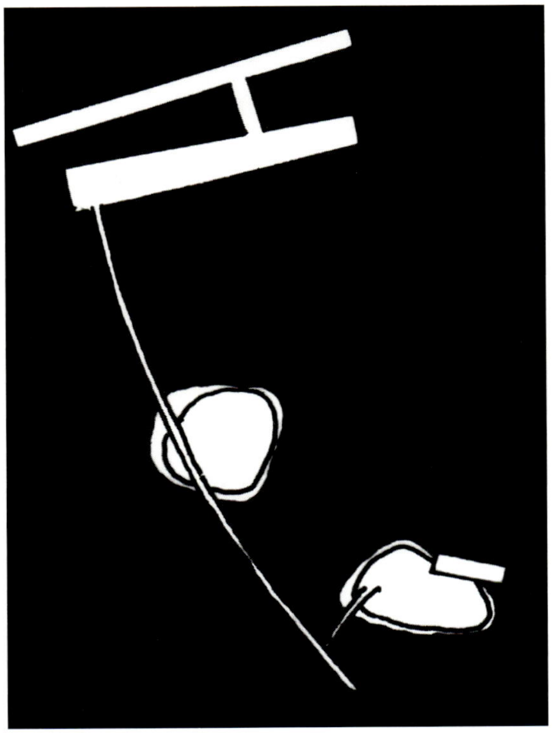

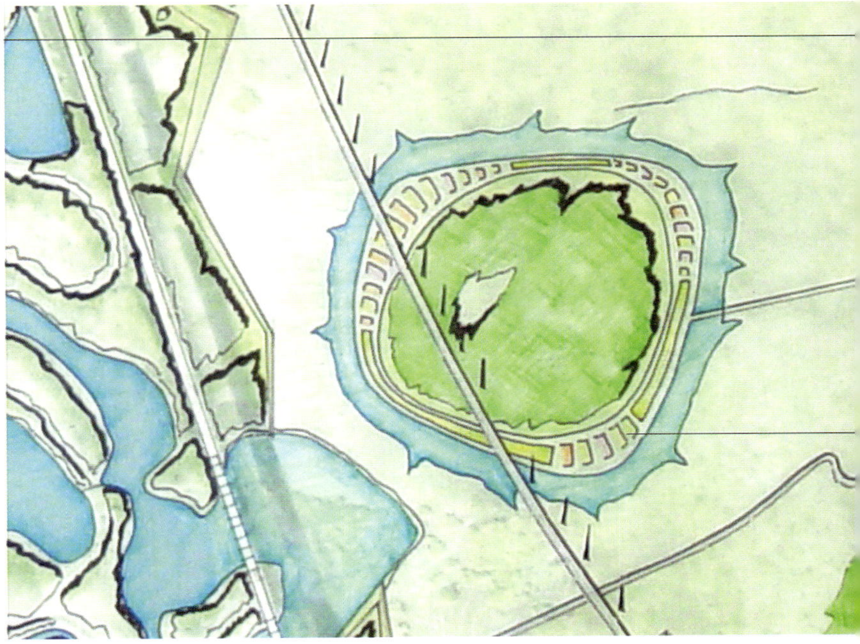

AUFGABE: Landschaftsplanerischer Wettbewerb, 2001, 1. Rang
LANDSCHAFTSARCHITEKTEN: Zhu Janing, Christoph Valentien, Dietmar Straub

VALENTIEN + VALENTIEN

XIN HUA GARTEN, SHEN ZHEN
XIN HUA GARDENS, SHEN ZHEN

Der städtebauliche Entwurf eines australischen Büros für das 17 ha große Grundstück in Shen Zhen war vorgegeben. Über vier Raumeinheiten, die mit Boulevard, Reliefpark, Ringallee und Seeterrassen bezeichnet werden, wird der Städtebau kommentiert.

Auf dem Boulevard liegen lichte Felder für Sport, Spiel und Aufenthalt zwischen schattigen Baumfeldern und Alleen. Dieser Baumzug ist die Schwelle zur Stadt.

Im Reliefpark befinden sich vertikales Wohnen und öffentliche Einrichtungen. Raumwirksame Bodenmodellierungen, lockere Baumgruppen und geschwungene Wege verdichten sich zu einer Landschaft, die als Park verständlich ist und dem Raum zwischen den Hochhäusern einen menschlichen Maßstab verleiht.

Die privilegierte Privatheit der Inseln wird umrahmt von einem öffentlichen Ring für Fußgänger und Radfahrer. Die laubenartig überdachte Ringpassarelle dient der Orientierung, Erschließung und dem Lustwandeln.

Die Seeterrassen sind ein grünes Foyer am Wasser, offen und weit. Eine Augenweide, wenn die Menschen aus der Dichte der Stadt treten, um den angrenzenden öffentlichen Park zu besuchen.

The urban design project of an Australian architectural partnership for the 17-hectare site in Shen Zhen was part of the brief. Our project is a running commentary, so to speak, of the four sections of our project which we have called 'boulevard', 'relief park', 'ring avenue' and 'ocean terraces'.

The 'boulevard' accommodates sports and games fields and recreational areas between shady groves and tree-lined avenues. These wooded areas and rows of trees form the threshold of the city.

The 'relief park' includes apartment high-rises and public facilities. The ground has been modulated to great spatial effect and combines with clumps of trees and curving paths to form a pleasant landscape park to human measure around the residential towers.

The privileged privacy of the islands is framed by a public pedestrian and cyclist ring path, covered like a bower. It gives orientation as well as access to and around the buildings, and people may also use it for going for walks. The 'ocean terraces' are like a green waterside foyer, open and vast – a delight to the eyes of the people who come from the densely built-up city to visit the park.

Die Terrasse (oberes Bild) im Boulevardband markiert den Anfang der nordöstlich einmündenden Straße. Von der Terrasse blickt man in den Reliefpark (rechtes Bild), der sich zwischen den Hochhäusern ausdehnt.

The terrace section (above) of the boulevard strip defines the beginning of the street which runs into it from the northeast. The terrace affords a view over the topographical relief park laid out between the high-rises.

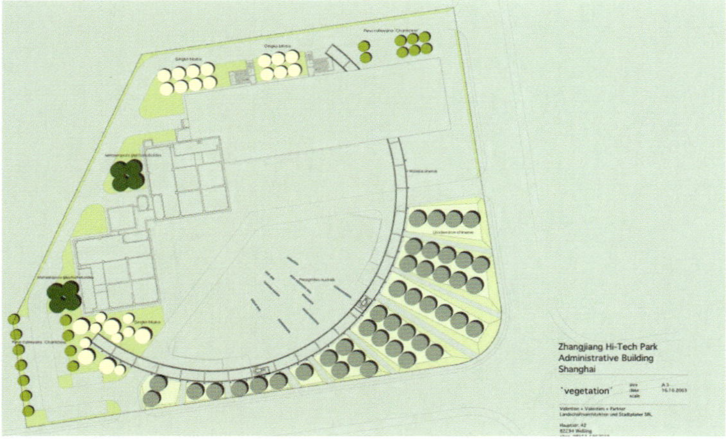
Zhangjiang Hi-Tech Park
Administrative Building
Shanghai
'vegetation'
size
date
scale
A 3
16.10.2003

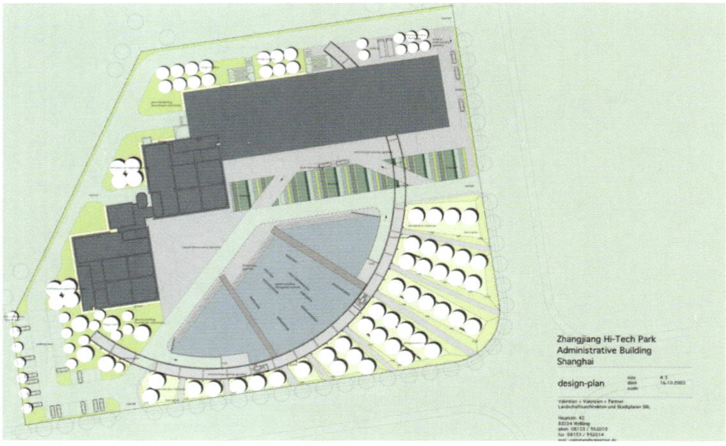
Zhangjiang Hi-Tech Park
Administrative Building
Shanghai
design-plan
size
date
scale
A 3

ARCHITEKTEN: AS&P –Albert Speer & Partner GmbH, Frankfurt am Main

VALENTIEN + VALENTIEN

ZHANGJIANG HIGHTECH-PARK

ZHANGJIANG HIGH-TECH PARK

Der Entwurf stellt eine strenge geometrische Lösung dar, in der die Gesamtstruktur (Wasser, Beläge, Vegetation) auf die Richtung und Koordinaten der Gebäude und des Grundstückes ausgelegt ist.

Das Zentrum der Anlage bildet eine Wasserfläche mit begrünter Pergola im „Rücken" und Sitzstufen an der Wasserkante zum Gebäude hin. Vor dem langgezogenen Ost-West-Riegel befindet sich ein „Parterre" mit einer einheitlichen Bepflanzung. Die Baumgruppen nördlich und westlich der Gebäude stellen den Übergang zur lockeren Pflanzung im benachbarten Park dar. Sie sind flächig mit Bodendeckern unterpflanzt. Südlich und östlich der Seefläche und der Pergola ist die Bepflanzung radial auf die Hochhäuser ausgerichtet. Schattige Rasenflächen unter den hier verwendeten Großbäumen laden zum Verweilen ein. Unterteilt wird die Rasenfläche von Fußwegen, die ebenfalls radial auf die Gebäude zulaufen und von denen sich zwei als Brücken über die Wasserfläche fortsetzen.

The design proposes a strictly geometrical solution in which the overall layout of water features, pavings and vegetation follows the orientation and configuration of both the buildings and the site.

A small lake – 'backed' by a green pergola and broad steps doubling as seats rising from the water's edge up to the elongated building – forms the centre of the complex. A garden parterre runs along the front of the building which is oriented east-west. Clumps of trees (under-planted with ground-cover plants) north and west of it form the transition to the sparsely planted adjacent park. South and east of the lake and the pergola, the plantings are arranged like spokes of a wheel all pointing to the high-rises. Lawns shaded by tall trees invite people to rest here. Radially aligned footpaths subdivide the lawn area and lead to the different buildings; two paths continue as bridges across the lake.

Aus dem Rasen ziehen sich Pflanzcontainer in die zentrale Wasserfläche hinein. Zwischen Wasser und Gebäude liegt die Hauptvorfahrt mit ihrem Asphaltbelag. Die Flächen direkt vor den Baukörpern und die platzartige Fläche östlich des Gebäuderiegels bestehen aus repräsentativen Natursteinplatten.

Plant containers project from the lawn into the water. The main drive, covered with asphalt, runs between the lake and the building. The areas directly in front of the different building sections and the plaza east of the structure are paved with high-grade natural stone slabs.

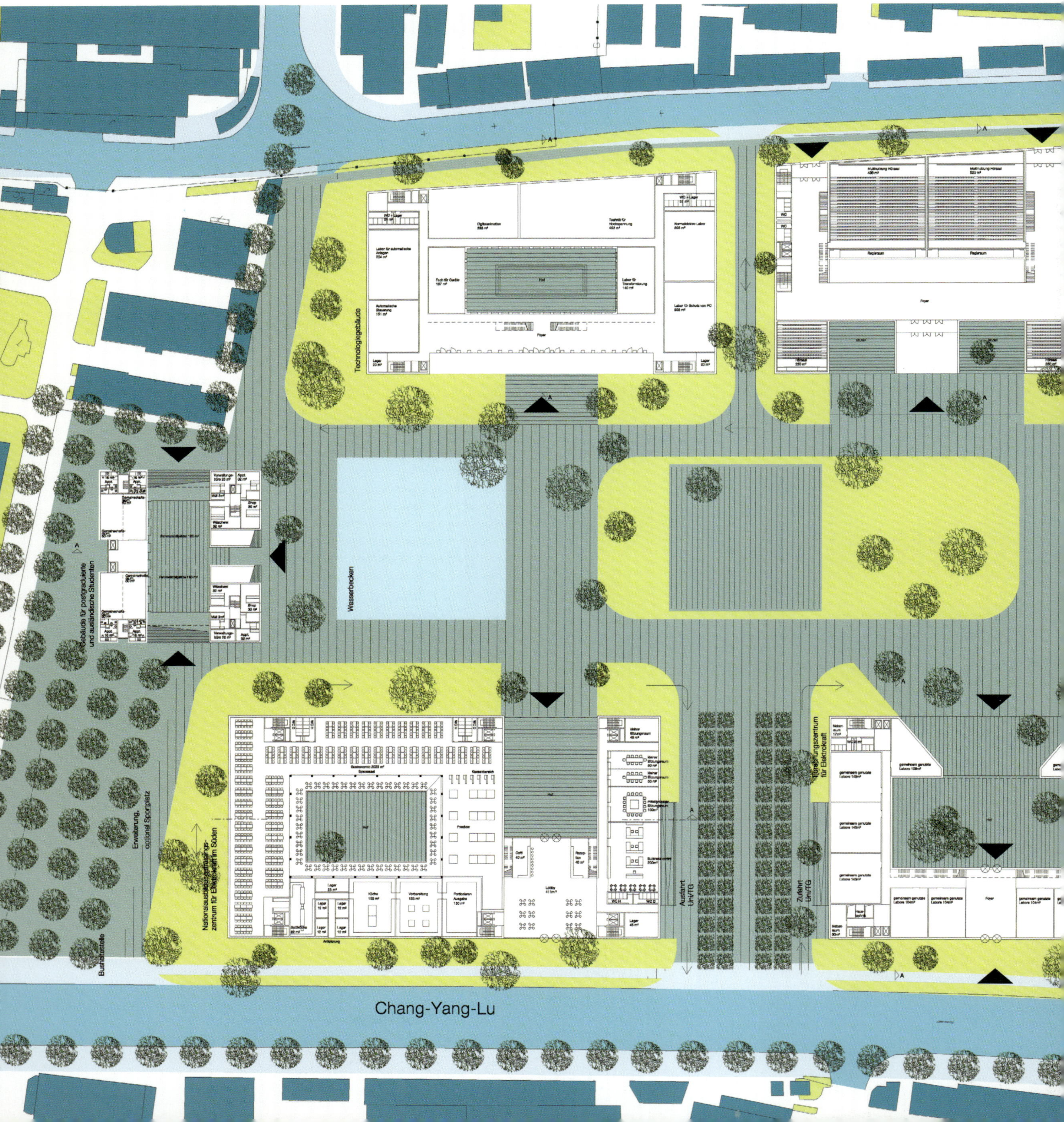

JO. FRANZKE ARCHITEKTEN

Shanghai University of Electronic Power

FLÄCHE: 76.000 m²
WETTBEWERB: 2005, 3. Preis

WES & PARTNER, HAMBURG
SHANGHAI UNIVERSITY OF ELECTRONIC POWER
SHANGHAI UNIVERSITY OF ELECTRONIC POWER

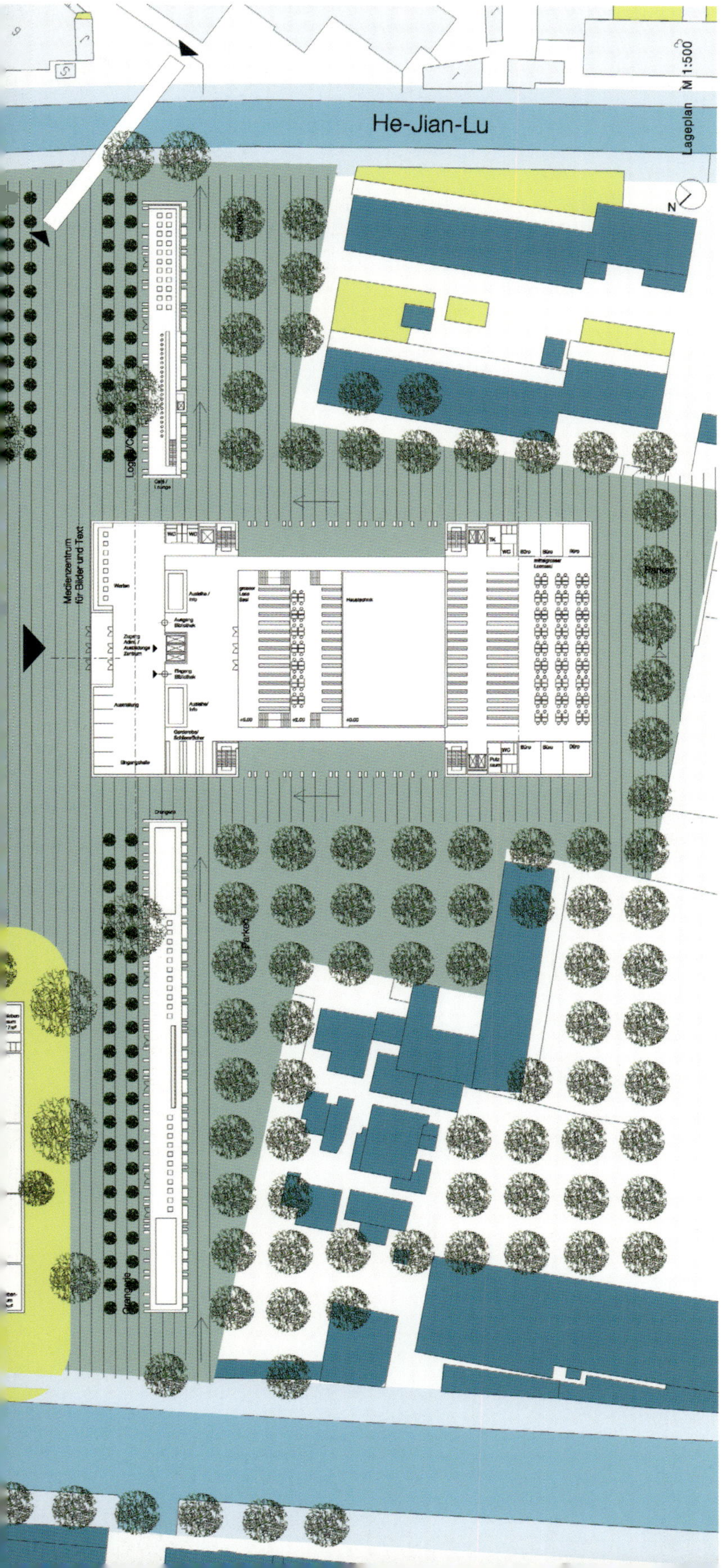

Ziel des Konzeptes ist die Entwicklung einer grünen Campusstruktur, die offen, hell und einladend ist. Die Abfolge von Räumen und Plätzen bietet eine hohe Nutzungs- und Aufenthaltsqualität.

Wichtig ist die atmosphärische Wirkung, geprägt von Licht, Luft und Himmel, die die Freiheit des Geistes animiert. Hauptthema sind große Rasenteppiche. Der Eingangsplatz von der Chang Yang Lu empfängt mit strenger Symmetrie: Vier Achsen mit Platanen, in der Mitte ein langer Wassertisch, der in den Campus führt.

Ein weiterer Hauptplatz ist der Bereich vor dem Medienzentrum. Die Bibliothek wird zu beiden Seiten von langen Fontänenreihen flankiert. Mit diesen Fontänenachsen vor den Flügelbauten entsteht eine repräsentative „schlossartige“ Vorzone. Die Mitte bildet die Mediensäule, die sowohl Bild- und Sprachinformationen bieten als auch Lichtskulptur sein kann. Von diesem Medienplatz aus gibt es fließende Übergänge in den theaterartigen Treppenhof des allg. Lehrgebäudes und durch das Tor des Forschungszentrums für Elektrokraft.

The design aimed for a green campus, open, light-flooded and welcoming with a sequence of high quality outdoor spaces for different uses.

An important aspect is the atmosphere, the result of light, air and the sky which is 'nourishment' for free spirits. Large carpets of grass are the main elements. The entrance area on Chang-Yang-Lu Road receives people with the strict symmetry of four rows of plane trees (sycamores) flanking a long water table which lead into the campus.

Another main area is the one in front of the media centre. Both side wings of the library are flanked by long rows of fountains which give the forecourt an impressive, palace-type appearance. In the middle is the 'media column' which serves as an IT information panel, but could also be seen as a light-emitting sculpture. There are flowing transitions from this media forecourt to the courtyard (with steps like in an amphitheatre) of the general teaching

Die Balance zwischen Platz und Park, umgesetzt in atmosphärische Wirkung und ergänzt durch Wasser und zeitgemäße Skulpturen, lässt ein Campusgelände von hoher Qualität entstehen.

The balance between sealed/paved and green areas – enhanced by water and contemporary sculptures – translates into a pleasant atmosphere and a generally high-quality campus.

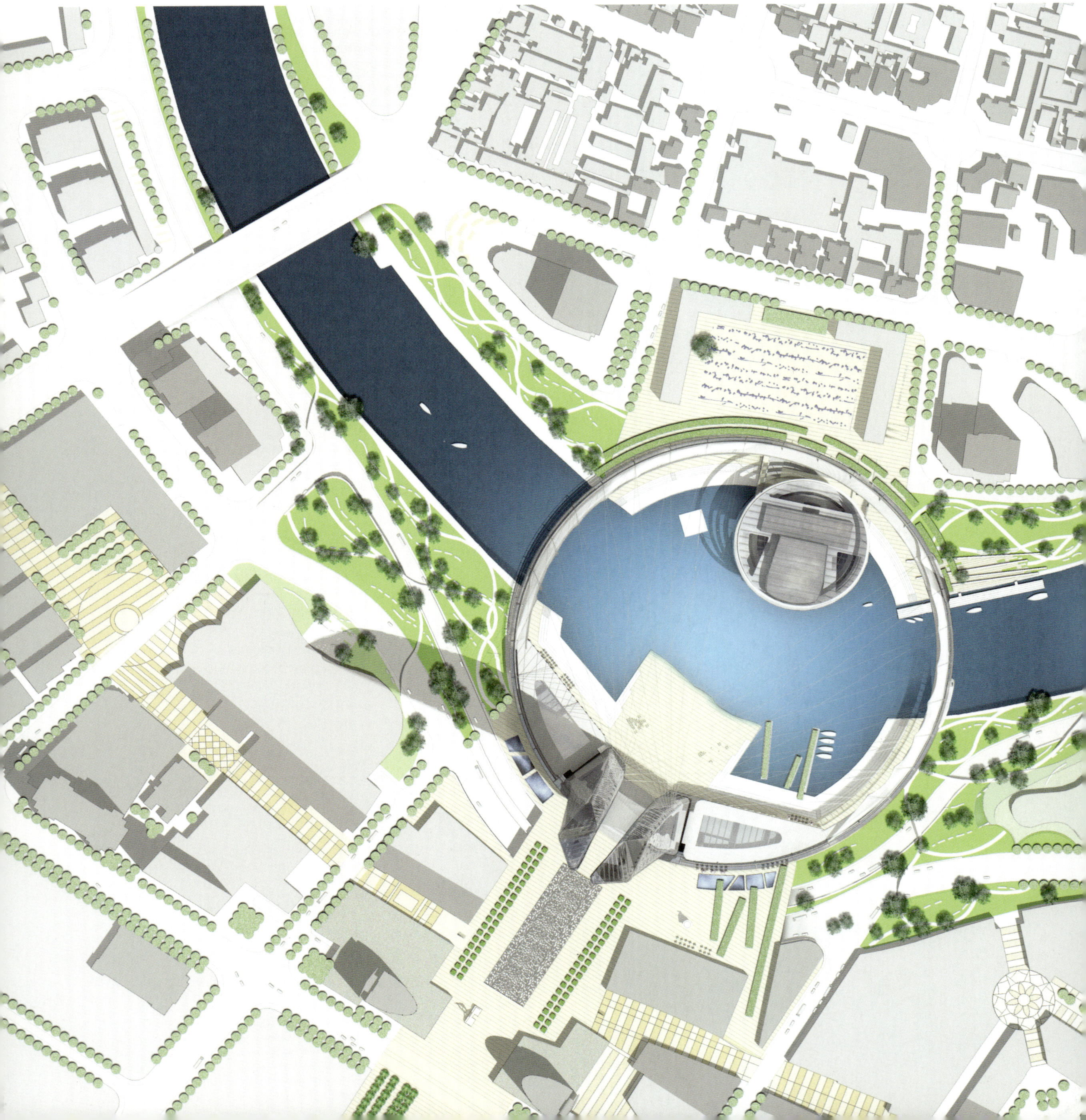

FLÄCHE: 120.000 m^2
WETTBEWERB: 2004, 1. Preisgruppe

WES & PARTNER, HAMBURG

TIANJIN NEUE STADTMITTE – FREIFLÄCHENPLANUNG

LANDSCAPE-ARCHITECTURAL DESIGN FOR TIANJIN'S NEW CITY CENTRE

Auf der Basis des Generalplans versuchten wir, in enger Anlehnung an die Grundzüge des Stadtplans von Tianjin ein besonderes Landschaftskonzept zu entwickeln. Der Entwurf sollte außerdem die Atmosphäre und Werte der Stadt Tianjin widerspiegeln. Hauptelemente der Anlage sind die Nord-Süd-Achse, der Park am Flussufer, der Friedensplatz und der zentrale Platz des „Wasserforums". Auf dem Weg zum „Torhaus" gelangen die Besucher auf den Friedensplatz. Hauptgestaltungselement ist hier das gemusterte Pflaster aus glänzendem schwarzem Marmor und grünem Mattglas.

Den Höhepunkt der Nord-Süd-Achse bildet der Bereich hinter dem „Torhaus", der zum Fluss hin sanft abfällt und mit Hunderten von Stühlen „übersät" ist. Aus der Luft gesehen wird er wie eine bunt bemalte Plastik wirken. Dieser zentrale Ort wird Besucher einladen, langsam herumzuschlendern und sich innerlich auf das bevorstehende Konzert einzustimmen oder einfach nur entspannt zu verweilen. Nachts wird er beleuchtet und wie ein glitzerndes Amphitheater vor der Konzerthalle aussehen.

Based on the masterplan, we attempted to develop a special landscaping design, closely linked to the basic urban design idea of Tianjin. The landscaping therefore also aimed to evoke an atmosphere which reflects the ideals of Tianjin. The major elements are the north-south axis, the river park, Peace Square and the central square, or 'Water Forum'. On approaching the 'gatehouse', people first reach Peace Square. Its main feature is the patterned paving of black polished marble and translucent green glass. The highlight of the north-south axis is the central open area behind the 'gatehouse', which slopes down to the river and will be dotted with hundreds of chairs. Seen from the air, it will appear like a colourful sculpture. Here people will be able to walk about at a leisurely pace so as to be in a receptive mood for the concert or just able to relax. At night, this central square will be lit as a glittering 'amphitheatre' in front of the concert hall.

Das kulminierende Element der neuen Stadt und Landschaft wird das „Water Forum" sein. Man könnte es auch „Water Square" oder „Water Plaza" nennen, da seine Mischung aus verschiedenen Elementen – Gebäude, landschaftlich gestaltete Flächen, plastisch geformte Räume, Wasser und nicht zuletzt Natur – den kraftvollen Geist des Ortes verkörpern wird, den Geist von Tian Jin.

The culminating element of the new town and landscape structure will be the Water Forum. One could also call it Water Square, or Water Plaza, because the combination of different elements – of architecture, landscape architecture, sculptured space, water and, not least, nature – will define the powerful spirit of the place, the spirit of Tian Jin.

Ansicht von Süden: Im Übergangsbereich zur offenen Landschaft erhält das Land eine neue Gestalt. Es schließen sich ein Sport- und Freizeitpark und danach die Central Avenue im Norden an.

South view: at the transition from the city to the open countryside, the area is given a new appearance. Behind it are a sports and leisure park, followed by the Central Avenue to the north.

AUSLOBER: Stadt Zhengzhou
GESAMTLÄNGE: – ca 25 km
KOSTEN: ca. 100 Mio. Euro

WITTIG & RIETIG, WEIMAR

ZHENGZHOU – CENTURY AVENUE

CENTURY AVENUE, ZHENGZHOU

Die Entwicklung wird die Stadt mindestens auf das Doppelte ihrer bisherigen Größe in Richtung Osten anwachsen lassen. Ein zentraler Identitätsbaustein ist ein neuer Central Business District und eine zentrale Avenue, die beide Stadtflügel miteinander verknüpft.

Unter Bezugnahme auf historische und kulturelle Bezüge wurde in einer Matrix eine Abfolge von Themen entwickelt: Im Norden und Süden werden Themen der Landwirtschaft aufgenommen, im Zentralbereich entsteht als urbaner Schwerpunkt eine zentrale Avenue, ein Stadtpark, weiterhin Entertainment und Sportparks, ein Wilderness Park wie auch ökologische Retentionsbereiche, Flächen zur Forschung, Bildung und Lehre.

The projected development will at least double its present urban area towards the east. One core element of the new urban identity is a new central business district on both sides of a central avenue which interconnects the two halves of the city.

With reference to historical and cultural factors, the design matrix was developed according to a series of themes. To the north and the south the subject of agriculture, at the centre the big avenue as an urban focus, then a public park, entertainment and sports centres, a wilderness park as well as ecological retention areas, research and educational facilities.

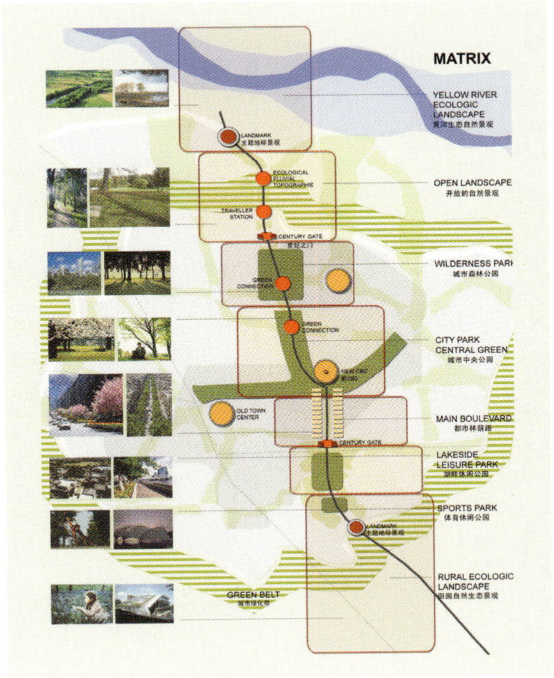

Die entwickelte Matrix – eine Abfolge von Themen – machte die enorme Dimension des Projektes beherrschbar.

The matrix of themes was the only way to control the enormous dimensions of the project.

Zhengzhou – Kreuzungspunkt bedeutender Verkehrsachsen in Chinas Mitte

The city of Zhengzhou lies in China's middle, at the crossroads of important na-tional traffic arteries

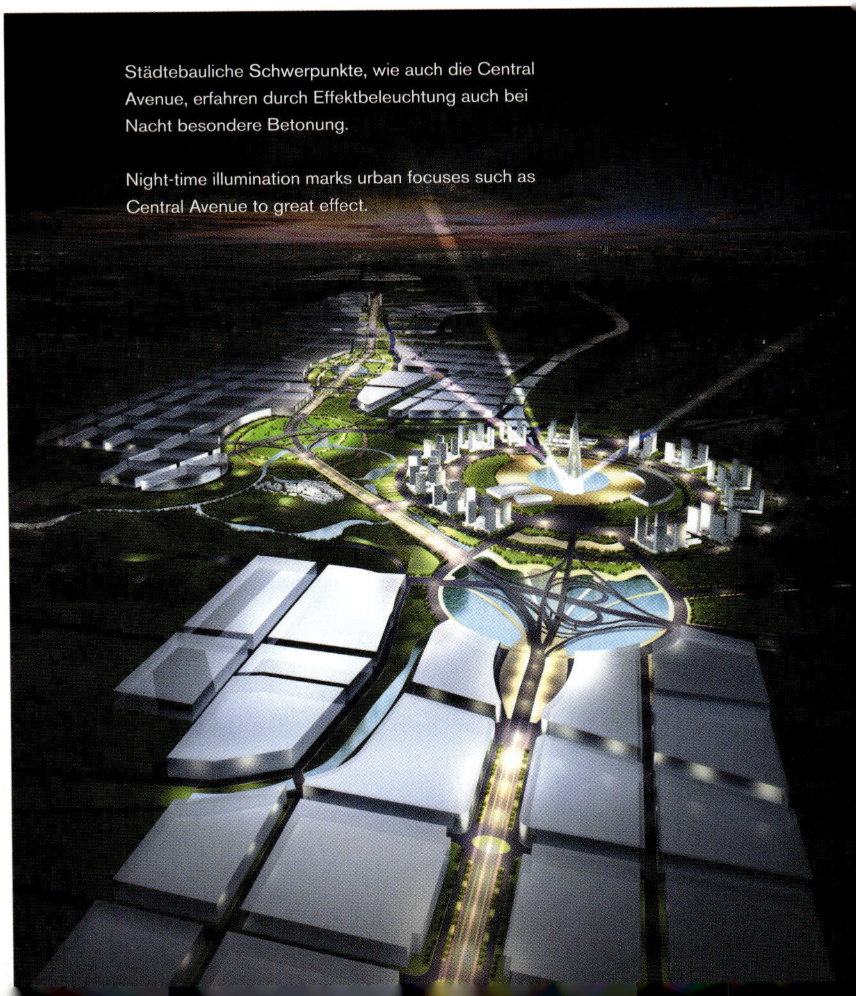

Städtebauliche Schwerpunkte, wie auch die Central Avenue, erfahren durch Effektbeleuchtung auch bei Nacht besondere Betonung.

Night-time illumination marks urban focuses such as Central Avenue to great effect.

Das Concept-Design für Anting New Town mit dem weitläufigen Green Belt – und die intensiv gestalteten Flächen des City-Parks. Augenfällig ist der hohe Wasseranteil – die Planung reagiert auf die sich ändernden Wasserstände

The design concept for Anting New Town shows the vast Green Belt and the carefully laid out City Park, large parts of which are planned as water gardens, in response to changing water levels in the region.

Gegenüber: Innerhalb der Model-Unit im Westen des Green Belt sind verschiedene Muster-Gärten und beispielhafte öffentliche Bereiche vorgesehen. Grünelemente, die sich im europäischen Siedlungsraum entwickelt haben, werden hier appliziert.

Opposite: Various model gardens and exemplary public zones are projected for the 'model unit' west of the Green Belt. Green elements developed in Europe have been applied in this design.

Gegenüber: Ausschnitte für Bootsanleger und moderne Pavillons im Green Belt.

Opposite: The 'cut-outs' of the Green Belt are used for boat piers and modern pavilions.

AUSLOBER: International Automobile City Real Estate Co. Ltd.
GESAMTFLÄCHE: ca. 150 ha
KOSTEN: ca. 160 Mio. Euro

WITTIG & RIETIG, WEIMAR

ANTING NEW TOWN – LANDSCHAFTEN
ANTING NEW TOWN – LANDSCAPES

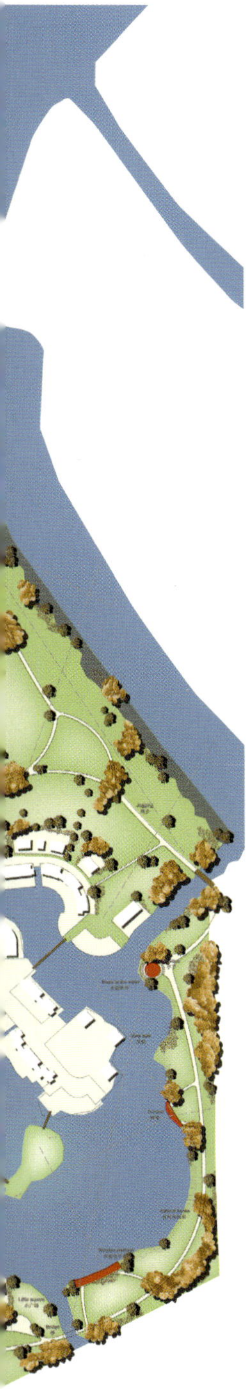

Für die Satelliten-Stadt im Norden Shanghais ist der „Green Belt“ von besonderer Bedeutung: Er übernimmt im Süden Schutzfunktionen gegenüber der Autobahn, ebenso werden ökologische Potenziale im Zusammenhang mit dem Angebot von Wasser und einer Revitalisierung von natürlichen Vegetationseinheiten geplant.

Der zentrale City-Park interpretiert klassische Kompositionsprinzipien des europäischen Landschaftsparks in moderner Form: Interessante Raumabfolgen und immer wieder wechselnde Sichtbezüge entstehen.

Im Norden wird im Green Belt ein vielseitiges Freizeitangebot entlang des Wuson-Rivers angeboten, während im Südosten vorrangig Sport- und Bildungsfunktionen die Gestaltung bestimmen.

The Green Belt is of special significance for the satellite towns north of Shanghai. For one thing, it is a protective barrier against the motorway to the south, for another it uses the the ecological potential of different water features and areas of natural vegetation that are to be revitalized.

The central City Park reinterprets the classical composition principles of the European landscape park in a modern language and thus offers interesting sequences of natural spaces and changing sight lines. Along its northern edge, formed by the river Wuson, the Green Belt includes a variety of leisure amenities, while sports and educational facilities dominate the layout and aspect of the southeast site corner.

Anting New Town – Satelliten-Stadt nordwestlich von Shanghai

Anting New Town – A satellite town northwest of Shanghai

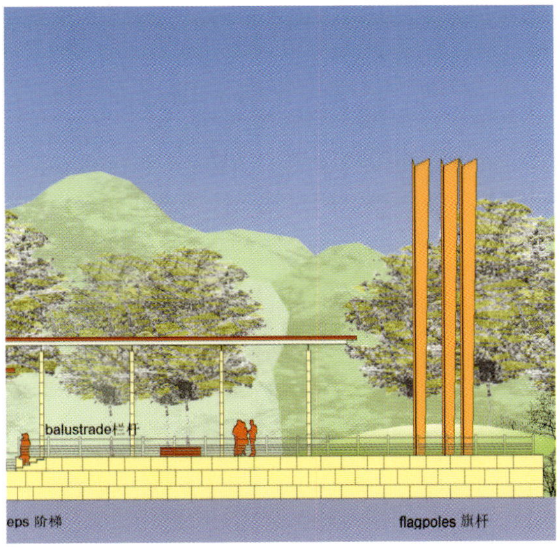

ARCHITEKTENREGISTER
LIST OF ARCHITECTS

AS&P – ALBERT SPEER UND PARTNER
Hedderichstr. 108-110, 60596 Frankfurt am Main
Tel +49 (0) 69.69 60 50 11 0
Fax +49 (0) 69.69 60 50 11 500
www.as-p.de / mail@as-p.de

BAU.WERK ARCHITEKTEN
Weseler Str. 35, 48151 Münster
Tel +49 (0) 251.53 95 40 0
Fax +49 (0) 251.53 95 40 4
bauwerk@t-online.de

EIKE BECKER_ARCHITEKTEN (AXIS-GROUP.DE)
Kochstraße 22, 10969 Berlin
Tel +49 (0) 30.25 93 74 0
Fax +49 (0) 30.25 93 74 11
www.eb-a.de / info@eb-a.de

BRANDENFELS LANDSCAPE + ARCHITECTURE
Herrenstr. 29, 48167 Münster
Tel +49 (0) 2506.36 17
Fax +49 (0) 2506.79 64
www.brandenfels.com / info@brandenfels.com

BRUNOBRAUN ARCHITEKTEN
Hansa Allee 42a, 40547 Düsseldorf
Tel +49 (0) 211.55 02 71 0
Fax +49 (0) 211.55 02 71 11
www.brunobraun-architekten
info@brunobraun-architekten.de

IRENE BURKHARDT LANDSCHAFTSARCHITEKTEN
Fritz-Reuter-Str. 1, 81245 München
Tel +49 (0) 89.82 08 55 40
Fax +49 (0) 89.82 08 55 49
www.Irene-Burkhardt.de / info@Irene-Burkhardt.de

PROF. DIPL.-ING. HARALD DEILMANN
Jessingstraße 11–13, 48149 Münster
Tel +49 (0) 251.41 88 0
Fax +49 (0) 251.41 88 18 8

FASKEL ARCHITEKTEN (AXIS-GROUP.DE)
Rheinstraße 45 Aufg. 3, 12161 Berlin-Steglitz
Tel +49 (0) 30.85 96 16 70
Fax +49 (0) 30.85 96 16 71
www.Faskel-Architekten.de
info@Faskel-Architekten.de

DEUTSCHE GOLF CONSULT
Grohs · Preißmann · von Wendt
Sabinastr. 27, 45136 Essen
Tel +49 (0) 201.25 88 1
Fax +49 (0) 201.25 08 88
www.golfconsult.com / goep.dgc@cityweb.de

JO. FRANZKE ARCHITEKTEN
Alte Gasse 27/29, 60313 Frankfurt am Main
Tel +49 (0) 69.13 81 20 0
Fax +49 (0) 69.13 81 20 29
www.jofranzke.de / info@jofranzke.de

gmp – VON GERKAN, MARG UND PARTNER
Elbchaussee 139, 22763 Hamburg
Tel +49 (0) 40.88 15 10
Fax +49 (0) 40.88 15 11 77
www.gmp-architekten.de
Hamburg-E@gmp-architekten.de

GTL – GNÜCHTEL · TRIEBSWETTER LANDSCHAFTSARCHITEKTEN
Grüner Weg 21, 34117 Kassel
Tel +49 (0) 561.78 94 60
Fax +49 (0) 561.78 94 61 1
www.gtl-kassel.de / kontakt@gtl-kassel.de

HENN ARCHITEKTEN
Augustenstr. 54, 80333 München
Tel +49 (0) 89.52 35 70
Fax +49 (0) 89.52 35 71 23
www.henn.com / info@henn.com

KOHL & FROMME ARCHITEKTEN
Dreilindenstraße 75-77
45128 Essen
Tel +49 (0) 201.10 56 30
Fax +49 (0) 201.10 56 31 0
www.kohl-architekten.de / info@kohl-architekten.de

KRAMM & STRIGL ARCHITEKTEN
Bad Nauheimer Straße 11
64289 Darmstadt
Tel +49 (0) 6151.97 52 0
Fax +49 (0) 6151.97 52 80
www.kramm-strigl.de / info@kramm-strigl.de

KSP ENGEL UND ZIMMERMANN
Hanauer Landstraße 287–289
60314 Frankfurt am Main
Tel +49 (0) 69.94 43 94 0
Fax +49 (0) 69.94 43 94 38
www.ksp-architekten.de
sekretariat@f.ksp-architekten.de

LÉON WOHLHAGE WERNIK ARCHITEKTEN
Leibnizstraße 65 . Metahaus, 10629 Berlin
Tel +49 (0) 30.32 76 00 0
Fax +49 (0) 30.32 76 00 60
www.leonwohlhagewernik.de
post@leonwohlhagewernik.de

NALBACH + NALBACH ARCHITEKTEN (AXIS-GROUP.DE)
Rheinstraße 45, 12161 Berlin
Tel +49 (0) 30.85 90 83 0
Fax: +49 (0) 30.85 11 21 0
www.nalbach-architekten.de
buero@nalbach-architekten.de

OBERMEYER PLANEN + BERATEN
Hansastraße 40, 80686 München
Tel +49 (0) 89.57 99 0
Fax +49 (0) 89.57 99 91 0
www.opb.de / info@opb.de

RAVE ARCHITEKTEN (AXIS-GROUP.DE)
Knesebeckstraße 13, 10623 Berlin
Tel +49 (0) 30.31 86 88 60
Tel +49 (0) 30.31 86 88 66
www.rave-architekten.de
office@rave-architekten.de

RKW · RHODE KELLERMANN WAWROWSKY
Tersteegenstraße 30, 40474 Düsseldorf
Tel +49 (0) 211.43 67 0
Fax +49 (0) 211.43 67 11 1
www.rkw-as.de / info@rkwmail.de

RAINER SCHMIDT LANDSCHAFTSARCHITEKTEN
Klenzestraße 57c, 80469 München
Tel +49 (0) 89.20 25 35 0
Fax +49 (0) 89.20 25 35 30
www.Schmidt-Landschaftsarchitekten.de
Mail@Schmidt-Landschaftsarchitekten.de

MARINA STANKOVIC ARCHITEKTEN (AXIS-GROUP.DE)
Schillerstraße 94, 10625 Berlin
Tel +49 (0) 30.31 50 53 17
Fax +49 (0) 30.31 50 53 19
www.stankovicarchitekten.de
mail@stankovicarchitekten.de

STEIDLE + PARTNER ARCHITEKTEN
Genter Straße 13, 80805 München
Tel +49 (0) 89.36 09 07 0
Fax +49 (0) 89.36 17 90 6
www.steidle-partner.de
architekten@steidle-partner.de

ARCHITEKTENREGISTER
LIST OF ARCHITECTS

tec ARCHITECTURE
Mittererstraße 3, 80336 München
Tel +49 (0) 89.54 54 38 0
Fax +49 (0) 89.54 54 38 38
www.tecarchitecture.de / office@tecarchitecture.de

TILKE GMBH
Krefelder Straße 147, 52070 Aachen
Tel +49 (0) 241.91 34 0
Fax +49 (0) 241.91 34 400
www.tilke.com / mailbox@tilke.de

VALENTIEN + VALENTIEN + PARTNER
Hauptstraße 42, 82234 Weßling
Tel +49 (0) 8153.95 20 10
Fax +49 (0) 8153.95 20 14
www.valentien.de / valentien@valentien.de

WES & PARTNER LANDSCHAFTSARCHITEKTEN
Jarrestraße 80, 22303 Hamburg
Tel.: +49 (0) 40.27 84 10
Fax: +49 (0) 40.27 06 66 8
www.wesup.de / info@wesup.de

WITTIG & RIETIG GMBH
Mozartstr. 16, 99423 Weimar
Tel.: +49 (0) 3643.88 66 0
Fax: +49 (0) 3643.88 66 12
www.wittig-rietig.de / info@wittig-rietig.de

STUDIO ZAMP KELP (AXIS-GROUP.DE)
Spanische Allee 70, 14129 Berlin
Tel +49 (0) 30.80 49 99 19
Fax +49 (0) 30.80 49 99 55
www.zamp-kelp.de / contact@zamp-kelp.de

Titelbild: TV- und Sightseeing Tower Guangzhou, China
Architekten: Léon Wohlhage Wernik Architekten, Berlin
Visualisierung: Léon Wohlhage Wernik Architekten, Berlin
Abb. Rückseite: Internationales Messe- und Kongresszentrum, Nanning
Architekten: gmp – von Gerkan Marg und Partner, Hamburg

Bibliografische Information der Deutschen Bibliothek
Die Deutsche Bibliothek verzeichnet diese Publikation in der Deutschen Nationalbibliografie; detaillierte bibliografische Daten sind im Internet über http://dnb.ddb.de abrufbar.

Gestaltungsraster: 3deluxe, Wiesbaden
Gestaltung, Satz und Bearbeitung: Lektorat Bernd Wylicil, Wiesbaden
Druck: Jütte-Messedruck Leipzig GmbH, Leipzig
Übersetzung: Annette Wiethüchter, Berlin

ISBN 3-932509-40-4 · © 2005 Verlag H.M. Nelte, Alwinenstraße 26, D–65189 Wiesbaden
www.nelte.de · verlag@nelte.de

Printed in Germany